SOCIAL CLASS IN LATER LIFE

Power, identity and lifestyle

Edited by Marvin Formosa and Paul Higgs

First published in Great Britain in 2015 by

Policy Press
University of Bristol
1-9 Old Park Hill
Bristol
BS2 8BB
UK
t: +44 (0)117 954 5940
pp-info@bristol.ac.uk
www.policypress.co.uk

North America office:
Policy Press
c/o The University of Chicago Press
1427 East 60th Street
Chicago, IL 60637, USA
t: +1 773 702 7700
f: +1 773 702 9756
sales@press.uchicago.edu
www.press.uchicago.edu

© Policy Press 2015

British Library Cataloguing in Publication Data
A catalogue record for this book is available from the British Library.

Library of Congress Cataloging-in-Publication Data
A catalog record for this book has been requested.

ISBN 978 1 44730 057 1 paperback

The right of Marvin Formosa and Paul Higgs to be identified as editors of this work has been asserted by them in accordance with the 1988 Copyright, Designs and Patents Act.

The statements and opinions contained within this publication are solely those of the editors and contributors and not of The University of Bristol or Policy Press. The University of Bristol and Policy Press disclaim responsibility for any injury to persons or property resulting from any material published in this publication.

Policy Press works to counter discrimination on grounds of gender, race, disability, age and sexuality.

Cover design by Policy Press
Front cover: image kindly supplied by www.alamy.com
Printed and bound in Great Britain by CMP, Poole
The Policy Press uses environmentally responsible print partners

Marvin dedicates the book to his son, Julian, for his support and appreciation.

Paul dedicates the book to his mother, Kathleen, whose determination to overcome obstacles has been an inspiration throughout his career.

Contents

List of tables and figures

Foreword

Malcolm Johnson

Social divisions in human societies have preoccupied social scientists in general, and sociologists in particular, since the beginning of these disciplines. From the original writings of Auguste Comte in the founding of sociology and the great giants of the nineteenth century, Karl Marx, Max Weber and Emile Durkheim, social class became a central and enduring theme. The class struggle characterised by Marx as between the owners of capital and those who sold their labour to them, ran through his entire published work. Weber's challenge in his seminal essay *Class, status and party* (1961) to Marx's dominating bifurcation of societies in *Capital* (1970) set the framework of discourse and analysis for a hundred years. In it Weber details the human desire for social power and how, through class, certain forms of power are achieved. Nevertheless, he shares with Marx the belief that property is the basic category that defines class situation.

The debates about class formation and the hierarchies of status and power continued in full force throughout the post-Second World War explosion of sociological enquiry. In the 1960s, when departments of sociology were flowering in many new universities across North America and Western Europe, the academic journals and textbooks were preoccupied with class, family and community. Economic growth and democratised modern societies developed new middle classes and gave rise to studies of social mobility and *embourgeoisement*. But as the 20th century moved into its final quarter, enthusiasm for social stratification waned. Modernism, postmodernism and feminism, among other new domains of interest, nudged class out of the way and until recently its proponents have spoken with small voices.

Two of the 'new' subdisciplines which became prominent as class lost its salience were the overlapping fields of gerontology and medical sociology. Both had roots in the inequalities of health and longevity which had grown out of public health and epidemiology. They were fuelled by the needs of governments and the desire of health professionals to understand the social, economic and lifestyle correlates of ill health at different stages of the lifepath. These imperatives generated empirical and public policy oriented enquiries which recognised social class as an important variable, rather than a subject of independent enquiry.

The reduction in interest in social class appears to have had several dimensions. As the 20th century moved to its close, opportunities for social mobility in Western Europe diminished, at a time when the principal engine of mobility, higher education, became available to increasing proportions of each cohort to reach their late teens. Concurrently interest expanded in dimensions of difference which had previously been subsumed in the great panjandrum of class analysis, women's studies, race and ethnicity, sexual identities, family breakdown and secularisation making the way for discourses about the corrosion of civic society. The work of Pierre Bourdieu (1984) opened up theoretical avenues which required new vocabularies and conceptual frameworks for what was personal and what might be considered social. Habitus became a more common point of reference than the much cruder constructs of categories based on birth, education and employment. And as the century turned, Robert Putnam's (2000) *Bowling Alone* provided a superlative analysis of the dissolution of civic engagement and the loss of social capital. Class distinctions had not vanished, nor were the economic foundations of class lost to social enquiry. It was the arrival of fresher and more penetrating modes of observation that shifted the spotlight.

Among the lengthening list of research domains was ageing and the lifespan. Essentially a post–Second World War development, the interdisciplinary field of gerontology developed as governments put resources into empirical studies of the consequences of increased longevity.: medical services, pensions, housing, retirement, social care, intergenerational relations and what became known as 'the burden of an ageing population'. Indeed, my own first piece of professional research in the late 1960s went under the compelling title 'The unmet social and medical needs of the elderly in the London Borough of Camden'. A strong emphasis was placed on public provision of services to alleviate poverty and disabling illness. Inevitably, the greatest recognition was given to medical research in all the countries of the then developed world. Social scientists were drawn into empirical studies which addressed a spectrum of socio-medical maladies. However, all too little effort went into conceptualisation. Theories of ageing were a minority field of scholarly activity. Social epidemiology was the central mode of enquiry, except for the few. In fact, it is far from surprising that in a chapter entitled 'Are theories of ageing important? Models and explanations in gerontology at the turn of the century' the authors, who included myself, wrote of gerontology as 'data rich and theory poor' (Bengtson et al, 1999).

As in the other developing domains of study, social status, occupation and income were significant factors in the constitution of old age as a problem. But class was seen as a variable for analytical purposes. In the UK, the Registrar General's Classification of Occupations was routinely used as the standard measure of class. Despite extensive dismay amongst sociologists, who wanted to promote more sophisticated calibrations, their dissenting essays were largely confined to scholarly journals. In gerontology, dissenters gathered under an umbrella network which eventually became known as 'critical gerontology'. Led in the US by the energetic standard-bearer Carroll Estes, supported by the colourful pressure group The Gray Panthers and their charismatic figurehead Maggie Kuhn, a movement emerged based on research and praxis. It was seen as radical and even subversive. In the UK, in an article in the very first issue of the journal *Ageing and Society* (of which I was the first Editor), Peter Townsend (1981) introduced the concept of 'structured dependency'. He articulated a view of the way nation states confined retired people into a restricted world of low incomes and severely limited opportunities for self determination and social engagement. In the same issue of the journal Alan Walker (1981) published an article 'Towards a political economy of old age'. Two issues later, Chris Phillipson (1982) wrote a review essay on 'state policies and the elderly'. Soon they were followed by Carroll Estes herself, Xavier Gaullier (1982) from France and Martin Kohli (Kohli et al, 1983) from Germany.

These key figures in the critical gerontology movement were rapidly joined by a rising tide of writers and researchers who sought to challenge the established paradigm, which characterised older populations as an economic and social problem and older people as individuals who had passed out of mainstream society into what Cumming and Henry (1961) had deemed the phase of disengagement. In the contests between the structural functionalists who observed 'old age' as the remnant of the lifespan and the parallel colleges of researchers who promoted successful ageing, one found the critical gerontologists, whose observations of later life left them more convinced of the boundaries to successful old age than its widespread achievement. The successful ageing studies stimulated by Glen Elder's (1974) landmark volume *Children of the great depression* engaged with class as an important variable in the exploration of life chances and the unexpected upward social migration which emerged from Elder's studies. But class remained a contextual issue, never the focus of enquiries.

Class was a much more central issue for the critical gerontologists. But for them it was sometimes a structural agency which delivered inequality in retirement and at other times a key feature of a polemic about institutional discrimination and what Robert Butler (1975) termed ageism. It is always hazardous to claim that there were no investigations into social class as a feature of old age, which was not simply a predetermined characteristic settled earlier in life, either by the lifetime occupation of the individual or a status gained by marriage or inherited from their family of origin. *But I can recall none.*

Undoubtedly, social status, income, occupation, education and other central dimensions of the class debate over one and a half centuries, have been present in the discourses about age and ageing. However, it is difficult to find – even in an era of electronic literature searches – serious discussion of, let alone empirical investigations into, social mobility beyond the point of retirement until recent times.

In his book *Class dynamics in later life*, Marvin Formosa (2009) combined a systematic review of the literature on the lived experience of older people and reported a sophisticated enquiry into the subtle shifts of social positioning that occur in the conservative and hierarchical arrangements of his own small island society of Malta. Through careful analysis of systematically gathered data, from interviews, group discussions and extensive observation, he produced a convincing account of the ways in which social capital is either accumulated or lost and measurable status shifts are achieved. It undermines the long-held presumption that the third age is one where all have a given designation and that place remains until death and beyond. Not that he claims the rest of us have failed to see rampant social mobility and simply not recognised it. Much more nuanced evidence is provided which lifts the cover on the nature of life lived in the third age. Limited but significant movement is observed and reported in this most status conscious of societies.

So how much more movement might there be in social systems which are looser, more in transition, more challenged by the impact of social and political change? Might closer inspection of the nations in Eastern Europe liberated from the oppression of Soviet governance and the least good influences of the Roman Catholic and Orthodox churches, reveal dynamics not seen in more settled nation states? In China, as the depopulation by the young of the rural areas in favour of urban living, one may well see new cultures of later life, to compensate for the slow collapse of the Confucian models of filial piety. In a different social and cultural context, the familial models of old age dependency across Africa may well reveal fitter, more self-confident older people innovating and managing new patterns of independent and socially mobile old age.

In his continuously fruitful work with Chris Gilleard, Paul Higgs (2000) has given to the study of ageing a new reflexivity, which was stifled by the earlier streams of thinking and research in the field of gerontology. Together they have put the established assumptive world of gerontology to critical scrutiny over more than a decade. In a series of highly regarded books and articles, they have created a stream of fresh thinking in the field of ageing studies. This body of work critiques the relatively static representations of old age encapsulated in the literature on the third and fourth ages and challenges them with new theoretical perspectives and a fresh look at emerging patterns of later life which are both varied and dynamic. In his book noted above, Formosa (2009: 45) is at odds with Gilleard and Higgs in their interpretation of the lives of older people 'because they see the growth of agency amongst the middle class third agers, but fail to recognise that others who are currently bounded by their economic and class limitations might also be liberated to greater autonomy and improved statuses, as old age becomes a more socially fluid domain'.

By bringing their differing interpretations together with their mutual regard for the seminal work of Pierre Bourdieu, Marvin Formosa and Paul Higgs add an imaginative flair and tension to this book which gives it a creative frisson that collections do not always achieve. In selecting authors, they have married the authority and depth of knowledge provided by Chris Phillipson and Christina Victor with the imaginative and forward-looking insights and empirical enquiries of younger scholars from a range of disciplines, nations and cultural traditions. The result is a collection of essays which embrace the rapidly changing worlds of old age and in so doing take a penetrating look into the emerging future. Having liberated the concept of social class from its moribund past, this volume looks critically at both the constraints placed on older people and the emerging cultures of later life which will ultimately leave behind the structured dependency which rightly troubled Peter Townsend over 40 years ago.

Here is a volume which benchmarks a renewal and transformation of a neglected form of social and economic analysis. It explores the still shifting sands of class in the context of old age, which most scholars believed were settled during the second age of lifetime employment and fixed at retirement.

References

Bengtson, V.L., Johnson, M.L. and Rice, C. (1999) 'Are theories of ageing important? Models and explanations in gerontology at the turn of the century' in V.L. Bengtson and K.W. Shaie (eds) *Handbook of theories of aging*, New York: Springer Publishing Co, pp 3-19.

Bourdieu, P. (1984) *Distinction: A social critique of the judgement of taste*, Cambridge, MA: Harvard University Press.

Butler, R.N. (1975) *Why survive? Being old in America*, New York: Harper and Row.

Cumming, E. and Henry, W. (1961) *Growing old: The process of disengagement*, New York: Basic Books.

Elder, G.H., Jnr. (1974) *Children of the great depression: Social change in life experience*, Chicago: University of Chicago Press.

Estes, C.L. (1979) 'Towards a sociology of political gerontology', *Sociological Symposium*, vol 26, Spring, pp 1-27.

Estes, C.L., Swan, J.H. and Gerard, L.E. (1982) 'Dominant and competing paradigms in gerontology', *Ageing & Society*, vol 1, no 3, pp 151-64.

Formosa, M. (2009) *Class dynamics in later life: Older persons, class identity, and class action in Malta*, Berlin: Lit Verlag.

Gaullier, X. (1982) 'Economic crisis and old age: Old age policies in France', *Ageing & Society*, vol 2, no 2, pp 165-82.

Gilleard, C. and Higgs, P. (2000) *Cultures of ageing: Self, citizen and the body*, Upper Saddle River, NJ: Prentice Hall.

Kohli, M., Rosenow, J. and Wolf, J. (1983) 'The social construction of ageing through work: Economic structure and life-world', *Ageing & Society*, vol 3, no 3, pp 23-42.

Marx, K. (1970) *Capital*, London: Lawrence and Wishart.

Phillipson, C. (1982) 'State policies and the elderly', *Ageing & Society*, vol 1, no 3, pp 427-32.

Putnam, R.D. (2000) *Bowling alone: The collapse and revival of American community*, New York: Simon & Schuster.

Townsend, P. (1981) 'The structured dependency of the elderly: Creation of social policy in the twentieth century', *Ageing & Society*, vol 1, no 1, pp 5-28.

Walker, A. (1981) 'Towards a political economy of old age', *Ageing & Society*, vol 1, no 1, pp 73-94.

Weber, M. (1961) *From Max Weber: Essays in sociology*, London : Collier-Macmillan.

Preface

This book provides a unique collection of chapters by authors who are committed to explore and improve our understanding of social class dynamics in later life. It focuses on the interface between social class and the latter stages of the life course, analysing why class relations remain an integral part of persons' lives even after they exit the labour market following either voluntary or mandatory retirement, and as they experience those life transitions associated with old age. The chapters document the widespread differences in resources available to various subgroups of older people, and how such variances in social, cultural and physical capital impact identities and lifestyles in later life. Focusing its attention on various spheres of class analysis, it provides the most up-to-date collection of new and emerging research relevant to emerging debates on the relationship between social class, power and ageing.

This collection of chapters arose from the editors' long-standing interest in the impact of social class on the quality of life of older people. Its genesis can be located in a symposium titled 'Theorising Social Class in Later Life: Power, Identity and Lifestyle' that the editors convened during the 19th World Congress on Gerontology and Geriatrics of the International Association of Gerontology and Geriatrics in July 2009 in Paris, France. This meeting generated so much interest that a follow-up symposium took place during the subsequent 20th Congress in June 2013 in Seoul, South Korea – as well as during the 2013 British Sociological Association Annual Conference (convened by Ian Rees Jones). These symposia included presentations by the convenors plus Martin Hyde, Kate Davidson, Trish Hafford-Letchfield and Christina Victor. The editors also take the opportunity here to thank a whole host of people who, in casual conversation and in more earnest dialogue, have influenced the direction and content of this book, as well as the contributors of chapters, all of whom respected deadlines and embraced various positive criticisms. Special gratitude goes to Malcolm Johnson who, for more than a decade, demonstrated unwavering support for the realisation of such a project, to Alison Shaw and Rebecca Tomlinson at The Policy Press for their production support, and to the independent reviewers who provided endorsements for the book.

Notes on contributors

Wendy Bottero is Senior Lecturer in Sociology at the University of Manchester, UK. Her research interests focus on how social inequalities are wound through people's personal ties and connections, and how this affects the way in which inequalities persist and reproduce. She has published a series of journal articles on questions of social mobility, class inequalities and class theory, and her publications include the book *Stratification: social division and inequality* (Routledge, 2005).

Marvin Formosa is a Senior Lecturer at the European Centre for Gerontology, University of Malta, Malta. In 1998 and 2008, he was appointed as a lecturer by the International Institute on Ageing (United Nations) on its missions to Thailand and Qatar, respectively. Marvin held the post of a Visiting Scholar at the Ontario Institute for Studies in Education, University of Toronto, Canada, and is on the UK National Executive of the Association for Education and Ageing. He has published extensively in the fields of educational gerontology, older adult learning and Universities of the Third Age, and his publications include the book *Lifelong learning in later life: a handbook on older adult learning* (Sense, 2010 – with Brian Findsen).

Trish Hafford-Letchfield is a Reader in Social Work at Middlesex University, London, UK. She has research interests in the lifelong learning of older people using social care and widening participation. Trish has published several books in the area of leadership, management and organisational development, sexuality, and interprofessional learning. She is on the UK National Executive of the Association for Education and Ageing and is co-chair of an international community of practice in relation to sexuality and sexual identities in social work.

Paul Higgs is Professor of the Sociology of Ageing at University College London, UK, where he teaches medical sociology. He is co-author of *Cultures of ageing: self, citizen and the body* (Prentice Hall, 2000) and, with Chris Gilleard, *Contexts of ageing: class, cohort and community* (Polity, 2005). A third volume, *Ageing, corporeality and embodiment*, will be published in 2013. In 2012, he was elected an academician of the UK Academy of Social Sciences.

Martin Hyde is the Deputy Director of the Epidemiology Unit at the Stress Research Institute at Stockholm University, Sweden. He has worked on several large studies, including the English Longitudinal Study of Ageing (ELSA) and the Swedish Longitudinal Occupational Study of Health (SLOSH). His main research areas include consumption and identity in later life, spatialities of ageing, and labour market exit trajectories and health. He has published around 30 papers and chapters, and co-authored, with Ian Rees Jones, Paul Higgs and Christina Victor, *Ageing in a consumer society: from passive to active consumption in Britain* (Policy Press, 2008).

Malcolm Johnson, who is currently Visiting Professor of Gerontology and End of Life Care at the University of Bath, has been Professor of Health and Social Policy (now Emeritus) at the University of Bristol since 1995. From 1984 to 1995 he was Professor of Health and Social Welfare and first Dean of the School of Health and Social Welfare at The Open University. Of his ten books and over 160 monographs, chapters and articles, more than half relate to ageing. He is a former Secretary of the BSA Medical Sociology Group and the British Society of Gerontology and Founding Editor of the international journal *Ageing and Society*. He is General Editor of *The Cambridge handbook of age and ageing* (Cambridge University Press, 2006).

Ian Rees Jones is Professor of Sociological Research at the Wales Institute of Social and Economic Research, Data & Methods (WISERD) at Cardiff University, UK. He is co-author, with Paul Higgs, of *Medical sociology and old age: towards a sociology of health in later life* (Routledge, 2009), and has published extensively in the fields of ageing, sociology and medical sociology. He is currently part of the editorial team for *Sociology of Health and Illness* and is the Monograph Series editor for the journal. He is a Fellow of the Learned Society of Wales.

Alexandra Lopes is a Lecturer in Sociology at the University of Porto, Portugal. Her research is in the field of public policies for ageing societies, with a particular focus on social care arrangements in familist countries and on theoretical and methodological instruments to address poverty in old age. She has published work on social class theories and ageing, on long-term care systems and arrangements, and on inequalities in old age. Up to 2010, she was the Director of the Department of Sociology of the University of Porto.

Chris Phillipson is Professor of Sociology and Social Gerontology at the University of Manchester, UK. The main focus of his research has been on issues relating to older people, covering issues concerned with retirement, changes in family and community life, and the impact of globalisation on policies for old age. He is involved in a long-term research programme exploring the relationship between demographic change and urbanisation. Recent books include *The Sage handbook of social gerontology* (co-edited with Dale Dannefer, Sage, 2010), *Work, health and well-being* (co-edited with Sarah Vickerstaff and Ross Wilkie, Policy Press, 2011) and *Ageing* (Polity, 2013).

Elizangela Storelli is a PhD candidate in the Department of Sociology at Boston College, US. Her research interests include aging, international development and comparative research in aging policy. She is currently working on the impact of changing policies and family structure on older adults across various countries in Latin America.

Christina Victor is Professor of Gerontology and Public Health at the School of Health Sciences and Social Care, Director of the Doctorate in Public Health and the Brunel Institute for Ageing Studies Programme Director for Health Ageing at Brunel University, UK. Her major research interests are in old age and later life and the use and evaluation of health services for older people. She has a particular interest in social relationships and later life and the experiences of ageing among minority ethnic elders. Christina has written over 200 journal articles and book chapters and has published eight books in the field of gerontology. Christina is Editor in Chief of *Ageing and Society*, the leading social gerontology journal in the UK.

John B. Williamson is currently a Professor in the Department of Sociology at Boston College, US. He is also affiliated with the Center for Retirement Research and the Sloan Center on Aging and Work, also at Boston College. He has authored or co-authored (or co-edited) 17 books and more than 140 book chapters and journal articles dealing with old age policy, older workers, poverty policy and the welfare state, among other issues. In recent years, his focus has been on comparative pension policy and generational equity issues.

ONE

Introduction

Marvin Formosa and Paul Higgs

The legacy of social class in gerontology

For many years, the concept of class constituted a fundamental touchstone of gerontological scholarship. This was especially true during the late 1970s and 1980s when the political economy and structured dependency perspectives on ageing argued strongly how class holds a crucial role in determining how people experience retirement and the quality of lives they lead (Townsend, 1981; Walker, 1981). Influenced by neo-Marxism, such standpoints revolved around the role of retirees within the capitalist economy and, therefore, embraced Wright's (1978) rationale that the best way to deal with class locations in later life is to treat them as 'parts of class-trajectories' – that is, as a lifetime structure of positions through which an individual passes in the course of a work career. Retirees, according to such a raison d'être, occupy post-class locations so that their class location can only be understood in terms of the trajectories of class positions to which they are linked. Although it was acknowledged that not all inequalities can be reduced to class, since the role of gender and race in promoting material and social forms of exclusion can never be underestimated, retirement was perceived as the final 'resolution' of the advantages and disadvantages attached to established class positions. In other words, once the advantages arising from a particular position are consolidated, they are sustained during later life. For political economists and structured dependency theorists, this was mostly due to the continued impact of the relative inequality between the level of state retirement pensions, which was the source of the majority of working-class elders' income, and the amounts paid out by the better-funded occupational pensions received by the middle class. This modernist drive to throw light on class relations in later life was instrumental in highlighting how the majority of working-class retirees tend to register a degree of distress that warrants social work intervention, following the 'problems [that] may arise through interaction between the physical and social contexts of ageing' (Phillipson, 1982: 111). However, this standpoint falls short by overlooking the effect of post-industrialisation and late modernity on the character of later life, class relations and society in general, and, hence, ignoring how classes are made and given value through cultural and symbolic processes. The key lacuna of structuralist standpoints on class dynamics in later life is perhaps its erroneous assumption that older persons occupy a 'pensioner' status defined by a confining dependence on state welfare when, presently, a rising number of retirees are taking an active part in the development of new later life identities.

In their quest to quantify the relationship between class and later life, gerontologists usually operationalise the former in terms of the classification of occupations. In fact, there is a strong body of empirical work demonstrating a positive correlation between socio-economic status on one hand, and levels of financial, social, cultural and physical capital on the other (Walker and Foster, 2006; Formosa, 2009). For instance, middle-class elders are generally found to own higher levels of financial capital due to more savings and better occupational pensions, and, hence, to live in more upmarket communities. Working-class peers, on the other hand, tend to enter retirement after careers in temporary and/or low-paying jobs, so that their pensions are insufficient to meet their everyday needs, a state of affairs that leads them to experience both absolute and relative poverty. Reminiscent of Bauman's (1998) point that although desiring comes free, the experiencing of desire as a pleasurable state requires resources, the literature reports that working-class elders are unlikely to be involved in sports clubs, formal volunteering, learning initiatives and leisure associations as many lack the resources that facilitate social involvement, such as income, access to a vehicle and online networking skills. Moreover, despite the increase in life expectancies in all high- and middle-income countries, class backgrounds continue to have a long-term effect on the patterning of morbidity, mortality, disability and emotional well-being. Victor concludes that:

> there is a significant health divide based around class in terms of achieving old age and in the amount of life to be enjoyed once having achieved old age, and there is no evidence to indicate that these life differentials have decreased over the past three decades. (Victor, 2010: 49)

Studies on class differentiation have generated important data on inequality in later life. Yet, similar to the wider field of social gerontology, theory-building has been a marginal feature. Researchers are quick to provide facts and figures without integrating them into an explanatory framework. This lacuna is serious since theory integrates findings into holistic totalities and explains how and why distinctly observed phenomena are related. Methodologically, it is also disappointing that most studies adopt a positivist standpoint that reduces external reality to observable patterns by operationalising 'class' either upon the job-status scale provided by the Registrar General (UK) or upon socio-economic status (SES). However, while the former is unreliable as its categories are vague and general, SES indicators are not theoretically grounded in ways that class is. Moreover, such approaches ignore how class in later life is shaped by biographical and subjective contexts. Even if occupation is deemed as a reliable source of class location, historicity can induce a 'mismatch' between the level of power decreed by a job in different time periods:

> occupational status is not a transhistorical concept ... the status ascribed to jobs held by the elderly will have changed over their lifetime ... the status ascribed to an office clerk in 1930 could have been very different from that in 1980. (Victor and Evandrou, 1987: 255)

This standpoint is also problematic for not allowing for any possibility for social mobility in retirement unless older persons re-enter the labour market in a diverse role. This is, however, misleading since relations of production serve only as catalysts, rather than determining mechanisms, for class mobility. This notion was emphasised by O'Rand (2001: 197) when highlighting how 'stratification operates across societal planes extending from the economy and state through the community and household to the individual'. Finally, serious problems arise when the conventional approach is applied to older women. Older women are highly susceptible to changes in their marital status, which, in turn, generate an apparent social mobility that may bear little or no relation to real change in mobility patterns: 'Are older women in their own, or their husband's class? And is this class of pre-retirement "origin" (i.e., in younger age) or the social class of destination in old age, based on retirement income and assets?' (Estes, 1999: 24–5).

In retrospect, the legacy of class in ageing studies is restricted by its adoption of a structuralist lens that overlooks 'what older people themselves make of who and what they are, as well as how they view their worlds' (Gubrium and Holstein, 2000: 3). This sensitivity is highly warranted since, even in later life:

class refers to much more than the individual's economic and social position. It implies an individual's self-concept and subjective understanding ... it focuses on intraindividual linkages across time as a central mechanism producing a type of continuity ... between work and retirement phases. (O'Rand and Henretta, 1999: 35)

As O'Rand (2001: 197) expands elsewhere, the crux of the issue when discussing patterns of inequality within older cohorts and their effects on life-course outcomes 'is the latent construct of stratification or inequality as a fundamental and pervasive, but complex, social condition that underlies the life course'. Indeed, the measurement of class inequality does not rest on some simple derivative strategy, but is actually both a multidimensional and multilevel exercise, consisting of a variety of indicators operating across societal planes, and extending from the economy and state through the community and household to the individual.

The evanescence of social class in ageing studies

The past two decades witnessed a resurgence of scholars arguing how class has become an obsolete concept in our efforts to make sense of inequality in industrial societies. The key argument is that following the 1980s, industrial societies have experienced profound economic, political and ideological changes that brought the 'classic' and 'modern' phases of industrialisation to a gradual end. Supporters of the anti-class brigade contend that such social change resulted in a radical transformation of societal dynamics so that 'class' is now an obsolete tool for social analysis: 'it is a capitalism without classes, but individualised social inequality and all the related social and political problems' (Beck and Beck-Gernsheim, 2002: 205). Influenced by the writings of Bell (1976), class sceptics argue that, presently, it is theoretical knowledge, rather than class, which constitutes the axial principle of differentiation. Stratification has become increasingly pluralistic, multidimensional and shaped by factors located outside the workplace, leading to a style of politics that embraces non-class divisions and issues. As a result, various theorists began making reference to the coming of a period of 'late', 'reflexive' or 'second' forms of modernity. A key denominator in such visions is an increasing scrutiny of the class concept as a means of understanding contemporary societies, with the consensus that late-modern societies have moved 'beyond class'. For Beck and Willms (2004: 107), 'society can no longer look in the mirror and see social classes ... all we have left are the individualized fragments'. Ascribed differences on the basis of race, ethnicity, gender, age, nationality and the like have superseded traditional identities rooted in class, family, religion and locality as the locus of social differentiation. The result, and a much-debated one, is that consumption has taken over class, with 'taste', 'fashion' and 'lifestyle' being the new bases of structural divisions and unities.

Such trends in social theory did not go unnoticed in social gerontology. During the last two decades the concept of class started to occupy an ambivalent position in the study of ageing lives, so that one finds hardly any efforts to conceptualise that interface between class and later life. The standpoints of structured dependency and political economy are currently out of favour, and the class concept is somewhat a *persona non grata* in ageing studies. It is not mere coincidence that Woodward (1999: x) went so far as to state that 'along with race, gender and age are the most salient markers of social difference', or that the recently published *Key concepts in social gerontology* (Phillips et al, 2010) includes no mention of 'class' either in the contents or index. It is also noteworthy that a recent edited publication, *Unequal ageing* (Cann and Dean, 2009), attempts to soften the link between class background and inequality, while emphasising that it is ageing per se that leads citizens to lower levels of quality of life. In its opening chapter – 'How social age has trumped social class?' – Dean (2009: 6, 4) puts forward the argument that by the turn of the 21st century, 'social age had replaced social class as a principle behind collective organisation', writing that 'growing older is a journey of loss' as the rise of the proportion of pensioners in poverty is widening across the whole board. For Dean, the key issue leading older adults to experience lower levels of successful ageing is age discrimination, a state of affairs that equally affects the large and diverse number of people aged roughly from 60 to 100. At the same time, it is also discouraging to note that mainstream class research tended to remain located in, and around, the younger and adult 'territories' of the life course, with class analysts arguing that older persons remain generally excluded from empirical research on the assumption that their class-related characteristics are not sufficiently unique to undermine the logic of class analysis (Formosa, 2009). Indeed, although sociologists have taken considerable pains to examine the 'interplay between gender and class ... and to a lesser extent between ethnicity and class ... very little has been made of the articulation of age and class' (Egerton and Savage, 2000: 24).

The evanescence of the role of class in shaping daily lives in old age is to be expected considering how the coming of late modernity has impacted retirement. Recent decades have witnessed the creation of a population of relatively affluent retirees whose income and expenditure have come close to, and in some cases even exceeded, those of younger people of working age. Moreover, the third age has been transformed from a demographic entity to a cultural field, whose dynamic derives from consumption, and whose boundaries are tied to the historical changes that provided the context for its gestation. However, this does not mean that class no longer has a role in influencing the outcome of retirement lives. Although the cultural significance of class in later life has declined, we should not go to the other extreme by overstating the power of agency. Despite the record levels of agency experienced by older persons – as they increasingly turn towards fashion, bodies and leisure as their preferred sites of cultural performance and identity creation – the coming of late modernity does not mean the end of traditional forms of inequalities, but only 'the growth of new inequalities alongside the continuation of traditional social divisions' (Phillipson, 1999: 323). Overstating human agency will only function to overlook how contemporary research demonstrates how inequalities generated by class still match other inequalities stemming from gender, race and ethnicity. Individuals with better resources early in life often continue to accumulate resources over time, while those with few or no resources experience no improvement (Dannefer and Kelley-Moore, 2009). This implies that there are significant disparities in financial, social and other resources in later life, putting older adults who do and do not have resources in positions and experiences that are worlds apart. Despite renewed claims that the old class structure of capitalism is steadily dissolving, critical sociology has no trouble in showing how the notion of 'capitalism without classes' is an illusion (Savage, 2000). Most contemporary critical gerontologists underline how attention to class is still a major issue for the study of ageing, only for this task to remain unaddressed in any detail. Such a state of affairs leads us to agree with Settersten and Trauten (2009: 460), who underlined that 'social class is at present remarkably absent in scholarship and policy-making in aging', a claim that was highlighted as long as 14 years ago:

> There is widespread confusion and ambiguity in the use of the term 'class'. This seems particularly so for those who have attempted analysis of ageing and class.... Gerontology from a political economy perspective demands attention to social class; nevertheless, *work on the topic is surprisingly underdeveloped*. (Estes, 1999: 23, emphasis added)

While there is no doubt that the efforts of critical gerontology to encompass globalisation, the deinstitutionalisation of the life course and the emergence of a consumer-driven one are all highly welcome, the significance of class in retirement is still a topic that needs addressing. Citing Settersten and Trauten (2009: 460, emphasis in original) again, 'understanding the growing diversity of the [older] population is ... not just about understanding *difference*; it is about understanding differences that generate and are generated by *inequality*'.

Renewing social class research in later life: goals and objectives

Social class in later life: power, identity and lifestyle seeks to develop an analytical and empirical understanding of the interface between social class and later life. We believe that the individual and collective experiences of growing old, as well as the very nature of age relations, differ so significantly by class that there is an urgent need for a unified analysis in which both age and class are taken into account. The fact that disparities related to class are increasing means that 'social class must therefore be a central point for theories of aging in all substantive areas' (Settersten and Trauten, 2009: 459). The chapters in this volume all strive to better understand how, despite the estrangement of older citizens from the productive process, retirees are not transformed into individualised beings who fly completely free of class identities. Attention is especially bestowed upon the ways in which the policies that have created and sustained the 'aging enterprise' and the 'medical–industrial complex' (Estes, 1979) constitute an important part of class dynamics in later life, as well as the extent that systems of social and health care services reinforce pre-existing class relationships. In this respect, the book's aim is to investigate the extent that social welfare policy continues to reinforce midlife patterns of class inequality. We hope that while the analysis of class and later life surely presents different challenges than does a more general analysis of the class dynamics of society, the chapters in this volume will illuminate the interconnections between class and age, and their consequences for future policies in social and health care for older persons.

This collection of chapters emerged from our quest to construct, theoretically and empirically, a developmental map of class structuring and action among older persons. Therefore, it endeavours to examine how the employment-to-retirement transition affects established patterns of class relations. The primary concern is not to fit older persons into a particular class schema, but to achieve a better grasp of class structuring and action in later life. Hence, its goal is not to construct a map of class positions, but to investigate if, and how, 'new' classes emerge following retirement, and how class background influences daily living in later life. *Social class in later life* seeks to shed light on the extent to which lifelong social class relations remain pervasive in later life so that older persons, despite their estrangement from the productive process, are still dynamically engaged in the dynamics of class structuring and action. Consequently, this study included a number of important objectives. First, to analyse the theoretical currents that provide a valid picture of how social class dynamics develop over the latter phases of the life course. Second, to examine the widespread assumption that older people's class position is directly correlated with past trajectories rather than analysing the interactions between past trajectories and ageing-related events on a series of outcomes that define how people live in later life. Third, to explore the extent to which class relations in later life are being transformed by the advent of globalisation, and, consequently, producing complex flows of people, activities, communities and networks that move beyond the confines of national borders. A fourth objective consisted in examining the links between class, politics and identities in later life by investigating the saliency of class for identity in later life through a range of cross-national data from well-established high-quality social surveys. However, the manuscript also includes a number of objectives that focus on the more pragmatic issues surrounding class dynamics in later life, in particular, the relationship between social class and income security, social work services and health care. The book also investigates the extent to which contemporary pension and social/health care policies create or maintain class differences in later life, and the degree to which such levels of inequality are being affected by the dismantling of the welfare state in favour of public–private partnerships and entrepreneurial care companies.

Social class in later life advances the analysis of class dynamics in later life by focusing on the three fundamental cornerstones of ageing studies – namely, theory, research and policy. First, the book provides a critical overview of the competing approaches and rationales underlying the explanation of class relations in later life. Nowadays, it is not just increased longevity that has had an impact on the character of population ageing. Various social and cultural currents – ranging from 'senior' lifestyle consumerism to bodily transformation – have multiplied the agentic options open to older people so that their lives are no longer bound by strict social, economic and biological reference points. The result is a blurring of the traditional life stages and a homogenising of aspirations in later life to what Featherstone and Hepworth (1993) identified early on in the debate as 'mid-lifestyles', which are maintained for as long as possible and sometimes deep into old age. This has major implications for the understanding of class dynamics in later life, and chapters will demonstrate that rather than calling for the class concept to be written off as an artefact of a superseded form of social organisation, it is more sensible to perceive it as a social category in need of considerable re-articulation.

The chapters in this book also endeavour to illustrate the unequal worlds that older people from various class backgrounds experience. These chapters will present empirical data that demonstrate how retirement reflects the advantages and disadvantages of class position in relation to resources and quality of life. Individual chapters will highlight the relationships between class, the ownership of financial capital, savings and occupational pensions, and participation in various social activities on the one hand, and caring, living with children, being in residential care, having extensive and stable social networks, and physical and psychological well-being on the other.

Last, but not least, *Social class in later life* seeks to illuminate the interconnection between class dynamics in later life and public policy for older persons. It addresses the paradox that while many retirees have benefited from the structures and stability of a first modernity, their current circumstances are much more contingent on what Beck calls the 'side effect principle', where decisions that affect their situations and opportunities are often the consequences of decisions and structures placed well outside nation state boundaries. Nowhere is this more true than in the financing of retirement, where shifts in the global economy have had dramatic effects on the values of the stocks and shares that underpin the profitability of pension funds, as well as reducing the rates of return on savings that many older people rely upon for important parts of their retirement income. For instance, in relation to health, there is now a complex picture of the interrelationships between income, health and disability. The 'accumulation of disadvantage' approach to health in later life has been contested in much the same way that the 'compression of morbidity' arguments have challenged the equation between chronological age and increased illness and infirmity. This is not to argue that there are no connections between earlier life-course events and circumstances, but rather to acknowledge that outcomes in later life might be as influenced by proximal factors as they are by distal ones. Chapters will address these debates but focus on the realisation that the changes that are occurring within later life are such that the conceptual tools of social policy of the past are no longer as effective as they once were and need modifying.

The structure of the book

Social class in later life includes a total of 10 chapters. Following this introduction, in Chapter Two, Wendy Bottero clears the ground for a holistic study of class dynamics in later life by dissecting the key debates in mainstream class research. She notes how over the past two decades, there has been a strong reaction against the continued relevance of class in understanding contemporary industrial societies. Bottero argues that while there can be no doubt about the important changes experienced by capitalist societies, and that 19th-century models of class are no longer theoretically adequate, it would be off beam to announce the death of class. She concludes that class is still very much alive and kicking, easily observable if one looks closely at the relationship between class on the one hand, and culture, lifestyle and taste on the other. In Chapter Three, Chris Phillipson explores the argument that class relations in later life are being transformed by the advent of globalisation, which is producing complex flows of people, activities, communities and networks that move beyond the confines of national borders. While the first section reminds the reader of broad definitions associated with the term globalisation, the second section addresses the discussion around globalisation that has been developed within critical gerontology. The third section develops a number of arguments and illustrations about the way in which globalisation is changing the landscape of class in old age, with the final section addresses the policy implications of using globalisation as a vantage point for understanding social changes affecting older people.

Chapter Four, by Alexandra Lopes, argues that although one could reasonably accept that older people's class position is directly correlated with past trajectories, such a standpoint suffers from various lacunae. For Lopes, a more fruitful approach involves analysing the interactions between past trajectories and ageing-related events on a series of outcomes that define how people live in later life. The starting question for such an exercise can be phrased as follows: does age act as a deterrent of past trajectories (either diluting or reinforcing its effects), or does it just reproduce those same past trajectories? Lopes answers this question by dissecting the relationship between class on the one hand, and well-being, social participation and socialisation milieus on the other. In Chapter Five, Martin Hyde and Ian Rees Jones turn the spotlight on the links between class, politics and identities in later life. The chapter investigates the salience of class for identity in later life through a range of cross-national data from well-established high-quality social surveys. While the first section reviews the literature, the second presents an empirical examination of the importance that older people themselves attach to class as a feature of their identity. The third section draws upon empirical data to explore the extent to which class and or age-class positions can be identified through older people's political ideas and actions. Finally, the chapter concludes by examining the results of the analyses in relation to the theoretical debates around the role of class and age in politics and identity in later life.

In Chapter Six, Elizangela Storelli and John B. Williamson develop an analytical and empirical understanding of the interface between class, pensions and financial security in old age. The authors outline different pension models, their effect on the economic position of older persons and their future implications on old-age financial security within a global context. Guided by the political economy perspective, Storelli and Williamson begin with a critical review of policies in the United States, examining how these pension policies create or maintain class differences in later life. Using country case studies, the authors also address the class implications of alternate models, including privatised pension systems, provident funds, defined notional contribution systems and social pensions. Chapter Seven, by Ian Rees Jones and Paul Higgs, discusses how it is best to describe and explain patterns of social class inequalities in health over the life course. Jones and Higgs point out that, to date, much socio-epidemiological research tends to treat class as a variable within standard log-linear models. As a result, considerations of the implications of the emergence of a relatively lengthy post-working life are not yet fully incorporated into studies of class and health in old age. To Jones and Higgs, this represents is an important gap in our knowledge because the generations in affluent countries entering retirement today are those who experienced the social changes that have led to debates about the salience of class in wider society.

Chapter Eight, by Christina Victor, examines the links between socio-economic status and care in later life through a typology of care developed by Zechner (2008) of 'caring about', 'taking care', 'care giving' and 'care receiving', which extends our understanding of the formal and informal care sectors, and how these dimensions of caring are linked to the key socio-structural factors of class, gender and ethnicity. While the first part briefly outlines the definition of 'care' and caring, subsequent parts consider the emergence of research examining the role of 'carers', while also discussing who cares, and their location within the broader care economy. Interwoven within such an analysis is the examination of the importance of class, gender and ethnicity in the provision and receipt of care in later life. In Chapter Nine, Trish Hafford-Letchfield discusses the links between social work, class and later life. She points out that the retreat of the government from its traditional role of provider/funder of care is posing enormous challenges for social work practice with older people, where evidence is beginning to emerge of widening inequalities and social exclusion. She maintains that little is known about the effect of socio-economic status on the take-up of social work services in later life, other than that opportunities for direct payments are disproportionately taken up by middle-class affluent people when research on the use of informal/formal sources of support shows that those most in need are in poor health, live alone and have poor access to financial resources. The final chapter sees the editors summarising and integrating the material covered in the book's chapters. This chapter also makes future projections about the likely bio-psychosocial contours relating to social class in later life.

References

Bauman, Z. (1998) *Work, consumerism and the new poor*, Buckingham: Open University.

Beck, U. and Beck-Gernsheim, E. (2002) *Individualisation*, London: Sage.

Beck, U. and Willms, J. (2004) *Conversations with Ulrich Beck*, Cambridge: Polity Press.

Bell, D. (1976) *The cultural contradictions of capitalism*, New York, NY: Basic Books.

Cann, P. and Dean, M. (2009) *Unequal ageing*, Bristol: The Policy Press.

Dannefer, D. and Kelley-Moore, J.A. (2009) 'Theorizing the life course: new twists in the paths', in V.L. Bengston, D. Gans, N.M. Putney and M. Silverstein (eds) *Handbook of theories of aging*, New York, NY: Springer Publishing Company, pp 389–411.

Dean, M. (2009) 'How social age trumped social class', in P. Cann and M. Dean (eds) *Unequal ageing*, Bristol: The Policy Press, pp 1–23.

Egerton, M. and Savage, M. (2000) 'Age stratification and class: a longitudinal study of the social mobility of young men and women, 1971–1991', *Work, Employment and Society*, vol 14, no 1, pp 23–49.

Estes, C.L. (1979) *The aging enterprise*, San Francisco, CA: Jossey Bass.

Estes, C.L. (1999) 'Critical gerontology and the new political economy of aging', in M. Minkler and C.L. Estes (eds) *Critical gerontology: perspectives from political and moral economy*, Amityville, NY: Baywood, pp 17–35.

Featherstone, M. and Hepworth, M. (1993) 'Images of ageing', in J. Bond (ed) *Ageing in society: an introduction to social gerontology*, London: Sage, pp 304–32.

Formosa, M. (2009) *Class dynamics in later life: older persons, class identity and class action*, Hamburg: Lit Verlag.

Gubrium, J. and Holstein, B.A. (2000) 'Introduction', in J. Gubrium and B.A. Holstein (eds) *Aging and everyday life*, Malden, MA: Blackwell Publishers, pp 1–12.

O'Rand, A.M. (2001) 'Stratification and the life course: the forms of life-course capital and their interrelationships', in R.H. Binstock and L.K. George (eds) *Handbook of aging and social sciences* (5th edn), San Diego, CA: Academic Press, pp 197–213.

O'Rand, A.M. and Henretta, J.C. (1999) *Age and inequality: diverse pathways through later life*, Boulder, CO: Westview Press.

Phillips, J., Ajrouch, K. and Hillcoat-Nalletamby, S. (2010) *Key concepts in social gerontology*, London: Sage.

Phillipson, C. (1982) *Capitalism and the construction of old age*, London: Macmillan.

Phillipson, C. (1999) 'The social construction of retirement: perspectives from critical theory and political economy', in M. Minkler and C.L. Estes (eds) *Critical gerontology: perspectives from political and moral Economy*, Amityville, NY: Baywood, pp 315–28.

Savage, M. (2000) *Class analysis and social transformation*, Buckingham: Open University Press.

Settersten, R.A and Trauten, M.E. (2009) 'The new terrain: hallmarks, freedom, and risks', in V.L. Bengston, D. Gans, N.M. Putney and M. Silverstein (eds) *Handbook of theories of aging*, New York, NY: Springer Publishing Company, pp 455–69.

Townsend, P. (1981) 'The structured dependency of the elderly: creation of social policy in the twentieth century', *Ageing & Society*, vol 1, no 1, pp 5–28.

Victor, C.R. (2010) *Ageing, health and care*, Bristol: The Policy Press.

Victor, C.R. and Evandrou, M. (1987) 'Does social class matter in later life?', in S. Gregorio (ed) *Social gerontology: new directions*, London: Croom Helm, pp 252–67.

Walker, A. (1981) 'Towards a political economy of old age', *Ageing and Society*, vol 1, no 1, pp 73–94.

Walker, A. and Foster, L. (2006) 'Ageing and social class: an enduring relationship', in J.A. Vincent, C.R. Phillipson and M. Downs (eds) *The futures of old age*, London: Sage, pp 44–53.

Woodward, K. (1999) *Figuring age: women, bodies, generations*, Bloomington, IN: Indiana University Press.

Wright, E.O. (1978) *Class, crisis and the state*, London: Verso.
Zechner, M. (2008) 'Care of older persons in transnational settings', *Journal of Aging Studies*, vol 22, no 1, pp 32–44.

TWO

Social class structures and social mobility: the background context

Wendy Bottero

Introduction

Class analysis is concerned with the patterning of inequality and its consequences on the lives of those who experience it. As we shall see, 'class' is a slippery concept, with disagreements about its precise meaning. Where there is agreement is that 'class' is a question of advantage and disadvantage – about who gets what, and how. Whether we see this in terms of money, property, occupational position, cultural assets or power and influence, the significance of class resources is in how they give those who possess them greater control over the external forces that affect us all, and open doors that might otherwise be closed. One aim of class analysis is to see how such inequalities persist and endure – over lifetimes and between generations. The question is: if we start off as unequal, are these disadvantages likely to accumulate and be reinforced? Are these disadvantages maintained over our lifetimes or from one generation to the next? However, we must also recognise that the passage of time (such as the life-course transitions associated with ageing, cohort changes from one generation to the next and the longer-term socio-economic changes associated with the shift from industrial to post-industrial societies) makes the question of how class inequalities endure a complicated one to answer. What does class inequality mean in an affluent, rapidly changing society?

Over the past two decades, there has been a strong reaction against the continued relevance of class in understanding post-industrial societies. The coming of a 'late' phase of modernity was characterised by swift and crucial socio-economic transformations. These included the restructuring of economies away from the manual sectors towards the service sectors, the expansion of educational and labour-market opportunities, and the rising significance of affluent, consumption-based lifestyles as the arena in which people's desires and hopes are fulfilled. It is sometimes argued that, as a result, post-industrial societies have become increasingly open, that is, more individualistic, more differentiated and more meritocratic, and that this openness undermines the basis of class inequalities. Supporters of the anti-class brigade argue that such social change has resulted in a radical transformation of societal dynamics so that 'class' is now an obsolete tool for social analysis since, it is argued, we now live in a 'capitalism without classes' (Beck and Beck-Gernsheim, 2002: 205).

Post-industrial societies have experienced major transformations, but a new wave of class theorists insist that these changes do not undermine the role of 'class', but instead open up new avenues for class competition and disadvantage. With the rise of knowledge-based and consumer-oriented economies, access to educational credentials and cultural knowledge is increasingly vital to maintaining or improving social position, so that education and cultural knowledge are assets, much like property or income. Because of this, accounts of class have increasingly looked to the role of cultural and educational resources (as well as economic 'capital') in placing people in the class structure and in reproducing class inequalities. The significance of cultural resources in class inequality also raises questions of class lifestyles, and of how class differences in everyday tastes (in things ranging from the types of food and clothing we like, to our preferences in music, art, decoration, gardening or sports) act as markers of class differentiation and serve as resources in the competition between classes.

This chapter examines the argument that contemporary societies require us to rethink the nature of class inequalities by taking a closer look at the relationship between 'class' on the one hand, and culture, lifestyle and taste on the other. It first considers how social change in post-industrial societies has created a challenge for how we think about 'class', and led some to claim that 'class is dead'. It then explores the counter-reaction by those class theorists who argue that, today, 'class' has a changed and increasingly cultural dynamic, with class inequalities reproduced through affluence and consumption practices and existing within processes of individualisation. Such theorists argue that contemporary times mean we 'need to reconsider the relationship between economic inequalities ... and specifically cultural differences springing from consumption and lifestyles' (Devine and Savage, 2000: 184).

Class inequalities across time

For some analysts, the passage of time in post-industrial societies has made 'class' irrelevant. Before we consider such arguments, just what are the social changes that have created this challenge for how we understand class inequalities? Class analysis is concerned with how inequalities persist and endure, how patterns of advantage (and disadvantage) are transmitted and reproduced *over time*. However, developed economies in the second half of the 20th century experienced a period of rising affluence and sustained economic growth, so many older people looking back over this time period saw an *improvement* in social conditions, personally as well as more generally (Pahl et al, 2007: 9). What has this meant for class inequalities?

Most people's lives are, materially at least, better than their parents' or grandparents': we live longer, experience better health, enjoy more comfortable lifestyles and face expanded opportunities in education and at work. In the post-Second World War period in countries like the US and the UK, an increase in higher-level occupations (in technical, white-collar, managerial and professional jobs) and a contraction in manual jobs (in heavy industry and manufacturing) created a shift to 'post-industrial' societies. This shift created 'more room at the top' in labour markets, so *everybody's* chances of achieving a higher-level job improved, and many studies show substantial social mobility for people from all social origins, including those from working-class backgrounds.[1] Large numbers saw their labour-market position improve in relation to that of their parents. In addition, this movement occurred within the context of a general rise in standards of living, and more affluent consumption-based lifestyles. Geoff Payne spells out the impact in the UK:

> Manual workers in this country now expect to own a car, and a television, to occupy a dwelling of several rooms in good physical condition, to take a holiday abroad, to have several sets of clothing. Such a lifestyle (even if still not available to more than, say, three-quarters of households) would in 1950 have been associated with the middle or upper classes, who made up about one quarter of society. In less than a single lifetime, manual workers have in consumption terms been upwardly mobile, 'even while we're standing still'.... If one compares 1921 with 1991, the contrast is even greater. Because we have continued to think of mobility as class movement in a monolithic way

> across a single dimensional social divide, we have ignored
> the very real change in material experience for the working
> class, a change which however imperfectly also extends to
> improved health, access to education and political rights.
> (Payne, 1992: 220)

Of course, if *most* people are better off, the *relative inequalities* between them may remain unchanged (Erikson and Goldthorpe, 1992). And, in fact, when we look carefully at the transformations in post-industrial societies, we can see remarkable continuities in the pattern of class inequalities and disadvantage. In countries like the UK and US, economic inequality has not only persisted, but increased, since the 1970s, and still has a decisive impact on people's lives. Despite affluence and rising standards of living, class inequalities continue to strongly influence life chances: shaping, among other things, people's life expectancy, their risk of serious illness or disability, their chances of educational success, the quality of their house and neighbourhood, and their risk of falling victim to crime. Class inequalities in one generation bleed over into the next, with the class position of parents influencing the prospects of their children, shaping their child's chances of infant mortality, their risk of ill health and disability, and their success in school and in the labour market. Despite the marked rise in affluence and increasing social opportunities that marked the post-war period, class inequalities persist within the fabric of change.

If one takes health as an example, one notes that despite dramatic improvements in general standards of living (and even where there is provision of free health care), there remain sharp class inequalities in health in most post-industrial societies, not only surviving the jump from absolute to relative poverty, but, in many countries, actually *increasing* over time (Wilkinson, 1996; Marmot, 2004). The lower your socio-economic position, the greater your risk of low birthweight, infections, cancer, coronary heart disease, respiratory disease, stroke, accidents and nervous and mental illnesses. Class inequality is – literally – written on the body. This is not an issue of deprivation alone, because health inequalities run right across society, with every rung in the social hierarchy having worse health than the one just above it. Increasing affluence has meant that the poor have got healthier, but so have the groups above them, and at about the same rate, so the class gap in health remains.

The same pattern exists in relation to expanding labour-market and educational opportunities (Erikson and Goldthorpe, 1992; Goldthorpe, 1996; Breen, 2004). During the period of expansion in higher-level jobs in the labour market, the *relative chances* of individuals from privileged class backgrounds (as opposed to those from more humble backgrounds) achieving a higher-level job remained significantly better. In both education and the labour market, class inequality persists because those from more privileged backgrounds remain more likely to achieve success. The link between social class background and educational attainment has also strengthened over time. Children from higher-class backgrounds are more successful in educational terms, and this is true even when we hold measured 'ability' constant. So, while less advantaged groups have taken up the new opportunities that have opened up in education, training and the labour market, they have still received an unequal share of them in comparison to more advantaged groups, so the relative gap between groups has persisted.

Despite enormous changes in contemporary post-industrial societies, there have been remarkable continuities in patterns of inequality. But this continuity in the face of change gives rise to a very complex picture of inequality, and one that can sometimes be hard to see. This is because class inequalities are not manifested in the *fixed attachment* of people to unequal positions, or in the straightforward *denial* of opportunities to the disadvantaged, but rather emerges in *unequal chances* of success and *lower relative rates* of social mobility. Of course, such relative inequalities, when summed up, amount to a massive gap in the opportunities, experiences and life chances between those at the top and the bottom of class structures. But how well are persisting relative inequalities (in access to education, the labour market, material possessions and income) understood, and do they matter to people?

The complexity of class inequality in the face of social change often means that people may not be fully aware of how such inequalities persist and continue to affect their lives. The concern is that such 'socially structured differences in life chances ... often have their effects "behind the backs" of the people involved and ... may not be reflected in their social awareness or the cultural meanings that they give to their lives' (Scott, 2001: 141). But if affluence and social movement mean that people are less *aware* of class inequalities, does this mean that the *social consequences* of class are also diminished? This is the argument of some thinkers, who claim that post-industrial societies have witnessed the 'death' of class as a social force.

The death of class?

For some thinkers, while people may still occupy class locations, 'the social meaning of inequality has changed' so that the 'attachment of people to a "social class" … has become weaker. It now has much less influence on their actions. They develop ways of life that tend to become individualized' (Beck, 1992: 92). For such theorists, 'class' is seen as a spent social force, with its social base – in the industrial factory production that dominated local communities in the early 20th century – apparently in terminal decline. Rising affluence and labour-market shifts have, so the story goes, given rise to a more diversified society, one based on services and consumption rather than manufacturing and production, and one organised around individual choice and achievement, not class constraints (Beck, 1992; Pakulski and Waters, 1996). Such theorists accept that *economic inequality* has not declined. For Beck (1992: 88), post-industrial society is both highly unequal and also classless: what we have is 'a capitalism without classes' but, instead, with 'individualized social inequality'.

For such critics, it is the translation of economic inequality into social awareness, collective groupings and social identity that is questioned. The claim is that society has become individualised and fragmented, so that the prospects of economic inequality giving rise to class communities, or to collectives who identify with their class interests or share a class consciousness, have receded. A range of class critics see a decline of 'class' in the post-industrial transformations (the decline of large-scale heavy manufacturing, the rise of smaller-scale service employment and the increasing significance of mass consumption and the diversity of consumption practices and lifestyles), which have resulted in a progressive process of *individualisation* that undermines 'class' as a collective, communal feature of social life. The model presented is one of the breakdown of older workplace divisions, and of rising affluence, leading to increasingly complex social differentiation on the basis of lifestyle and consumption choices. Classes are 'crumbling communities of fate' in which 'class communities, neighbourhoods and cultures are eroded and fragmented' (Pakulski and Waters, 1996: 66). For these theorists, while economic inequality remains high, it is experienced in such highly individualised ways that the social meaning of such inequality is minimal. Class critics claim that a 'shifting relationship between class divisions and their social consequences' (Pakulski and Waters, 1996: 66) means that class inequalities no longer give rise to systematic and patterned differences in social identity or to classes as collective social groups.

The increased significance of such consumption differences in social life, and the suggestion that such lifestyle differences result in more fleeting and fragmented social groupings and affiliations, is said to undermine 'class' as the basis of people's social identities, affiliations and communities:

> People with the same income level, or put in the old-fashioned way, within the same 'class', can or even must choose between different lifestyles, subcultures, social ties and identities. From knowing one's 'class' position one can no longer determine one's personal outlook, relations, family position, social and political ideas or identity. (Beck, 1992: 131)

This is not just a question of affluence and rising standards of living, but also the notion that the increasing centrality of consumption in social life allows for the fashioning of a much wider, more fragmented and more transient array of cultural identities than lives centred on production did. Central to such accounts is the notion that 'class' is a collective, communal phenomenon that has been undermined by affluence and individualisation. In the past, it is claimed, classes were not simply economic categories with shared life chances, but also cultural communities, with workmates living alongside and socialising with each other, sharing a common culture and lifestyle. The mining valley or the steel town would be the classic examples of such occupationally formed class *communities*. However, with the rise of service economies and more flexible and fragmented labour markets, 'such communities have progressively disappeared from modern societies' (Pakulski and Waters, 1996: 90), leaving in their wake highly differentiated and ever-changing lifestyles based on consumption.

These arguments have been fiercely disputed. It has been pointed out that while lifestyles may now be individualised and highly differentiated, they remain systematically related to social inequalities, so that:

> Hardly any aspect of human experience – the clothes one wears, the number of siblings one has, the diseases one is likely to contract, the music to which one listens, the chances that one will serve in the armed forces or fall prey to violent crime – is uncorrelated with some dimension of social rank. (DiMaggio, 1994: 458)

On this basis, a newer generation of class theorists reject the claim that affluence, social change and individualisation undermine the relevance of 'class' inequalities. As we shall see, they do concede that 'class' needs to be conceived rather differently in contemporary societies, but argue that 'class' inequalities continue to be reproduced *through* affluence and mass consumption and exist *within* processes of individualisation. They argue that class critics are only able to claim the 'death of class' by adopting a narrow, unduly restricted version of 'class', seen only in terms of economic relations and working-class occupational communities. To understand how 'class' works *now*, they insist, we must stop seeing 'class' in solely economic terms, and recognise that 'class' divisions go beyond the issue of collective social groups.

This alternative framing is sometimes called 'cultural class analysis', because of its broader emphasis on 'class' inequalities as generated in *every* sphere of social life (not just in production or workplace relations) and transmitted through both economic *and* cultural resources (Bottero, 2004; Devine and Savage, 2005). There is less emphasis on class consciousness or class communities as signs of the continuing relevance (or irrelevance) of class inequalities, with analysts instead looking at how ordinary social activities are shaped by class processes, often in an unremarked fashion. *Cultural* class analysis takes as its focus the question of how 'in various settings of social life, processes of inequality are produced and reproduced routinely and how this involves both economic and cultural practices' (Devine and Savage, 2000: 196).

Rethinking 'class' inequalities

In the last 20 years or so, 'class' analysis has been reconfigured into a 'new paradigm' (Savage, 2003). These newer approaches redefine 'class' to include both economic *and* cultural and lifestyle divisions, in effect, fusing class and status elements. Drawing inspiration from the work of the French sociologist Pierre Bourdieu (1984), they see post-industrial societies as providing a very different landscape for 'class' processes to operate, but insist that affluence and cultural differentiation are themselves mechanisms of class inequalities. Bourdieu argues that cultural resources are increasingly important to how inequality works in post-industrial societies, because the consumer-oriented nature of such societies creates 'a social world which judges people by their capacity for consumption, their "standard of living", their life-style, as much as by their capacity for production' (Bourdieu, 1984: 310). Consumption-based economies have resulted in new occupations (in sales, public relations, marketing, advertising, medical and social advice and assistance, cultural production, etc) in which the possession of cultural knowledge is a marketable commodity. Social advancement in such jobs depends less on economic resources than on cultural competences and social connections. Increasingly, cultural knowledge and educational credentials are valued assets in the competitive struggle for class advantage, with cultural resources playing an equivalent role to economic resources in generating class position. This, according to Bourdieu, has 'precipitated a shift in upper-class inheritance practices from one of direct transfer of property to reliance upon the cultural transmission of economic privilege' (Swartz, 1997: 181). More generally, access to educational qualifications has become vital to maintaining position in the social hierarchy, and investment in education and cultural knowledge is a key strategy in class competition.

By making this argument, Bourdieu greatly expands the concept of 'class' to include social and cultural formations, and reconfigures the causal model that historically underpinned older versions of class analysis (class position leads to consciousness and action). Using French data, Bourdieu (1984) shows that – even in an age of affluence – cultural tastes remain systematically and enduringly related to class position, but that the relationship is more complicated than the 'economic cause leading to social effects' model of conventional class theory. For Bourdieu, culture is not an *effect* of class location, but rather a central mechanism by which class positions are *constituted*. Conventional class theory has always maintained that there is a good association between (economic) class location and cultural tastes and lifestyles, but Bourdieu's approach:

> goes beyond the mere demonstration of their association, to explore the ways in which taste may be seen to be a resource which is deployed by groups within the stratification system in order to establish or enhance their location within the social order. (Crompton, 1998: 147)

Such approaches see 'class' operating in the varying ability of individuals to draw on different kinds of resources or 'capitals'. Bourdieu distinguishes four main types: economic capital (material resources: wealth, income, property); cultural capital (cultural knowledge, educational credentials); social capital (social connections, networks, patronage); and symbolic capital (symbolic legitimation). Symbolic capital is rather different from the other main forms of capital, which derive from 'material' resources of different kinds, as it is the power that emerges from the symbolic recognition of other resources (ie from the acceptance of certain types of cultural, material or social resources as being of greater value than others): being the 'prestige, reputation, renown, etc., which is the form in which the different types of capital are perceived and recognized as legitimate' (Bourdieu, 1991: 232).

Bourdieu sees symbolic capital as the disguised form of other types of capital, since it 'produces its proper effect inasmuch as it *conceals* the fact that it originates in "material" forms of capital which are also, in the last analysis, the source of its effects' (Bourdieu, 1977: 183). Bourdieu also mentions other variant types of capital, such as physical capital – work on the body to produce bodily forms with different kinds of symbolic value, such as the toned or muscular body or different kinds of deportment. Bourdieu sees economic and cultural capital as the most important, believing that people 'tend to draw disproportionately from either cultural or economic resources in their struggle to maintain and enhance their positions in the social order' (Swartz, 1997: 137). However, people can also use resources in one kind of capital to convert into resources in another kind (for example, investing in education to convert into economic assets, or using social networks to gain access to cultural resources or economic opportunities).

Bourdieu's model is of people occupying broad regions of the class structure, finely differentiated from each other by their access to different kinds of resources, rather than one of bounded social class 'groups' based on a shared economic situation. Differences in both the *amount* and *type* of capital give rise to different 'class' positions, and people in these positions exhibit systematic differences of lifestyle and taste, which serve as both *markers* of class difference and *resources* in the competitive differentiation of class fractions, since they can act as barriers in processes of social inclusion and exclusion. The complex interplay between variations in the amount and type of capital that people possess gives rise to a large number of class 'fractions' positioned differently and constantly attempting to distinguish themselves from each other. Bourdieu's (1984) analysis of the French class structure identifies a 'dominant' class with high overall levels of capital, but this category is internally differentiated into subgroupings with different combinations of assets. The *bourgeoisie* (business owners and financiers) have high economic capital but lower cultural capital, and exhibit different lifestyles from and limited contact with *intellectuals* (writers, artists, university professors), whose high social position is the result of their high cultural capital. Both are differentiated from a third group of *professionals and senior managers*, who have more balanced levels of cultural and economic capital. There are similar differentiations, or 'fractions', within the 'middle class' (those with more modest overall levels of capital), while the 'working class' is defined by a relative lack of either cultural or economic assets. Other studies, in other countries and at different times, have shown rather different empirical configurations and class relations, but confirm Bourdieu's general point about the role of both economic and cultural resources in generating and differentiating complex class 'fractions' (Savage et al, 1992; Bennett et al, 1999, 2009).

In such approaches to class inequality, cultural tastes and lifestyles are a product of our class backgrounds, a marker identifying our class difference from others, but also a mechanism that helps to maintain social divisions between and within classes. From this perspective, 'class' continues to shape people's social identity (even if perceived in highly individualised ways) because class cultures are now viewed as 'modes of differentiation rather than as types of collectivity' (Savage, 2000: 102). Hence, 'while collective class identities are indeed weak, people continue to define their own individual identities in ways which inevitably involve relational comparisons with members of various social classes' (Savage, 2000: xii). This 'cultural' version of class analysis abandons the notion of distinct class groups or cohesive class identities, and focuses instead on how class inequalities exist in processes of individualised hierarchical differentiation, with people using different valued resources in competitive strategies to advance or maintain their social position, distinguishing themselves from others in the process. On this basis, Savage (2000) argues that far from individualisation entailing the death of class, it actually represents a *shift in how class operates*. Conventional class models that 'focus on class as a collective process [have] neglected how class identities and class processes are bound up with individualised processes' and have missed social changes that have led to 'the reforming of class cultures around individualized axes' (Savage, 2000: xii). For Savage, Bourdieu's arguments 'lead not to an emphasis on class as heroic collective agency, but towards class as implicit, as encoded in people's sense of self-worth and in their attitudes to and awareness of others – on how they carry themselves as individuals' (Savage, 2000: 107).

What this potentially means is that the persistence of inequality is not simply a matter of material advantage and disadvantage; along with it goes a range of attitudes, social relationships and styles of life, so that the persistence of inequality over time is partly about the continual reproduction of these social relationships and styles of life. For cultural class analysts, class inequality is about more than just the economic conditions of people's lives, because – as a question of uneven access to a range of valued social and cultural resources – class relations are also about how some people come to be judged as less prestigious, less worthwhile and less valued or esteemed than others.

Cultural class analysis suggests that processes of lateral or 'sideways' differentiation are centrally bound up with vertical class distinctions, as groups *within* the dominant and middle classes 'are engaging in endless though reasonably genteel battles to assert their own identities, social positions and worth' (Savage et al, 1992: 100). Such battles vary according to the social arenas in which they are played out. Bourdieu argues that social relations are differentiated into a series of 'fields' (eg the political field, the education field, the arts field), each with their own 'stakes' around which contestants struggle and compete for position. The value of different kinds of capital partly depends on the stakes of the field in which one is engaged (eg economic resources may be less helpful for success in the arts field than having the right cultural knowledge or social cachet). So, class advantage is also a question of having the *right* kind of resource for a given field, or else of having the ability to convert another kind of 'capital' into the right kind (being able to convert economic assets into cultural cachet or connections or vice versa).

For analysts influenced by Bourdieu, then, 'class' processes are not simply a question of which groups get access to valued resources, but also reflect symbolic conflicts between groups over the appropriate value to place on different kinds of activities and resources. For example, it is clear that educational credentials are very significant assets in post-industrial societies, but, for Bourdieu, this is the result of social struggles in which groups with a vested interest in education have been able to establish qualifications as increasingly valuable and necessary in social life. A key issue in class relations, then, is the struggles between people to establish *their* resources and practices as the ones that should be recognised and socially valued within different social arenas. Bourdieu argues that the educational success of 'cultural' fractions of the dominant class is not simply a function of their greater access to cultural capital (the advantage of growing up in families with 'serious' books, or being taken to museums as a child), but also because of their ability to ensure that the education system enshrines *their* cultural practices and tastes as the legitimate ones (by placing a higher educational value on, say, the works of Shakespeare or museum culture than on TV or football). Cultural class analysis, then, not only goes beyond the 'economic' by incorporating the effects of culture, but also explores how this is central to the making of class difference, generating new ways of attributing value and producing new forms of exploitation (Skeggs, 2004).

Cultural class analysis sees both cultural and economic resources as central to how people are placed in the class structure, and also redefines 'class' identity from explicit attachment to collective class groups, to much more implicit processes of individualised differentiation and social distance within class hierarchies. This represents a significant break with older, 'conventional' models of class (which saw people's 'class' location as a reflection of their labour-market and employment relations) and rejects the older analytical model in which economic class structure *gives rise to* status (or cultural) differences, to 'instead focus on how cultural processes are embedded within specific kinds of socio-economic practices' (Devine and Savage, 2000: 194). For the newer generation of class theorists, this helps tackle the paradox that class remains structurally important in shaping people's lives in post-industrial societies but often does not seem to translate into consciously 'claimed' cultural or political identities. Class cultures are here viewed as modes of differentiation rather than as types of collectivity, and 'class' processes operate through individualised distinction rather than in social groupings (Savage, 2000: 102).

Conclusion

The need to understand how inequality works in affluent, individualised, consumption-driven economies has led to a range of new ways of thinking about 'class' in post-industrial societies. Such 'cultural' approaches to class have been influential, but result in a very different understanding of how 'class' operates. What are the implications of this for how we think about class processes? The focus of new class theory is on how specific cultural practices are bound up with the reproduction of class inequalities. People do not have to explicitly recognise class issues, or identify with discrete class groupings, for class processes to operate. The emphasis is not on the development (or not) of class consciousness, but rather on the classed nature of a wide range of social, economic and cultural practices.

It is also worth pointing out that not all analysts approve of this move to 'rethink' class analysis into a 'new paradigm'. Such approaches have met with significant criticisms. Chief among these is the claim that 'cultural class analysis' overstates the significance of 'cultural' resources in class processes. Even theorists sympathetic to Bourdieu have suggested that he underestimates the significance of *social* capital (or social networks and connections) in class inequalities (Devine, 2004; Bottero, 2005, 2009). Rather more critical, however, are analysts from conventional approaches to class analysis who argue that it is *economic* relations, not cultural relations, which are central to understanding class inequalities (Goldthorpe, 2007).

Conventional class analysis continues to insist that class positions derive from social relations in *economic life*, particularly from employment relations. Such approaches – often characterised as 'employment aggregate approaches' to class analysis (Crompton, 2006) – categorise people into class groups according to their position in the workplace division of labour. For conventional class theory, class locations are defined by employment conditions, which offer sharp differences in people's economic security, stability and prospects. For those who continue to see 'class' in economic terms, while cultural assets may be significant in *allocating* people to employment positions, the class *locations* themselves are still largely (though not entirely) generated by economic processes (Crompton, 2006).

This, of course, is the issue that is in debate, since the avowed aim of cultural class analysis is to reject the idea that class structures are predominantly generated by economic processes. The question becomes the relative significance that analysts accord to economic versus other factors in explaining class processes. Most analysts would accept that the 'cultural turn' in class analysis has served to point out that 'social classes cannot be adequately conceptualised as economic or material categories alone, but are also characterised by cultural and normative practices that themselves serve to maintain differentiation from other classes and to reproduce class inequalities' (Crompton, 2006: 662). However, there are those who suggest that the 'cultural turn' has gone too far. The relative weight afforded to cultural factors in cultural class analysis is criticised by those who suggest that:

> an over-emphasis on the causal significance of 'culture' in the construction of social life … may lead to what Fraser (2000) has described as 'vulgar culturalism', in which material factors are disregarded and inequalities are seen as being largely a consequence of misrecognised or devalued 'identities'. (Crompton, 2006: 662)

On the other hand, proponents of cultural class analysis argue that the great advantage of their approach is that it allows us to think more broadly about the role of *different kinds* of 'capitals, assets and resources' in processes of inequality (Savage et al, 2005: 43). This, they suggest, allows researchers to look in more complex detail at how class inequalities work, and, in particular, to examine how people's ability to convert *one kind* of resource or asset *into another* (to convert economic assets into cultural cachet or connections, or vice versa) can be used to 'accumulate, store and retain advantages' across different arenas or within periods of rapid social transformation (Savage et al, 2005: 43).

Cultural class analysis directs our attention to how different 'capitals, assets and resources' come to be seen as valuable and how this depends on the stakes of struggle in different social fields. So, for example, there may be some social arenas in which economic assets are decisive for determining social position and prospects, but in other social arenas, cultural assets or social connections may be of more significance. Some resources – such as economic assets – may be more easily converted into others, but there are often limits and restrictions on the accumulation and conversion of advantage. This directs our attention to how processes of general social change, as well as individual social transitions, may affect the accumulation and transmission of inequality, since the advantages that specific assets may bring in one social arena may not translate well to others, and since our investments in certain kinds of assets may become less relevant as their value depreciates over time.

The complicated nature of 'class' in affluent, rapidly changing societies raises some important questions for how we think about the impact of class inequalities in the latter stages of the life course. Clearly, economic resources remain very significant for class inequalities, and the question of how material advantage (and disadvantage) accumulates over the life course and affects the experiences of people in later life and post-retirement is a crucial one. But while it is necessary to consider people's trajectories through occupational class positions and their access to income and wealth over the life course, we must also remember that 'class' inequalities are not solely a question of economic resources or employment relations. Lifestyle inequalities, cultural resources and social connections are clearly very important aspects of the class inequalities in contemporary, affluent, post-industrial societies, and people approaching retirement now will typically have spent their adult lives in societies dominated by affluence, but also by unequal access to consumption-based lifestyles. What is the impact of retirement, or physical ageing, on social lifestyles, and how does later life affect people's access to valued social assets, such as social connections and networks, or cultural knowledge and resources? Do these forms of capital acquire more social value in later life, and how does this depend upon the changing social arenas that people negotiate as they age? In reflecting on the interrelationship between class and ageing, we must take into account the acquisition and conversion of different *kinds* of 'capitals, assets and resources': in acquiring and maintaining social position as people age; in affecting forms of social competition and differentiation among older people; and, more broadly, in confronting the opportunities and challenges that the changes of later life present.

This chapter started by asking what 'class' inequality means in an affluent, rapidly changing society. For some, the challenge of change means that we must reframe the answer to this question, with a new wave of analysts conceptualising 'class' advantage in new and more differentiated ways. However, the central task of this new form of class analysis is not to focus on specifically *cultural* forms of advantage, but rather to explore how inequality continues to be reproduced by people's (varying) ability to draw on a *variety* of valued social currencies (or 'capitals, assets and resources'), which can be accumulated and converted for social advantage within changing social environments.

Note

[1] The slowing expansion of post-industrial economies has led to speculation that intergenerational social mobility has also slowed or declined in the last 20 or so years. However, there is disagreement as to whether the empirical evidence on intergenerational mobility patterns actually supports such claims (Blanden et al, 2004; Ermisch and Nicoletti, 2007; Erikson and Goldthorpe, 2010; Li and Devine, 2011). The long time frame needed to assess mobility across the lifetimes of parents and their children makes such issues difficult to assess for very recent periods, so the jury is still out on this question (Lambert et al, 2008).

References

Beck, U. (1992) *Risk society*, London: Sage.

Beck, U. and Beck-Gernsheim, E. (2002) *Individualization*, London: Sage.

Bennett, T., Emmison, M. and Frow, J. (1999) *Accounting for taste*, Cambridge: Cambridge University Press.

Bennett, T., Savage, M., Silva, E., Warde, A., Gayo-Cal, M. and Wright, D. (2009) *Culture, class, distinction*, London: Routledge.

Blanden, J., Goodman, A., Gregg, P. and Machin, S. (2004) 'Changes in intergenerational income mobility in Britain', in M. Corak (ed) *Generational income mobility in North America and Europe*, Cambridge: Cambridge University Press.

Bottero, W. (2004) 'Class identities and the identity of class', *Sociology*, vol 38, no 5, pp 979–97.

Bottero, W. (2005) *Stratification: social division and inequality*, Cambridge: Polity.

Bottero, W. (2009) 'Relationality and social interaction', *British Journal of Sociology*, vol 60, no 2, pp 399–420.

Bourdieu, P. (1977) *Outline of a theory of practice*, Cambridge: CUP.

Bourdieu, P. (1984) *Distinction: a social critique of the judgement of taste*, London: Routledge & Kegan Paul.

Bourdieu, P. (1991) *Language and symbolic power*, Cambridge: Polity.

Breen, R. (ed) (2004) *Social mobility in Europe*, Oxford: OUP.

Crompton, R. (1998) *Class and stratification* (2nd edn), London: Polity.

Crompton, R. (2006) 'Class and the family', *The Sociological Review*, vol 54, no 4, pp 658–77.

Devine, F. (2004) *Class practices*, Cambridge: Cambridge University Press.

Devine, F. and Savage, M. (2000) 'Conclusion: renewing class analysis', in R. Crompton, F. Devine, M. Savage and J. Scott (eds) *Renewing class analysis*, Oxford: Blackwell, pp 184–99.

Devine, F. and Savage, M. (2005) 'The cultural turn, sociology and class analysis', in F. Devine, M. Savage, R. Crompton and J. Scott (eds) *Rethinking class: culture, identities and lifestyles*, Basingstoke: Palgrave Macmillan.

DiMaggio, P. (1994) 'Stratification, life style, and social cognition', in D. Grusky (ed) *Social stratification: class, race and gender in sociological perspective*, Boulder, CO: Westview Press.

Erikson, R. and Goldthorpe, J. (1992) *The constant flux: a study of class mobility in industrial societies*, Oxford: OUP.

Erikson, R. and Goldthorpe, J.H. (2010) 'Has social mobility in Britain decreased? Reconciling divergent findings on income and class mobility', *British Journal of Sociology*, vol 61, no 2, pp 211–30.

Ermisch, J. and Nicoletti, C. (2007) 'Intergenerational earnings mobility: changes across cohorts in Britain', *The British Journal of Economic Analysis and Policy*, vol 7, no 1, pp 1–37.

Fraser, N. (2000) 'Beyond recognition', *New Left Review*, vol 3, May/June, pp 107-120.

Goldthorpe, J.H. (1996) 'Class analysis and the reorientation of class theory: the case of persisting educational differentials', *British Journal of Sociology*, vol 47, no 3, pp 481–505.

Goldthorpe, J.H. (2007) 'Cultural capital: some critical observations', *Sociologica*, vol 1, no 2, pp 1–22.

Lambert, P., Prandy, K. and Bottero, W. (2008) 'By slow degrees: two centuries of social reproduction and mobility in Britain', *Sociological Research Online*, vol 13, no 1. Available at: http://www.socresonline.org.uk/12/1/prandy.html

Li, Y. and Devine, F. (2011) 'Is social mobility really declining? Intergenerational class mobility in Britain in the 1990s and the 2000s', *Sociological Research Online*, vol 16, no 3. Available at: http://www.socresonline.org.uk/16/3/4.html

Marmot, M. (2004) *Status syndrome: how your social standing directly affects your health*, London: Bloomsbury Press.

Pahl, R., Rose, D. and Spencer, L. (2007) *Inequality and quiescence: a continuing conundrum*, ISER Working Paper 2007-22, Colchester: University of Essex.

Pakulski, J. and Waters, M. (1996) *The death of class*, London: Sage.

Payne, G. (1992) 'Competing views of contemporary social mobility and social divisions', in R. Burrows and C. Marsh (eds) *Consumption and class*, Basingstoke: Macmillan.

Savage, M. (2000) *Class analysis and social transformation*, Buckingham: Open University.

Savage, M. (2003) 'A new class paradigm', *British Journal of Sociology of Education*, vol 24, no 4, pp 535–41.

Savage, M., Barlow, J., Dickens, P. and Fielding, T. (1992) *Property, bureaucracy and culture*, London: Routledge.

Savage, M., Warde, A. and Devine, F. (2005) 'Capitals, assets, and resources: some critical issues', *British Journal of Sociology*, vol 56, no 1, pp 31–47.

Scott, J. (2001) 'If class is dead, why won't it lie down?', in A. Woodward and M. Kohli (eds) *Inclusions and exclusions in European societies*, London: Routledge, pp 127–46.

Skeggs, B. (2004) *Class, self and culture*, London: Routledge.

Swartz, D. (1997) *Culture and power: the sociology of Pierre Bourdieu*, Chicago, IL: The University of Chicago Press.

Wilkinson, R. (1996) *Unhealthy societies: The afflictions of inequality*, London: Routledge.

THREE

Ageing and class in a globalised world

Chris Phillipson

Introduction

Discussions about the role of social class in the lives of older people have, it might be argued, occupied a tenuous position in social research into ageing. This might seem a surprising statement given the concerns of many researchers with issues focused around financial resources, inequality and social exclusion (Scharf and Keating, 2012). Despite the importance of such themes, the tendency has been to examine these only loosely through the lens of social class, with researchers often preferring to emphasise individual characteristics or life histories, other major social statuses (eg gender and ethnicity), or general features associated with the social organisation of age. In consequence, social class has been somewhat marginal to the range of concepts deployed to understand the lives of older people (see Formosa, 2009, for a discussion of the relevance of class analysis to ageing). This chapter develops a number of arguments as to why this might be the case. In addition, it considers whether it tells us anything of wider significance about the way social gerontology has developed. Would a fuller appreciation of social class add anything to our understanding of later life?

Social class and social gerontology

Taking class out of analysis

A starting point – at least in the case of the UK – concerns the position of class analysis within the social sciences and sociology in particular. Debates about social class were of considerable significance in the early history of sociology, drawing upon pioneering surveys undertaken by Charles Booth and Seebohm Rowntree in the 19th and early 20th centuries, together with the economic and political theories of Karl Marx and Max Weber. Savage (2000: 5) argues that adoption of the techniques associated with social class allowed the relatively new discipline of sociology access to a 'recognizable tradition of social scientific enquiry'. This focus served to provide legitimacy to sociological research as well as access to a wider political debate about the social consequences of class-based inequalities, discussions that were especially important in Britain in the 1950s and 1960s (Sandbrook, 2005). The role of social class was an important theme running through work in the field of social policy and was reflected in research on ageing populations during the 1950s. Class inequalities in occupational benefits underpinned the warning from Titmuss (1958) about the likely emergence of 'two nations in old age'. In particular, he contrasted the majority of older people having pensions supplemented by National Assistance with a small group of affluent older people supported through an occupational pension – the gap between the two, he argued, growing wider over time. Social class was a major dimension in Townsend's (1957) *The family life of old people*, where the injustices associated with class position were reflected in the problems faced by working-class men in adjusting to life in retirement.

One can only speculate on the characteristics of social gerontology in the UK today if work on ageing had been a major part of sociology as it developed in the 1950s and 1960s. Certainly, it is conceivable that class analysis would have played an important role in terms of how the lives of older people were studied (Townsend's work was exceptional in this regard), with this research forming a significant legacy for subsequent development in the 1970s and beyond. However, research on social aspects of ageing (beyond that with a welfare and policy orientation) was – at least up until the 1970s – somewhat limited and conducted mainly outside the discipline of sociology. When research in social gerontology did start to expand – through the 1970s and beyond – class theory and analysis was undergoing a period of crisis, gradually losing what had been its central position within British sociology. The precise reasons for this are not the direct concern of this chapter and have in any event been reviewed in some detail by Savage. Briefly, underpinning what Savage (2000: 19) refers to as the 'impasse of class theory' was what he views as 'the exhaustion of the classical tradition', with the failure of Marxist and Weberian perspectives to provide a 'clear theoretical explanation as to how and why class matters'. Instead, the shift in focus in sociology, as reflected in the work of writers such as Beck (1992) and Giddens (1991), was towards what were viewed as processes of 'individualisation', these undermining ascribed positions such as those associated with social class (see also Gilleard and Higgs,

2005). This discussion contributed to ideas about the emergence of the self as a 'reflexive project' (Giddens, 1991: 5), with the emergence of new sources of identity reflected in social and political movements linked with women, gay and lesbian, and black and minority ethnic groups.

Such trends were to become influential – in different ways – to social gerontology as it emerged in the UK. Leaving aside the value and importance of these developments within sociology, they confirmed the limited influence of class analysis within studies of ageing. But the importance of this is less about the narrow issue of class per se and more about the wider structural debates to which class analysis might have contributed. These were absent in much of the social gerontology of the 1970s and 1980s, as reflected in some of the concerns raised by critical gerontology in the 1990s (Phillipson, 1998; Minkler and Estes, 1999). Ideas about class were, in any event, somewhat difficult to assimilate within social gerontology given its focus on what was 'defined *en masse* as a "decommodified" pensioner population' (Gilleard and Higgs, 2005: 60). Despite acceptance of differences within the older population, there was limited acknowledgement of the lifelong effects of given class positions or, indeed, that these might become more pronounced (certainly not less) as the individual moved into old age.

Such characteristics can be related to another important feature of social gerontology in the UK and elsewhere. Hagestad and Dannefer (2001), in an influential essay, highlighted that while concerns with social structure had been central to social gerontology in its early phase of development (notably so in the US), this had become increasingly less the case. They pointed to what they described as the 'persistent tendency towards microfication in social science approaches to aging' (Hagestad and Dannefer, 2001: 4), defining this process as referring:

> to a trend in the substantive issues and analytical foci, what we might call the ontology of social research in aging. Increasingly, attention has been concentrated on individuals in micro-interactions, to the neglect of the macrolevel. Apart from population characteristics, macrolevel phenonomena of central interest to social scientists, such as social institutions, cohesion and conflict, norms and values, have slipped out of focus or been rendered invisible. (Hagestad and Dannefer, 2001: 4)

Life-course analysis emerged as a major theme of work in the 1990s and into the 2000s and, in theory at least, offered the opportunity of integration with structural issues such as social class. However, the emphasis of much of this work – in the UK, US and elsewhere – tended to be upon individual biographies and life histories, these often poorly integrated with broader issues of social structure (Dannefer and Uhlenberg, 1999). Hagestad and Dannefer (2001: 15) pointed to multiple causes behind the emphasis on ageing individuals, these including: 'late modernity's emphasis on individuals and their agency, a steady medicalization of old age, [and] strong pressures from problem-orientated professionals'. Against this, by the 1990s, critical gerontology had emerged to reassert the importance of macro- (and meso)perspectives in the study of ageing, these seemingly bringing to the fore new opportunities for class analysis (Minkler and Estes, 1999). It is to the contribution of critical and related approaches that we now turn.

Bringing class back in

If gerontology (at least in the UK) was largely 'classless' in its assumptions, then the 'turn' towards critical gerontology made some inroads into restoring the concept of class to a more central place in studies of ageing. This was certainly the case in political economy approaches, which pointed out that forms of stratification, such as social class, gender and ethnicity, influenced growing old in numerous (and invariably unequal) ways. Even though older people may have left full-time employment or previously had only a limited role in the labour market, the effects of particular work settings were seen to endure into late old age (Walker, 1980; Phillipson, 1982; Formosa, 2009). This insight was further developed in the *cumulative advantage/ disadvantage* theory of ageing (Dannefer, 1988; Crystal and Shea, 1990; Dannefer and Kelly-Moore, 2009), which highlighted the extent to which predictable patterns of inequality developed as cohorts moved through the life course. This model drew upon a life-course approach but emphasised the interaction between the individual life course, the social structure, economic relations and social policy, these seen to determine the material realities around which later life was constructed.

Following this approach, Crystal (2006) examined the issue of health inequalities and their development over the life course. He argued that while early advantages and disadvantages, such as parental status and formal education, have long-persisting influences, 'it is the resources and events of midlife that are the immediate precursors to late-life economic and health status' (Crystal, 2006: 207). He went onto suggest that:

> By midlife, as well, the relationship between the economic
> and health domains becomes more apparent. The cumulative
> consequences of differences in socio-economic status on
> health are often long-term in nature; they become more
> marked in midlife after decades of exposure to differential
> stresses and risks. Disparities are generated through multiple
> pathways, including socio-economic differences in risky
> health behaviour; differences in access to healthcare ...; and
> differences in occupational stress and occupationally based
> coping resources. (Crystal, 2006: 207)

Social class also re-emerged as an important variable as researchers
moved towards embracing intra- as well as inter-cohort analysis.
Cohort-level analysis had been especially important in demonstrating
the extent to which patterns of ageing could vary over time, allowing
researchers to challenge ideas about later life having a 'normative' or
'natural' trajectory. Nonetheless, emphasis on cohort experiences of
ageing neglected the extent of inequalities (especially those relating to
social class) *within* particular birth cohorts. Here, Dannefer and Kelly-
Moore (2009: 393) make the point that:

> Thus while the analytic tactic of comparing cohorts
> demonstrated the importance of context, it also allowed
> cohorts to stand as virtually *coterminous* with context so
> that the role of social forces operating within each context
> (e.g. regulating heterogeneity and homogeneity) received
> little attention.

The move back to focusing on the role of the social structure within
cohorts provided a way back for recognising the importance of social
class as a factor generating inequalities through the life course. This was
not, it might be argued, entirely incompatible with ideas associated with
what were viewed as trends towards 'individualisation' (Beck, 1992),
the development of new identities associated with what came to be
characterised as 'the third age' (Laslett, 1989), and the importance of
consumption for groups such as the baby-boomer cohort (Gilleard
and Higgs, 2011). Notwithstanding these developments, social class
has continued to play a significant role in influencing life chances in
older age – even more so given the growth of inequalities that have
followed periods of economic growth and subsequent recession in
Western economies (Dorling, 2012). However, the influence of social
class in the lives of older people remains somewhat unclear, with

political economy perspectives and cumulative advantage/disadvantage theory often imprecise about the way in which class operates in the lives of elderly people. For example, how does attachment to particular social classes change over time? What is the intersection with gender and ethnicity? What is the role of broader political processes such as globalisation? This is a major agenda that can only be partially developed in this chapter. The next section, however, develops an argument about changes in the UK context before developing some new areas where a social class analysis might be applied.

The re-emergence of social class

As already suggested in this chapter, the development of social gerontology (in the UK, but elsewhere as well) was based around a 'classless' view of growing old. Clearly, some affluent elders were encountered in studies but these were treated as an exceptional case to a general rule of pensioners tending to share similar economic hardships and often a similar fate of isolation and loneliness. This perspective was subsequently challenged by trends beginning in the 1980s, which suggested both substantial variations in the incomes of older people and importantly also an overall decrease in poverty. One conclusion from this, put forward by Gilleard and Higgs (2005: 60), was that: 'Later life is no longer a site of conflict because of its endemic poverty'. They go further to argue that: 'There is poverty in later life, but poverty is not a defining condition. Rather, the contemporary crisis is over a new image of later life, a crisis of meaning that is exemplified in and by the third age'. According to this line of argument, it is not that class is unimportant, rather, it is simply one of a number of areas of conflict between capital and labour. Gilleard and Higgs conclude that:

> Other sites [of conflict] have emerged, between the interests of global and national capital, between the lifecourses of men and women, between economic prosperity and social legitimation, and between the moral responsibilities of the state and the moral responsibilities of its citizens. The issue of inequality in later life is important *per se*. but it is the changing contexts affecting the (social) nature of later life that are ... of principal concern for the contemporary study of ageing. (Gilleard and Higgs, 2005: 61)

Despite the importance of these arguments, notably, in reminding us about the significance of social and cultural change over the decades of the 1990s and 2000s, it may still be the case that social class remains central in driving the allocation of resources and, hence, the distribution of life chances for older people. Indeed, it could be argued that the restructuring of the life course over the past 20 years has made class *more* rather than less important in respect of its influence upon later life. The reason for this, it might be argued, lies in changes to the life course over the past three decades, these introducing or exacerbating divisions and inequalities within and between groups of older people. From the 1950s to the 1970s, economic prosperity and full (male) employment in Western economies formed the basis of what Best (1980) termed the 'three boxes' of the life course formed around education, work and retirement. Kohli and Rein (1991: 21) subsequently described this regime as follows:

> The modern tripartition of the life course in a period of preparation, one of 'active' work, and one of retirement had become firmly established. Old age had become synonymous with the period of retirement: a life phase structurally set apart from 'active' work life and with a relatively uniform beginning defined by the retirement age limit as set by the public old-age pension system. With the increasing labour participation of women, they too have increasingly been incorporated into the life course regime. (Kohli and Rein, 1991: 21)

By the late 1970s and 1980s, however, the development of a stable life course was brought to an abrupt halt by two interrelated trends: first, the spread of mass unemployment; and, second, the fiscal crisis affecting the welfare states of industrialised countries. The former, while initially strengthening the spread of early retirement, had the more general effect of undermining the idea of stable periods of 'preparation', 'activity' and 'retirement'. The latter called into question the idea of reciprocity between generations, with governments 'talking up' the potential economic burden attached to ageing populations. Both these characteristics become more pronounced with the slide into economic recession following the banking crisis of 2008 – notably, with moves to force longer working (through the raising of pension ages) and through predictions of intergenerational conflict around pressures on the welfare state (Howker and Malik, 2010; Willetts, 2010).

One argument arising from these trends is that the emergence – for a short historical period – of a 'stable' (albeit highly gendered) life course contained (in some cases, concealed) the operation of class forces within old age. Indeed, it was the gendered rather than class-based nature of ageing that was probably the most striking feature of the period from 1950 to 1980 (see further Arber and Ginn, 1991; Estes, 2006). Conversely, developments since the late 1980s might be said to have reconfigured the operation of class-based forces (intersecting with gender and ethnicity) as sites of inequality in old age. This, it might be suggested, is a by-product of what Guillemard (1989: 177) termed the 'deinstitutionalisation' of the life course. She described this process as follows:

> The life course as a process is coming undone. Retirement is no longer a central means of socialisation that determines the identities and symbolic universes of individuals. There is less and less of a definite order to the last phase of life. The life course is being de-institutionalised.

The sociological consequences of this process have yet to be fully appreciated or analysed within social gerontology. In terms of social class, however, it has been highly disruptive – not least in respect of work and retirement transitions. The changes associated with the 'de-standardisation' of the life course served to transform working-class and middle-class work attachments in respect of a stable progression through the life course. In the case of the former, the demise of major branches of manufacturing and the extractive industries undermined the idea of an orderly transition either into work (through apprenticeships or associated routes) or into retirement (Jones, 2011). In the case of the latter, there is what Savage (2000: 140) refers to as the 'individualizing' of the middle-class 'career', with the 'decoupling' of careers from their 'anchorage in bureaucratic hierarchies'. Savage highlights the development of a new model of the career that has now opened up:

> one which is less organized around transitions across class-based thresholds. This new model of career can be seen as breaking from older established class cultures at the same time that it re-encodes class in new, though implicit rather than explicit, ways. While the traditional career linked occupational movements to class thresholds and to life course shifts, so anchoring careers in biographies, contemporary restructuring has disembedded the career from the life course. (Savage, 2000: 139)

One implication of this development is that we are seeing not the demise, but the 're-encoding', of social class in the way that it operates across the life course and within retirement and old age in particular. The next section provides an illustration of this process through the example of pension provision and the potential for new class inequalities to arise from the spread of stock market-based/defined contribution plans. It is an examination of this important area that forms the subsequent section.

Pensions and the social construction of inequality

One argument referred to in this chapter is that the financial circumstances of pensioners have now improved substantially in comparison with previous decades. It is certainly possible to identify positive trends, notably, in relation to the position of older people in relation to other groups in the population. In the UK, for example, on the standard measure of relative poverty, defined as earnings below 60% of contemporary household income, the period over the last two decades has seen fairly consistent falls in pensioner poverty in countries such as the UK. Using a poverty line of 60% of median income, 1.8 million people aged 60–65 are living in poverty after housing costs (AHC) and 2.1 million before housing costs (BHC) (2009/10 figures). From these figures, Jin et al (2011: 55) comment that:

> Pensioner poverty is at its lowest level since the first half of the 1980s. In particular, the rate of pensioner poverty has been lower in 2009–10 in only two years since the start of [a consistent time series] in 1961 using incomes measured AHC and in only three years … using incomes measured BHC.

Class-based inequality remains, however, a significant dimension in social ageing. Property ownership and different sources of income continue to serve as the basis for class divisions in later life similar to that at earlier stages in the life course, reinforced by the class-based nature of occupational benefits. The general point is illustrated in findings on financial and health resources around retirement age in the review by Hills et al (2010), where they demonstrate that, by age 55–64, the top 10% of managerial and higher professionals owned on average £2.1 million in property and pensions, while the bottom 10% of routine/semi-routine workers owned less than £13,000. The distribution of pensioners' incomes in the UK has in fact become wider since 1979, with the increasing value of non-state sources of income leading to a faster growth in incomes towards the top end of the income distribution (DWP, 2008a). As an illustration, median net income per week for retired couples in the bottom fifth of the income distribution was £185 AHC over the three-year period 2007–10, compared with £762 for the top fifth; equivalent figures for single retirees were £95 and £348 (DWP, 2011). The contrasts between groups narrowed somewhat over the 2000s, with a more even distribution of occupational pensions; nonetheless, in 2008/09, 56% of income from such pensions together with annuities were taken up by the top income quintile.

Class inequalities are also likely to grow through changes in non-state pension provision, in particular, the decline of defined benefit (DB) and the corresponding growth of defined contribution (DC) pension schemes. Active membership of occupational pension schemes (both public and private) has reduced from 10.1 million in 2000 to 8.3 million in 2010 – the lowest level since the 1950s (ONS, 2011). There has been a substantial (and – in terms of rapidity – largely unforeseen) decline in membership of DB schemes. In 2000, active members – that is, current employees accruing new benefits – in non-government (private sector) DB schemes totalled *4.1 million*; this figure had dropped to *1.0 million* by 2010 (ONS, 2011). This figure was actually below the modelling assumptions used in the UK Pensions Commission's (2004) first report, which suggested a long-term floor of around 1.6–1.8 million members. Of final salary DB schemes in the private sector, 79% are now closed to new employees (2012 figures), compared with just 17% in 2001 (Phillipson, 2013).

Stock market-based DC plans (occupational and personal) have thus become highly important in transforming the landscape of pensions. However, there is considerable potential in this development for creating new forms of class-based inequalities in old age. Blackburn (2006: 117) summarises the besetting problems of DC schemes in terms of 'uneven coverage, high charges and weak employer commitment'. Wolff (2007) in the US highlights research linking the rise of DCs with greater wealth inequality and limited coverage among low-wage, part-time and minority ethnic workers. Women have particular problems with DCs, with the longevity risk transferred to individual contributors rather than pooled among different groups. Here, Zaidi (2006: 9) observes that although:

> countries have tended to legislate that gender-neutral mortality tables are utilised, there have been practical problems of implementing these annuity regulations with

insurance companies reluctant to offer them and the market proving difficult to kick-start. Thus, the net outcome of these reforms increases the risk that women will continue to have lower pension incomes. (See, further, Blackburn, 2006)

Timmins (2008) highlights the views of one UK investment provider that hundreds of thousands of employees who have been switched out of final-salary pension schemes and into money-purchase products could be on their way to being 'private pension paupers' in old age – with these schemes only replacing around 38% of current salary. This reflects the extent to which employers often contribute fewer resources to their DC plans than is characteristic of traditional DB schemes (see, further, ONS, 2011). Indeed, the switch to DCs is invariably accompanied by a review of contribution levels – usually to the detriment of employees (see Timmins, 2008). DC schemes are a particular problem given findings on the limited understanding about pensions generally – with research in the UK reporting that two thirds of respondents claiming their knowledge as 'very patchy' or that they 'know little or nothing' about pensions (cited in DWP, 2008b). In the US, Munnell (cited in Greenhouse, 2008: 286) observes that:

> Workers have to decide whether to join the [DC] plan, how much to contribute, how much to allocate to what plan, when to change contribution formulas, how to handle things when they move from one job to another. The data show very clearly that many people make mistakes every step of the way.

Zaidi (2006: 10), summarising evidence from Hungary and Poland on the switch from DB to DC schemes, cites surveys showing how most people felt that they were well informed and that information on pension reform was readily available, but the surveys also showed that 'knowledge of the pension system was limited to slogans rather than a deep understanding'. Research conducted by the World Bank also concluded that 'a significant proportion of people simply joined the pension of the first agent they came across' (cited in Zaidi, 2006: 10).

One conclusion from these examples is that instabilities in pension provision look set to introduce new forms of inequality into old age. DC pensions introduce distinctive forms of risk in financial planning for old age, require greater knowledge about the management of pensions and provide more uncertainty given the likelihood of greater insecurity and volatility in employment. These elements – interacting with factors linked to biography and human and social capital – are likely to produce class-related distinctions in pension outcomes for people at the end of their working lives. On the one hand, the daily reality for many groups within the older population remains that of living on a very narrow range of income that almost certainly limits participation within the community: among pensioner couples, 28% have no savings or less than £1,500; among single female pensioners, the figures rises to 45% (DWP, 2011). For single retired households, expenditure on housing, fuel and power, and household goods and services comprises around one quarter of household expenditure, compared with one sixth for two-adult non-retired households with children (2008 figures). Fuel poverty looms as an important issue in the context of climate change and escalating fuel costs. Over 30% of the households of single people aged 60 or over in England (1.0 million) are defined as 'fuel-poor' (Department of Energy and Climate Change, 2009), with, for the very poorest households, evidence that food expenditures in periods of very low temperatures are reduced to pay for extra heating costs (Beatty et al, 2011).

Yet, in contrast with the foregoing, it is also the case that pensioner households – especially those representing part of the baby boom generation of the late 1940s and early 1950s – are using their wealth and assets to transform many aspects of growing old. Gilleard and Higgs (2011: 365) refer to the way in which older people have become engaged in what they term 'complex' forms of consumption, with many retired households able to access a wide variety of domestic goods and build leisure-based lifestyles around these. Indeed, evidence for this is compelling, with examples such as the rise of the 'second-home industry', tourism and the extensive involvement of older people in cultural and educational activities (the latter illustrated by the growth of the University of the Third Age and associated activities).

The social distinctions introduced by complex forms of financial provision in old age underline the point that social class will increase in importance over the coming decades. Moreover, this is likely to be enhanced by the economic and social forces associated with globalisation, some of the key dimensions of which are summarised in the following section.

Understanding class in later life: globalisation and economic change

The argument of this chapter has been that changes to the life course have the potential to introduce new forms of class-based inequalities into old age. The nature of these are, in many respects, still unclear and will almost certainly depend on the way in which economic recession and welfare state restructuring change the lives of those entering as well as those experiencing old age. Intra- as well as inter-cohort variation will be crucial here. Indeed, one conclusion is that understanding the dynamics of the former will become increasingly important for drawing a comprehensive picture of the lives of older people.

Social class must also be positioned within the context of the complex changes introduced by globalisation and the potential of these to enhance inequalities based around class, gender and ethnicity. Debates around the impact of globalisation on aging have been extensive both within the social gerontology literature (see, eg, Baars et al, 2006; Dannefer and Phillipson, 2010) and in studies of social welfare (George and Wilding, 2002; Yeates, 2001). One argument emerging from within gerontology concerns the extent to which globalisation has itself become an influential factor in the construction of old age, notably, in the design of policies aimed at regulating and managing population aging. Although the impact of globalisation remains 'highly contested' (Diamond, 2010), there seems no question that an interdependent world such as that associated with more fluid labour markets and transnational forms of governance creates distinctive pressures and influences across the life course. Much work has still to be done in working out more precisely what these might be and the relative influences on the particular policies of national and global actors. Yeates (2001: 2), for example, suggests that the relationship between globalisation and social policy is best conceived as 'dialectical' or 'reciprocal' and that 'far from states, welfare states and populations passively "receiving" [and] adapting to globalisation ... they are active participants in its development' (see, further, Diamond, 2010). This may be especially the case in the context of the present economic recession, where the role of nation states in managing the crisis, over and against global bodies, appears to have been enhanced.

The processes associated with globalisation have assisted the development of a new approach to ageing societies, based around what Ferge (1997) refers to as the 'individualization of the social'. On the one side, ageing is presented as a global problem and concern; on the other side, the focus has moved towards individualising the various risks attached to growing old. In this context, Young (1999: 6) has interpreted such developments as part of a wider shift from an:

> *inclusive* to an *exclusive* society. That is from a society whose accent was on assimilation and incorporation to one that

> separates and excludes. This erosion of the inclusive world
> … involved processes of disaggregation both in the sphere
> of community (the rise of individualism) and the sphere of
> work (transformation of … labour markets). Both processes
> are the result of market forces and their transformation by
> the human actors involved.

From a sociological perspective, however, writers such as Bauman (1998) have presented the 'human consequences' of globalisation in terms of new forms of exclusion and segregation, especially affecting those in deprived and peripheral communities. Furthermore, Sennett (2006) linked aspects of globalisation – for example the rise of flexible labour markets – to the 'erosion of social capitalism', with older workers increasingly disadvantaged within corporations that emphasise low-wage and low-skill work environments.

All of the preceding carries significant implications for understanding the landscape of social class in later life. The impact of globalisation, alongside and interacting with a transformed life course, has redefined the social context of ageing. The trajectories set by membership of a given social class now have the potential to determine significant areas of life in old age. Population ageing now has to be 'managed' within what has been described as a fluid and deregulated social order (Elliott and Lemert, 2006), opening the possibility for class inequalities to find new forms of expression. Risks once carried by social institutions have now been displaced onto the shoulders of individuals and/or their families. Dannefer (2000: 270) summarises this process in the following way:

> Corporate and state uncertainties are transferred to citizens
> – protecting large institutions while exposing individuals
> to possible catastrophe in the domains of health care and
> personal finances, justified to the public by the claim that
> the pensioner can do better on his or her own.

At the same time, the evidence suggests the widening of inequalities within and between different countries, produced as a consequence of global forces. Rather than leading inexorably to minimum levels of social protection (Moseley, 2007), globalisation has been implicated in the rise in income inequality produced as a consequence of falling relative demand for unskilled labour and the weakened power of labour organisations (Glyn, 2007). The increase in incomes at the very top of the income distribution has been a feature of advanced industrial societies throughout the 1990s and 2000s (Judt, 2009; Dorling, 2012). For those less fortunate, however, there has been the growth of what Sennett (2006) refers to as 'underemployment', this coming alongside constraints on wages and salaries, and both these coming alongside the contraction of jobs accompanying economic globalisation (see, further, Blossfield et al, 2006).

Conclusion

The arguments put forward in the preceding section suggest that globalisation is having a profound impact on the landscape of ageing, not least in terms of influencing new forms of inequality in the structure of daily life. Class, it would appear, along with the other factors identified in this chapter, has returned to play a major role in the experience of ageing. Settersten and Trauten go so far as to suggest that:

> In the future, social class will almost certainly become the most powerful factor in determining aging and life course experiences and in creating 'cleavages' within societies.... Disparities related to social class are growing on indicators of all kinds; inequalities generated by social class will likely trump inequalities that stem from gender, race, and ethnicity and will yield additional power *through* these other statuses. Individuals with adequate resources early in life often accumulate resources over time and those with few or no resources stay the course at best....This results in significant disparities in financial, social and other resources by old age. The chasm between those who do and those who do not have resources leaves people in positions and experiences that are worlds apart. This chasm is likely to persist – and even grow – in the future. (Settersten and Trauten, 2009: 459)

All of this suggests an important research agenda in terms of assessing the way in which social class will influence the quality of life in old age. Some key questions here include: how far will different class trajectories affect patterns of care and support in old age (likely to be a key area given the crisis in funding for residential and social care; for evidence on this point, see Forder and Fernández, 2010). To what extent will class position influence patterns of consumption and access to different forms of leisure? Will the increased role for stock market-based pensions widen inequalities in old age? Will the attempt to extend working life (supported by the raising of pension ages) itself generate new class inequalities based around differential access to remunerative employment? These and many other questions will be important for researchers to address over the coming years. They indicate that we are moving some distance beyond the 'classless' social gerontology that developed over the course of the 1970s and 1980s. Social class has returned to transform daily life in old age; equally, it looks set to change many of the theoretical and policy debates within gerontology itself.

References

Arber, S. and Ginn, J. (1991) *Gender and later life*, London: Sage Books.

Baars, J., Dannefer, D., Phillipson, C. and Walker, A. (eds) (2006) *Aging, globalization and inequality: the new critical gerontology*, Amityville, NY: Baywood.

Bauman, Z. (1998) *The human costs of globalization*, Cambridge: Polity Press.

Beatty, T., Blow, L. and Crossley, T. (2011) *Is there a 'heat or eat' trade off in the UK?*, Working Paper 09/11, London: Institute of Fiscal Studies.

Beck, U. (1992) *Risk society*, London: Sage.

Best, F. (1980) *Flexible life scheduling*, New York, NY: Praeger.

Blackburn, R. (2006) *Age shock: how finance is failing us*, London: Verso.

Blossfield, H.-P., Mills, M. and Bernandi, F. (eds) (2006) *Globalization, uncertainty and later careers*, London: Routledge.

Crystal, S. (2006) 'Dynamics of later-life inequality: modeling the interplay of health disparities, economic resources, and public policies', in J. Baars, D. Dannefer, C. Phillipson and A. Walker (eds) (2006) *Aging, globalization and inequality: the new critical gerontology*, Amityville, NY: Baywood, pp 205–14.

Crystal, S. and Shea, D. (1990) 'Cumulative advantage, cumulative disadvantage and inequality among elderly people', *Gerontologist*, vol 30, no 4, pp 437–43.

Dannefer, D. (1988) 'Differential gerontology and the stratified life course: conceptual and methodological issues', in G.L. Maddox and M.P. Lawton (eds) *Annual review of gerontology and geriatrics*, New York, NY: Springer, pp 3–36.

Dannefer, D. (2000) 'Bringing risk back in: the regulation of the self in the postmodern state', in K.W. Schaie and J. Hendricks (eds) *The evolution of the aging self: the societal impact on the aging process*, New York, NY: Springer, pp 269–80.

Dannefer, D. and Kelly-Moore, J. (2009) 'Theorising the life course: new twists in the paths', in V.L. Bengston, D. Gans, N. Putney and M. Silverstein (eds) *Handbook of theories of aging* (2nd edn), New York, NY: Springer, pp 375–88.

Dannefer, D. and Phillipson, C. (2010) (eds) *Handbook of social gerontology*, London: Sage Books.

Dannefer, D. and Uhlenberg, P. (1999) 'Paths of the life course: a typology', in V.L. Bengston and K.W. Schaie (eds) *Handbook of theories of aging*, New York, NY: Springer, pp 306–26.

Department for Energy and Climate Change (2009) *UK fuel poverty strategy – the annual report*, London: DECG.

Diamond, P. (2010) *How globalisation is changing patterns of marginalisation and inclusion*, York: Joseph Rowntree Foundation.

Dorling, D. (2012) *Injustice: why social inequality persists*, Bristol: The Policy Press.

DWP (Department for Work and Pensions) (2008a) *Pensions Bill – impact assessment*, London: DWP.

DWP (2008b) *The pensioners' income series 2006–07*, London: DWP.

DWP (2011) *Family resources survey 2009/2010*, London: DWP.

Elliott, A. and Lemert, C. (2006) *The new individualism: the emotional costs of globalization*, London: Routledge.

Estes, C. (2006) 'Critical feminist perspectives, aging and social policy', in J. Baars, D. Dannefer, C. Phillipson and A. Walker (eds) *Aging, globalization and inequality: the new critical gerontology*, Amityville, NY: Baywood, pp 81–102.

Ferge, Z. (1997) 'The changed welfare paradigm: the individualization of the social', *Social Policy and Social Administration*, vol 31, no 1, pp 20–44.

Forder, J. and Fernández, J.-L. (2010) 'The impact of a tightening fiscal situation on social care for older people', PSSRU Discussion Paper 2723, Kent University.

Formosa, M. (2009) *Class dynamics in later life: older persons, class identity and class action*, Hamburg: Lit Verlag.

George, V. and Wilding, P. (2002) *Globalization and human welfare*, London: Palgrave.

Giddens, A. (1991) *Modernity and self-identity: self and society in the late modern age*, Cambridge: Polity.

Gilleard, C. and Higgs, P. (2005) *Contexts of ageing: class, cohort, community*, Cambridge: Polity Press.

Gilleard, C. and Higgs, P. (2011) 'Consumption and aging', in R. Settersten and J. Angel (eds) *Handbook of sociology of aging*, New York, NY: Springer, pp 361–78.

Glyn, A. (2007) *Capitalism unleashed*, Oxford: Oxford University Press.

Greenhouse, S. (2008) *The big squeeze: tough times for the American worker*, New York, NY: Knopf.

Guillemard, A-M. (1989) 'The trend towards early labour force withdrawal and the reorganisation of the life course', in P. Johnson, C. Conrad and D. Thomson (eds) *Workers versus pensioners: Intergenerational justice in an ageing world*, Manchester: Manchester University Press, pp 163-180.

Hagestad, G. and Dannefer, D. (2001) 'Concepts and theories of aging: beyond microfication in social science approaches', in R. Binstock and L. George (eds) *Handbook of aging and the social sciences* (5th edn), San Diego, CA: Academic Press, pp 3–21.

Hills, J., Brewer, M., Jenkins, S., Lister, R., Lupton, R., Machin, S., Mills, C., Modood, T., Rees, T. and Riddell, S. (2010) *An anatomy of economic inequality in the UK: summary*, London: Government Equalities Office/Centre for Analysis of Social Exclusion.

Howker, E. and Malik, S. (2010) *How Britain has bankrupted its youth*, London: Icon Books.

Jin, W., Joyce, R., Phillips, D. and Sibieta, L. (2011) *Poverty and inequality in the UK: 2011*, London: Institute for Fiscal Studies.

Jones, O. (2011) *Chavs*, London: Verso.

Judt, T. (2009) *Ill fares the London*, Land: Allen Lane.

Kohli, M. and Rein, M. (1991) 'The changing balance of work and retirement', in M. Kohli, M. Rein, A-M. Guillemard, and H. Van Gunsteren (eds) *Time for retirement: Comparative studies of early exit from the labour force*, Cambridge: Cambridge University Press, pp 1-35.

Laslett, P. (1989) *A fresh map of life*, London: Weidenfield & Nicolson.

Minkler, M. and Estes, C. (eds) (1999) *Critical gerontology*, Amityville, NY: Baywood Press.

Moseley, L. (2007) 'The political economy of globalization', in D. Held and A. McGrew (eds) *Globalization theory*, Cambridge: Polity Press, pp 106–25.

ONS (Office for National Statistics) (2011) *Occupational pension schemes survey 2010*, London: ONS.

Pensions Commission (2004) *Pensions: Challenges and choices. First report of the Pensions Commission*, London: The Stationery Office.

Phillipson, C. (1982) *Capitalism and the construction of old age*, London: Macmillan Books.

Phillipson, C. (1998) *Reconstructing old age*, London: Sage Books.

Phillipson, C. (2013) *Ageing*, Cambridge: Polity Press.

Sandbrook, D. (2005) *Never had it so good: a history of Britain from Suez to the Beatles*, London: Little Brown.

Savage, M. (2000) *Class analysis and social transformation*, Buckingham: Open University Press.

Scharf, T. and Keating, N. (eds) (2012) *From exclusion to inclusion in old age: a global challenge*, Bristol: The Policy Press.

Sennett, T. (2006) *The culture of the new capitalism*, New Haven, CT: Yale University.

Settersten, R. and Trauten, M. (2009) 'The new terrain of old age: hallmarks, freedoms and risks', in V.L. Bengston, D. Gans, N. Putney and M. Silverstein (eds) *Handbook of theories of aging* (2nd edn), New York, NY: Springer, pp 455–69.

Timmins, N. (2008) 'Paupers warning over private pensions', *Financial Times*, 30 May, p 4.

Titmuss, R. (1958) *Essays on 'the welfare state'*, London: George Allen & Unwin.

Townsend, P. (1957) *The family life of old people*, London: Routledge & Kegan Paul.

Walker, A. (1980) 'The social creation of dependency in old age', *Journal of Social Policy*, vol 9, no 1, pp 45–75.

Willetts, D. (2010) *The pinch*, London: Atlantic Books.

Wolff, E. (2007) 'The adequacy of retirement resources among the soon-to-be-retired', in D. Papadimitriou (ed) *Government spending on the elderly*, London: Palgrave.

Yeates, N. (2001) *Globalisation and social policy*, London: Sage Publications.

Young, J. (1999) *The exclusive society*, London: Sage Publications.

Zaidi, A. (2006) *Pension policy in EU25 and its possible impact on elderly persons*, Vienna: European Centre for Social Welfare Policy and Research.

FOUR

Measuring social class in later life

Alexandra Lopes

Introduction

The interaction between later life and social class has been measured from two opposite standpoints. The first tends to place 'old age' on the side of the independent variables and highlights how retirement arises as a trigger of loss and a factor of downward social mobility. This loss is substantiated in different aspects, not only the loss of income and material security as a direct result of exiting the labour market, but also loss as an indirect result of: growing unmet needs for material resources; declining health and needs for care; rising costs of living coupled with the deterioration of pension systems; loss of social status as a result of the weakening of social networks and social participation; loss of energy and enthusiasm, often as a result of deteriorating health; as well as dissolution of workplace-based networks, leading to isolation. The second approach to how later life intersects with social class tends to place the latter on the dependent variable side. It highlights the social trajectories of becoming 'old' and is more focused on how past class trajectories become determining factors of the way individuals experience the ageing process. This view is more concerned with analysing how the material and social conditions associated with different class positions act as significant discriminators in retirement, and explaining inequalities and differences in a variety of aspects of individual and group life. Irrespective of the functional role assigned to social class in social theory on ageing, most scholars tend to base their operational definitions of the concept in the well-established typologies of social class, and without taking into consideration the need to assess how well those typologies perform when applied to older groups. The starting question of this chapter is: 'How can we measure social class in later life?'. It is a question worth asking at the current stage of development of social theories on ageing, even though we do not have a straightforward answer.

The goal of this chapter is to discuss the concept of social class in its appropriateness to analyse inequalities and social divisions with the specific goal of clarifying how well existing empirical measurement tools of the concept perform when addressing older people's lives. We are fully aware of the ideological baggage carried by the concept of social class and the contentious vocabulary that marks deep divides among social class scholars. We will not take sides in such disputes, but instead try and work with different approaches to the conceptualisation of class in an effort to identify what dimensions of analysis perform better when analysing social class dynamics in later life. This chapter is organised into three sections. It starts with a general overview of how the concept of social class has been used in the field of ageing studies and a summary about the schools of thought that have been more influential in the way the concept of social class has been called into the analysis of inequalities in old age. The second section of the chapter takes us to a discussion about the main difficulties and paradoxes one finds in the way traditional social class typologies perform when used to measure the class position of older people, and the structural reasons underlying such choices. The third and last section opens up to alternative ways of thinking about social class measurement in old age. It puts forward calls for a multidimensional approach to the measurement of social class in old age, one that remains faithful to the main theories on social class analysis while expanding the empirical analysis of class to accommodate two key operational elements. The first captures the relationship between social class and well-being, and, therefore, tackles the material dimension of social class. The second highlights the relationship between social class and social participation, and, hence, is more related to viewing social class as power and prestige.

The concept of social class in ageing studies

The foundational theories of social class and stratification that developed in the early 20th century were motivated by the problems of new modern societies emerging from industrial capitalism. Not surprisingly, they restricted their empirical universe to workers and capitalists, agents actively engaged in production, and therefore the population of individuals of active age. Other groups, such as the older, but also the physically impaired or the mentally disabled, were left to the margins of social class analysis, either because they had a meagre weight in the overall demographic composition of the population or because they were excluded from the labour market. In the specific case of older people, and considering the disproportional weight of women in this group of the population, the traditional difficulties of social class theories to accommodate the gender issue have further contributed to a general lack of interest from scholars in older people as an object for social class analysis and development.

Despite this age-aversion in its foundational moment, the concept of social class remains a resilient leading concept in the broad field of ageing studies (Formosa, 2009). Indeed, we can easily spot it playing a central role in many studies even outside the scope of sociological analysis. However, and even though everybody acknowledges that contemporary societies have been experiencing dramatic changes in their demographic composition, namely, with the intensification of demographic ageing (and all that entails for the broad social system), social class theorists have not felt challenged by the need to improve the performance of the concept of social class to revise it to accommodate the specificities of growing shares of older people in the population. On the contrary, what we have been witnessing in the broad scope of social theory is a rather uncritical use of the concept of social class. This can be seen in research carried out in disciplines such as gerontology, social policy, health policy and even sociology of ageing, where researchers have been systematically bringing on board the research designs of the mainstream formats of social class typologies and analysis.

A large number of scholars, namely, those closer to the North-American school of thought, have been using the Marxist-inspired typologies of class, with a clear dominance of the proposals of Olin Wright (Krieger et al, 1999). Herein, social classes are conceptualised as stable positions in the social space that are structurally determined by the sphere of social relationships of production. This means that measuring the class position of older people, namely, of those that are already out of the labour market, involves the identification of the last registered situation in the labour market. It also means that the empirical indicators with which one works are those that classify the relation each individual had with the means of production, and with the instruments of control and authority, while actively engaged in the labour market. On the other hand, among authors that are more influenced by the European tradition, we more often see the use of typologies of class inspired by the Weberian view, although with some Marxist influence as well, as is the case with the so widely used Goldthorpe scale (Matthews et al, 2006). Herein, social class is mainly derived from classifications of professions and is often labelled as socio-economic status. The assumption is, of course, that modern societies are hierarchical systems of power and prestige that determine to a very large extent the conditions of existence of individuals. Yet, similar to the typologies influenced by the work of Olin Wright (1979), these occupational scales are also translated into last recorded job when the measurement of social class is done among older people.

It is not the aim of this chapter to go into much depth in the discussion about the roots and the doctrinal implications of all these different theories, and even less to go into the more specific issue of how these theories have been incorporated into research taking place in different national contexts. The argument put forward in this chapter is that the use of social class typologies as they were originally developed, considering that they were conceived by reference to the active age population and the blooming period of industrial capitalism, is replete with paradoxes and difficulties that necessitate some theoretical and methodological revision of the concept of social class itself. The next section addresses some of these challenges and paradoxes.

Paradoxes in social class typologies as applied to older groups

One of the first questions that needs to be asked if we are to discuss what is so specific about measuring social class in later life is the following: what is the rationale of measuring social class from a set of indicators that are directly related to trajectories and positions in the labour market, even after the individual has left the labour market? Social class measurement is grounded in the assumption that individuals are connected in distinct manners to mechanisms of income and power creation as a result of their place in the sphere of economic production. These different manners in turn translate, objectively and subjectively, into different economic opportunities and/or into different levels of control over resources, material and immaterial. It is in these opportunities and resources that rest the origins of differences in living conditions, in ways of social participation, in interests and so on. The last registered occupation as an indicator to classify the social class position of retired older people is argued to be the best proxy to capture the set of opportunities each individual had (or did not have) to acquire control over a set of resources (material and immaterial) originated in the sphere of economic production. Therefore, this almost quintessential tie between social class and relationships of social production/professions applied to the older population draws on a critical premise, namely, the reproduction of the conditions that describe the moment when the individual exits the labour market throughout the rest of his/her life, irrespective of how long that last phase of life lasts and irrespective of what happens to the individual throughout that period of time. It is this premise that we want to question in this chapter. Three main reasons motivate us to do so.

The first reason concerns the growing tensions in labour-market dynamics that impose radical changes on the traditional mechanisms of labour-market exit for older workers. Up to the middle of the 1990s, we could identify across the majority of the developed nations three main exit trajectories for older workers: unemployment social benefits, disability social benefits and early retirement benefits. These different mechanisms, isolated or combined, were frequently used as a strategy for a smooth move from the labour market to the status of pensioner with access to full pension entitlements. In the last two decades, and despite some contradicting political discourses, we have been experiencing, especially at the European level, a significant pressure to put an end to this 'exit culture', which ends up translating into a growing diversity of ways of exiting the labour market, especially among older workers (Conen et al, 2012). Measuring social class from the last recorded position in the labour market becomes, as a result, a risky exercise. In times where the changes in labour-market dynamics are so profound and when traditional notions of career and professional trajectory are being questioned (both being traditionally taken as stable in nature by classic typologies of social class), it is expected that the last recorded position in the labour market will show a weak discriminatory capacity to identify in a satisfactory manner the core characteristics of the ties each individual had with the labour market throughout the life course and the paths of opportunities and disadvantages that were accumulated throughout.

This brings us to a second line of questioning. Changes in labour-market dynamics are strongly associated with another type of changes, the ones taking place as a result of the general movement towards the retrenchment of social policies and the welfare state. This has prompted some researchers to estimate the impacts that will be felt by the older population as a result of the weakening of the traditional systems of social protection, and of pension systems in particular, all evidence suggesting that the ability of older groups to adapt to the withdrawal of social benefits will largely depend of their ability to generate resources outside the framework of public social protection (Rosnick and Baker, 2012). The traditional social class typologies were firmly grounded in the premise that the institutional framework of social protection systems, themselves forged in the milieu of social relations of production, guarantees to a large extent the reproduction of the conditions that characterise the place of individuals in the labour market even after their exit from the labour market due to mandatory retirement policies. The changes that have been accumulating in the traditional mechanisms of social protection across Europe suggest that older people will be asked to shoulder more responsibilities for their income and well-being, accommodating to lower benefits and generating resources outside the social protection framework. To fully grasp the relative position of older people in the social class hierarchy, it is increasingly important to bring on board the concept of the degree of ability individuals hold to protect their status outside the framework of public social protection.

A third issue concerns the structural changes experienced by contemporary societies, and, more specifically, changes in family dynamics. Underlying most typologies of social class is an ideal-type of family structure – that is, the stable married couple (mother and father) with dependent children – a model of family formation that remains very important statistically but that one can hardly argue remains the norm. If anything, scholars interested in analysing family dynamics have been showing how things have changed in the field of family formation, with the emergence of a plurality of family models. Classic social class analysis has always been grounded in the premise that social class defined throughout the life course is reproduced in old age via stable family structures, a premise that will hold with increasing difficulty for growing shares of the older population.

On the basis of the aforementioned three issues, one must ask: how can we enrich the concept of social class to describe the relative position of older people in the hierarchical systems of inequalities of contemporary societies? Attempting to come to terms with such a query is the goal of the remaining sections in this chapter.

A multidimensional approach to measuring social class in old age

To formulate alternative operational definitions of social class that take into consideration the challenges of using the concept applied to older persons, it is important to start by asking what could be considered the foundational question for the entire debate on social class analysis – 'Why do we want to measure social class?' – a candid but, nevertheless, complex question to counter.

One possible solution is to research the distribution of inequality in later life, with a strong emphasis on material disparities. This involves measuring social class as a gradient that translates into resources that are unevenly distributed. Underlying this approach is the belief that social class is a building block of the opportunities individuals have (or do not have) throughout the life course and the premise that the trajectories of accumulation of advantages/disadvantages that social class embeds are essentially determined by individual trajectories in the labour market. Researchers call for the concept of social class in their research designs by looking for a measurement of the degree of control over resources older individuals display using as a proxy the trajectories of accumulation of advantages and/or disadvantages associated with previous positions in the labour market. However, we argue that if that is the purpose of measuring social class, then the concept has to evolve to measuring more objectively and directly the degree of control over resources. Indeed, the conceptualisation of social classes as paths of opportunities forged in the labour market measured as last recorded job does not allow to measure directly the amount, composition and durability of the material and social resources each individual controls.

A better, and more comprehensive, solution as to why gerontologists may want to measure social class is to develop an operational definition of social class that combines a dynamic approach to trajectories in the labour market with indicators of control over resources, material and immaterial. The rationale is to extend the underlying assumptions of classic social class analysis and look for functional equivalents in old age to what individuals collect from their status as active members of the labour market when they are younger. In order to illustrate our arguments we have run some empirical demonstrations using data from the *European Quality of Life Survey* (EQLS) for the year 2007 (Eurofound, 2009).[1] Considering the overall purpose of this chapter, the empirical material introduced in the next paragraphs serves the exclusive goal of illustrating some theoretical and methodological arguments, and at no point can be used to identify trends in the composition of the European older population.

Material resources: measuring financial vulnerability

The indicator we suggest to measure material-built capacity and financial vulnerability is to combine last recorded job with mechanisms of income protection. The underlying argument for this can be stated in the following manner: if it is true that the place of individuals in the social spectrum defined as professions determines to a large extent the opportunities and strategies they have at their disposal to accumulate and control resources, it is also true that the extent to which those opportunities actually materialise into objective conditions is unaccounted for if one rests the measurement solely on the identification of the profession. More than the subjective scenarios of opportunities that are created within the universe of professional groups, it is the material expression of those opportunities that will determine living conditions in old age and the ability of individuals to protect their status throughout the increasing number of years that they are expected to live outside the labour market. The purpose is not to include the individual drivers that may influence behaviours or any effect of professional socialisation in the decisions individuals make throughout life (although one could easily accept this approach as a promising one). The argument is of a different nature and aims at highlighting the way professional status is embedded in institutional frameworks of social protection that are very important to describe in a satisfactory manner the resources older people actually control. We suggest considering in particular the material capacity that has been built using two indicators: income from savings/investments to top up pension income and home-ownership.

The EQLS2007 data set we have analysed shows a distribution of income sources of older people and shows that pensions rank high as the main source of income (87.7% of respondents declared that they are the main source of income for the household). Moreover, some 21% of the respondents declared that they also have income from savings/investments to top up pension income. Looking in particular at these 21% (see Table 4.1), the relatively clear matching with the distribution of last job recorded along trends that follow what could be considered the expected direction for the statistical association is noticeable (with a peak of 63.5% among employed professionals and a low of around 11% among manual workers, both skilled and unskilled). This certainly reinforces the idea that different statuses in the labour market translate into different income opportunities. The same holds for home-ownership, which, as several authors have already demonstrated, is a very important asset that can be mobilised to cushion for age-related demands, namely, in the field of care servicing (Elsinga and Mandic, 2010). In times of retrenchment of welfare benefits, it is a statement that bears additional relevance.

Generally, the data for the two indicators provide evidence for the general hypothesis of positive association between socio-economic status in the labour market and the capacity to build mechanisms of income protection and wealth. A more detailed analysis, though, points to some elements worth considering. On the one hand, overall, there is a high dependence of older people who were 'employees' on public mechanisms of income protection. It is among those that were either proprietors or liberal professionals that we see significant shares of income coming from savings and/or investments. On the other hand, the relative high weight of home-ownership across the different professional groups is noticeable, differences across groups most likely stemming from differences in terms of type and market value of properties. This is an indicator to use with some caution and that should be complemented by information on the value of property in terms of potential to turn into an active resource. In the absence of that information, we suggest combining the indicators on built material capacity with the assessment of the financial capacity of the individual in terms of liquidity.

Table 4.1: Proportion of older people who own their homes and have additional sources of income, defined by last recorded job

Last recorded job	% who have additional sources of income from savings/interests	% who are home-owners
Business proprietor	46.88	87.70
General management	45.06	78.90
Professionals	37.21	74.40
Employed professionals	63.49	84.10
Middle management	30.71	73.10
Self-employed	33.33	89.40
Employed position at a desk	24.40	71.60
Employed position, not at a desk, but travelling	17.50	63.30
Employed position, not at a desk, but in a service	17.50	69.60
Supervisor	24.75	78.20
Skilled manual worker	11.05	72.20
Other (unskilled) manual worker, servant	11.34	58.60
Total	21.00	74.40

Source: Author's calculations based on data from EEQLS, 2007, in Eurofound, 2009.

Following arguments previously introduced (Lopes, 2011), we also contend that social class analysis should find ways to include in its empirical formulations a series of indicators of financial material support, in line with the proposals of Townsend (1987). These indicators also represent trajectories of opportunities (or lack of them) to accumulate resources, but they provide a more clear measurement given that they are observed at the arrival point of those trajectories. We have argued before and maintain that there is a wide potential for cross-fertilisation between social class theories and the social indicators approach (Lopes, 2011). If there is some underdevelopment in terms of empirically oriented tools to the first, there is some frailty in the theoretical foundations of the second. Combined, they can provide a clearer picture about the depth and social origins of the inequalities that can be observed in the material conditions of the lives of individuals.

Table 4.2: Proportion of individuals in extreme positions on deprivation index in each social group, defined by last recorded job

Last recorded job	% with no essential item missing	% with five or six items missing
Business proprietor	92.30	0.50
General management	91.30	1.30
Professionals	86.00	0.90
Employed professionals	84.40	–
Middle management	85.70	1.20
Self-employed	75.40	2.50
Employed position at a desk	77.50	2.00
Employed position, not at a desk, but travelling	68.10	1.80
Employed position, not at a desk, but in a service	67.20	2.50
Supervisor	79.00	0.20
Skilled manual worker	61.30	4.40
Other (unskilled) manual worker, servant	48.30	2.90
Total	**70.50**	**2.40**

Source: Author's calculations based on data from EEQLS, 2007, in Eurofound, 2009.

From a more detailed reading of the results displayed in Table 4.2, we would pinpoint one element that we find particularly meaningful. It should be noticed that it is among 'employees' (manual workers in general and employed positions) that we find the lowest shares of non-deprivation, pointing to a more likely state of financial vulnerability of some sort. This means that the discrimination operated by professional group will inflate the social differentials that in fact exist among individuals at the lowest quadrant of the social scale, which are otherwise much more similar if classified according to their financial vulnerability.

All empirical trends in the selected indicators seem to converge on the belief that some social groups are better equipped than others in terms of the material resources individuals control, which one could argue reinforces the validity of traditional social class typologies. Our argument is complementary rather than opposing this. We propose measuring directly the built material capacity and the financial vulnerability that professional trajectories have made available in an attempt to provide for a better operational predictor of how social class positions influence a series of aspects of the lives of older people. This approach, however, will remain incomplete if it is not combined with the assessment of the immaterial resources that individuals build up throughout their lives and that can operate as important cushions for the material vulnerabilities associated with old age.

Social and symbolic capital: measuring social deprivation

It is particularly relevant to include in the concept of social class some considerations about the density of the available social networks (family, neighbourhood, former work colleagues) that individuals may activate in pursuit of answers to their needs and objectives. Additionally, the concept of social class should also find room to accommodate indicators of participation in the community, for example, participation in voluntary organisations. This is a critical dimension of differentiation among individuals that are no longer integrated in the labour market but not entirely deprived from the possibility to invest in creating opportunities to generate resources (although of an immaterial character) that may translate into opportunities.

To illustrate this argument, and using the indicators available in the EQLS2007 data set, we suggest composing an index of social capital that involves the consideration of three layers of social networking: the close family network (children in particular); the proximity network of friends and neighbours; and the community network understood in terms of participation in community organisations (Table 4.3). Contrary to what resulted from the distributional inequalities in material assets, which are highly aligned with the hierarchy of socio-economic status as measured by occupational status, the distributions of relational capital seem more even when it comes to close family and proximity networks. This confirms the general argument about the importance of family and a close network of friends and neighbours in people's lives irrespective of their social class, but less so when it comes to the indicator of participation in community/voluntary organisations, where the reproduction of the occupational divide is more clear.

Hence, our proposal involves plotting social life conditions to understand outcomes in old age as social class differentials. It is, we believe, a methodologically promising approach that adds multidimensionality to material indicators of social class. It is in this multidimensionality that rests the explanation for the full discrimination potential of social class in old age rests: older people have their life chances defined by the path of accumulation of (dis)advantages that characterise their social trajectories in a social–occupational group, but the materialisation of those (dis)advantages will have different compositions and durability and therefore offer different opportunities in their ability to protect the socio-economic status of the individual as age progresses.

Table 4.3: Descriptives for dimensions of social networks within social groups, defined by last recorded job

Last recorded job	% who have no children	Contacts with children		Contacts with friends and neighbours		% engaged with voluntary organisations
		Strong	Weak or none	Strong	Weak or none	
Business proprietors	7.7	64.60	12.30	81.80	3.00	32.30
General management	9.8	51.90	17.20	76.10	1.20	53.70
Professionals	11.4	69.70	11.60	75.00	15.90	34.90
Employed professionals	6.3	49.20	7.90	85.70	–	50.80
Middle management	13.5	48.40	17.10	87.00	1.70	39.60
Self-employed	8.2	64.90	18.30	77.00	6.70	19.70
Employed position at a desk	17.4	57.70	21.60	82.60	6.90	31.30
Employed position, not at a desk, but travelling	11.7	71.10	12.40	85.70	7.60	19.30
Employed position, not at a desk, but in a service	11.4	65.80	15.80	86.80	2.50	27.60
Supervisor	7.9	68.40	9.20	85.10	2.00	25.00
Skilled manual worker	13.4	68.10	16.00	85.20	3.40	16.40
Other (unskilled) manual worker, servant	10.3	66.00	16.00	84.40	3.60	16.90
Total	**11.9**	**61.90**	**16.40**	**83.90**	**3.90**	**27.00**

Source: Author's calculations based on data from Eurofound (2009).

Multidimensional predictors

The argument that we have been trying to sustain consists of two main points. On the one hand, we argue that social class in old age, understood as material opportunity, is very helpful to unravel how some individuals become trapped in a pathway of accumulation of disadvantage (if considering those in weaker positions in terms of the resources over which they have some control), and how little room they have to improve their situation and deal with the age-specific hazards that may occur. On the other hand, we contend that material opportunity needs to have its impacts controlled by non-material opportunity. This last factor can either diminish or increase the vulnerability of the older person and therefore becomes a building block of the relative position the individual holds in the hierarchical community. This argument, however, will only hold if this multidimensionality proves efficient as a predictor in fields where traditional typologies of social class have been somehow fuzzy.

For the purpose of demonstration, we have adjusted three logistic regression models to explain the likelihood of three conditions being observed: the older person declaring chronic illness or disability; the older person declaring having difficulty paying for medical care; and the older person declaring feeling happy about life (Table 4.4). For each outcome variable, the same set of independent indicators were considered: age; social group defined from last recorded job; social capital; built material capacity; and financial vulnerability.[2] The hypothesis to be tested concerns the performance of each of the indicators of control over resources we have presented (built material capacity, financial vulnerability and social capital) when controlled among them, but also when controlled by occupational group as last job recorded.

The results show that the classification produced by last job recorded bears no statistical significance when controlled by the alternative indicators we have suggested. In other words, the assumption that the last recorded job is a good enough proxy for past trajectories that translate into different levels of control over resources in old age does not fully hold. As a matter of fact, if anything, we conclude from the results that the impact of how past trajectories translate into real control over resources can operate in varied ways within the same occupational group. The most significant impact comes from the material dimension of social class positions measured as built capacity (assets) and financial vulnerability (financial capacity to keep up with the standard lifestyle). These are the variables that show the highest impact in all outcome

Table 4.4: Logistic regression models for the impact of different measurements of social class on: having a chronic illness or disability; having difficulties paying for care from a medical doctor; and feeling happy

Predictors	Likelihood of having chronic illness and disability		Likelihood of having problems paying a medical doctor		Likelihood of declaring being happy	
	Odds ratio	Wald test	Odds ratio	Wald test	Odds ratio	Wald test
Age (in years)	1.036**	30.226	.975**	9.748	1.009	1.074
Built capacity (base = low)						
Moderate	.628**	21.911	.744*	6.473	1.405**	7.506
High	.788+	3.466	.537**	13.849	2.763**	25.582
Financial vulnerability (base = very low)						
Low	1.420**	10.941	2.315**	48.131	.596**	14.142
Moderate	2.634**	31.757	2.513**	25.307	.257**	54.135
High	1.741**	4.679	3.482**	22.118	.114**	67.809
Social capital (base = very low)						
Low	1.030	.006	2.071	2.319	.566	1.689
Moderate	1.314	.574	1.657	1.182	.969	.005
Strong	1.100	.074	1.635	1.169	1.093	.045
Very strong	1.239	.353	1.831	1.695	2.634**	4.690
Social group as last job (base = unskilled manual workers)						
Skilled manual workers	1.096	.442	.968	.039	1.168	.738
Supervisor	1.371	1.776	1.612	2.879	.484*	6.276
Employed position in service	1.155	.808	.859	.589	.871	.425

Predictors	Likelihood of having chronic illness and disability		Likelihood of having problems paying a medical doctor		Likelihood of declaring being happy	
	Odds ratio	Wald test	Odds ratio	Wald test	Odds ratio	Wald test
Employed position travelling	.962	.030	.845	.353	.906	.117
Employed position at desk	1.213	1.587	1.005	.001	.806	1.151
Self-employed	1.094	.218	1.966**	9.688	1.424	1.449
Middle management	1.100	.393	1.192	.928	.800	1.176
Employed professional	.706	1.335	.296*	4.420	1.337	.289
Professional	1.051	.021	2.791**	7.312	2.777	1.800
General and top management	.771	1.577	.609+	3.037	.737	1.106
Business proprietors	.984	.003	1.068	.028	.438*	4.753
Constant	−2.928		.133		.897	

Notes: ** Significant at .01; * significant at .05; + significant at .10.

Source: Author's estimates based on data from EQLS2007.

indicators. Social capital, on the other hand, does not perform well as a discriminator in all the three events considered. Although the notion of social capital itself is ambiguous (and these results may be just the side effect of a bad operational approach to social capital), these results can very well be pointing to the critical role of material resources in old age. Additional investment may be required if we are to capture the importance of social capital in old age as a discriminator of relative positions in the social hierarchy, but, for now, the conclusion to be drawn suggests that social classes in old age should be seen primarily as trajectories of accumulation of material advantage/disadvantage.

Conclusions

Analysing social classes understood as hierarchical systems of inequalities involves a starting assumption: individuals can be differentiated in a hierarchical manner, according to one or several criteria, into classes or strata. Irrespective of the theoretical streams one brings to their research, the central goal for all scholars interested in social class analysis is to discriminate in a satisfactory way the conditions of existence that have a social origin and that turn into opportunities and inequalities. Following that, the challenge social class analysis faces at this stage is that of finding ways to develop the concept of social class to make it more sensitive to the specific factors that produce effects of the same nature and magnitude as those traditionally understood as effects of position in social relationships of production and that are particularly central in the lives of older people who have already left the labour market.

The classic measurements of social class draw on the assumption that individuals sharing the same profession will most likely share or display similarities in terms of their objective, subjective and symbolic conditions of existence, which will also make it more likely that they will show similarities in the way they behave and perform in the social space. We have contended that extending this approach to the measurement of social class after retirement poses validity problems, especially given the changes that have been experienced in the structural assumptions of labour-market dynamics and the increasing number of years individuals are expected to live after retirement. The premise that the end point of trajectories in the labour market captured as last recorded job will be durable to the point of sustaining a static measurement of social class among older people is far too stretched.

Our proposal was inspired by an understanding of the social space as a multidimensional space, where each individual takes a position with coordinates defined by the amount and combination of resources that are effectively controlled at each point in time. This means that there is room for social mobility in old age, depending on how durable the resources are and how effectively they perform when it comes to protecting the status of the individual in face of a series of hazards that are likely to come with old age. It involved measuring two types of resources. The first concerned the material dimension of resources and translated into the financial capacity to keep up with the standard lifestyle (allowing for the identification of different social positions according to different levels of access to the standard lifestyle of developed societies). We have named that as 'financial vulnerability'. It also translated into what we have labelled as 'built material capacity', resulting from investments and savings that were made throughout the life course and that can give some leverage to the individual. The second type of resources took us to the space of social relations and networks in an attempt to assess how effectively networks of proximity can introduce some leverage that compensates for or reinforces unequal positions in the social space. Contrary to our initial hypothesis, and under the format we have chosen to empirically assess social capital, the level of control of immaterial/social network resources did not show any discriminatory effect.

The main conclusion to be drawn from our discussion seems to be that material deprivation indicators bring to social class analysis in old age a more accurate measurement of the extent of the social class differentials built throughout the life course as a result of employment trajectories. Measuring the possession of and control over material resources discloses pathways of accumulation that are certainly related to labour-market dynamics but that bear consequences in terms of their capacity to protect the status of the older individual. That capacity may be more resilient or less durable and therefore able to produce effects that go beyond what would be expected at the moment when the individual exited the labour market. The erosion of the resources the individual controls over the years after reaching old age can in fact be an interesting approach to discuss social class changes among older people.

Notes

[1] The EQLS has been carried out every four years since 2003 by Eurofound and offers a wide-ranging view of the diverse social realities in the 27 member states of the EU, as well as covering Norway and the candidate countries of Turkey, Macedonia and Croatia. It includes 35,000 respondents aged 18 years or older who were interviewed in most countries in face-to-face interviews. For most countries, the sample size is around 1,000, with the exception of the UK (1,500) and Germany and Turkey (2,000 each). Random samples

were drawn to represent adult persons who were living in private households during the fieldwork period in each of the countries covered. In most countries, the EQLS sample followed a multi-stage, stratified and clustered design with a 'random walk' procedure for the selection of the households at the last stage. Only one person from the same household was interviewed. Sample data were re-weighted by age, sex and region to conform to national population patterns. Fieldwork for the 2007 data set was carried out in the last four months of 2007. The overall response rate was 57.9%, although there are significant country variations (a low of 33.5% in the UK and a high of 88% in Romania). For our empirical analysis, we have retained data for the EU15 group of countries and for individuals aged 65 or more at the time of the interview. The final data set comprises 4,001 cases, which were weighted for EU15 population patterns.

[2] Ordinal indicators were computed from the original variables. Social capital combined data from intensity of contacts with children and friends/neighbours as well as from participation in community organisations (none = very low; no children/proximity networks = low; one close/proximity network = moderate; both close/proximity networks = strong; all three dimensions = very strong). Built material capacity combined data for income from savings/investments and home-ownership (none = low; one = moderate; both = strong). Financial vulnerability was computed following the methodology of EQLS2007 (no items missing = very low; one or two items missing = low; three or four items missing = moderate; five or six items missing = high) (Eurofound, 2009).

References

Conen, W.S., Henkens, K. and Schippers, J.J. (2012) 'Are employers changing their behavior toward older workers? An analysis of employers' surveys 2000–2009', *Journal of Ageing & Social Policy*, vol 23, no 2, pp 141–58.

Elsinga, M. and Mandic, S. (2010) 'Housing as a piece in the old-age puzzle. The role of housing equity in eight countries', *Teorija in Praksa*, vol 47, no 5, pp 940–58.

Eurofound (2009) *Second European Quality of Life Survey overview*, Luxembourg: Office for Official Publications of the European Communities.

Formosa, M. (2009) *Class dynamics in later life: older persons, class identity and class action*, Hamburg: Lit Verlag.

Krieger, N., Chen, J.T. and Selby, J.V. (1999) 'Comparing individual-based and household-based measures of social class to assess class inequalities in women's health: a methodological study of 684 US women', *Journal of Epidemiology and Community Health*, vol 53, no 10, pp 612–23.

Lopes, A. (2011) 'Ageing and social class: towards a dynamic approach to class inequalities in old age', in M. Sargeant (ed) *Age and discrimination: multiple discrimination from an age perspective*, Cambridge: Cambridge University Press, pp 89–110.

Matthews, R.J., Jagger, C. and Hancock, R.M. (2006) 'Does socio-economic advantage lead to a longer, healthier old age?', *Social Science and Medicine*, vol 62, no 10, pp 2489–99.

Rosnick, D. and Baker, D. (2012) 'The impact of the housing crash on the wealth of the baby boom cohorts', *Journal of Ageing & Social Policy*, vol 22, no 2, pp 117–28.

Townsend, P. (1987) 'Deprivation', *Journal of Social Policy*, vol 16, no 2, pp 125–46.

Wright, E.O. (1979) *Class structure and income determination*, New York: Academic Press.

FIVE

Social class, age and identity in later life

Martin Hyde and Ian Rees Jones

Introduction

This chapter will examine social class identity and age identity in later life in the context of social change. As previously noted in the introductory chapter, it is important for research to be sensitive to the subjective as well as the objective elements of social class in later life. Thus, while it is critical to look at how the material structures of class can impact on the life chances and living conditions of those in later life, as has been done by the other contributors to this volume, it is equally important to see whether older people themselves see class as a meaningful source of identity in later life. Much gerontological research has operated with a materialist definition of class. This approach has been criticised for not giving sufficient consideration to how older people themselves relate to or identify with class as a salient source of their own identity (Gubrium and Holstein, 2000). Thus, there is an argument that research that focuses on social class inequalities in later life would benefit from being supplemented by research that takes a more culturalist approach and that explores class as part of an 'individual's self-concept and subjective understanding' (O'Rand and Henretta, 1999: 35). This issue is not specific to gerontological research, but resonates with wider issues within sociology around the meaning and materiality of class in contemporary, late-modern, society (Bourdieu, 1984; Beck and Beck-Gernsheim, 2002; Savage et al, 2010).

Class identity in late modernity

Although there is no agreement over the precise starting point of late modernity, those scholars that have described, evaluated and attempted to explain the social, economic and political transformations of the last 40 years agree that there have been profound changes in individuals' lives and social relations. Key aspects of late modernity and its accompanying transformations have been identified in terms of increasing individualisation (Beck and Beck-Gernsheim, 2002), cosmopolitanism (Beck, 2002), risk and uncertainty (Giddens, 1990), and liquidity (Bauman, 2000). A striking feature of these social changes is that individual and social identities become more contingent, changeable and fluid. Social class identities in particular have been subject to much theorising and empirical research as a consequence; with some authors referring to the 'death of class' (Pakulski and Waters, 1996) and Ulrich Beck (2007), for one, arguing that class has become a 'zombie category' devoid of sociological and social meaning. In response, some scholars have developed critiques of the individualisation thesis, providing alternative interpretations of social change that highlight changes in forms of class identity and class expression but emphasise the continued salience of class and forms of class distinction (Skeggs, 2004; Atkinson, 2010). Here, class has not disappeared, but is present in emotional frames, albeit increasingly expressed at individualised levels (Savage, 2000). Indeed, there remain deep and long-standing moral dimensions to class and class relations permeating the fabric of individual lives. Yet, much theoretical and empirical work remains to be done in this area (Sayer, 2011).

Evidence from the US indicates that individuals recognise and can locate class labels and class categories clearly and that these have meaning for individual lives (Gilbert, 2003). However, studies have also shown that self-reported class position is not a good indicator of objective class position (Oddsson, 2010). Crudely, in the US, there is a tendency for people to identify as middle class, with both working-class and upper-class individuals aligning with the middle (Evans and Kelley, 2004). In the UK, there appears to be a phenomenon of not identifying with a social class category at all or at least there is a tendency towards 'dis-identification'. Ethnographic research has shown that working-class people tend to refer to themselves as 'ordinary' rather than explicitly referring to a class position (Skeggs, 2004). Further testing of this 'dis-identification' thesis has thrown up ambivalent and varying accounts of class position. But the evidence also suggests that this goes hand-in-hand with a wider recognition of the cultural aspects of class, including forms of distinction based on snobbery and elitism that are implied in the use of class idioms (Savage et al, 2010).

While acknowledging that there have been radical changes to social life, we need to recognise that this is also an area of profound disagreement among social theorists and researchers. In particular, disputes have revolved around the role of individual agency and consequent changes in modes of reflexivity (Archer, 2007, 2010). Contra the individualisation thesis, Archer has argued that we have entered a period of morphogenesis characterised by radical structural transformations at social and cultural levels. In such conditions, social life becomes more contingent, and individuals are faced with shifting temporal and institutional conditions. These conditions include new modes of connectivity, mobility and technological change and changes in political and social rights and to family structures, to name but a few. One consequence of this is that diversity becomes the norm; in effect, variety engenders more variety and the individual is faced with a reflexive imperative (Archer, 2012). This has implications for how identities (including class identities and age identities) are formed and reproduced. Building on this work, Pierpaolo Donati (2011) distinguishes between three semantic codes that define changes in the ways in which identity is formed. First, there is a classical symbolic code, where identity is understood as an essential, immediate unity; identity is *monistic*. Second, there is a modern symbolic code, where identity is formed in a process of negation or opposition to what it is not; identity is *dualistic*. Finally, there is an after-modern symbolic code, where identity is defined through and by social relations; identity is *relational*. If we are to understand the social phenomena that accompany late modernity, Donati argues, we need to view and study identity in relational terms. Thus, he sees the rise of new forms of multiple citizenship, post-secularism, conflict over environmental and human relations (including intergenerational relations), new forms of community and association, and the demise of traditional cultural identities (including class identities) as better understood within a relational paradigm. From this perspective, one of the interesting aspects of identity in later life is the extent to which different forms of identity arise as a consequence of changes in social relations that are themselves related to profound changes in life expectancy, well-being in later life and the demographic structure of late-modern societies. It seems that class identities and age identities may be related and that changes to both may reflect wider social change.

In what follows, we provide an overview of gerontological approaches to class and later life, consider key theoretical approaches to identity and social change, and examine evidence at national and cross-national levels for the relationship between class identity and age identity. In so doing, we discuss the methodological and data issues associated with cross-national research before presenting an analysis of global comparative data from the International Social Survey Programme

(ISSP) and also analysis of changes in identity over time using the UK Citizenship Survey.

Gerontological approaches to class and age in later life

Social class occupies an ambiguous position within social gerontology. On the one hand, there is an abundance of empirical research on how social class location (earlier in life) impacts on mortality and morbidity in later life. On the other hand, attempts to develop a class-based theory of old age have, arguably, been less successful. A number of writers have sought to integrate old age into a general, Marxist, theory of class and capitalism. This is perhaps most obvious in Phillipson's (1982) *Capitalism and the construction of old age*, in which he argued that labour-market participation rates of older workers are dependent on the demands of capital and, therefore, in the early part of the 20th century at least, highly variable. During periods of lower labour-market supply, like war, older workers will be retained or rehired to fill gaps in the workforce. During times of economic constraint, such as a recession, companies will seek to lay older workers off to maintain their rate of profit. Other writers from the political economy approach have also pointed to the link between early retirement policies, such as the Job Release Scheme introduced in the UK in 1977, and mass unemployment (Dex and Phillipson, 1986; Maule, 1995; Desmond, 2000; Taylor, 2002, 2003). Hence, the demands of (international) capitalism are seen as a threat to the labour-market position of older people in the UK. From this perspective, older workers are seen very much as a reserve army of labour who appear to occupy a special position within the class system based on their age. Some writers have extended these analyses further to argue that the interests of older people and those of the working classes are essentially the same:

> The only way old people can keep pace with rising prices is by aligning themselves with the workers, who in turn can only benefit if they align themselves with pensioners and espouse their cause.... Otherwise organised workers will eventually find themselves in the same position as today's pensioners. (Elder, 1977: 123)

According to such arguments, not only does class remain an important determinant of life chances in later life, but also older people should self-consciously identify with the working class to promote their collective interests. However, attempts to establish a class analysis of old age are inherently problematic as most measures of class are occupationally based and the majority of older people are no longer in the labour market.

Ironically, perhaps, age itself has also become a much more problematic term in the study of later life. Chronological age, in later life at least, has become a very unstable measure of a person's health, labour-market position or social activity. Instead, it must compete against an ever-growing number of other temporal schema, such as emotional age (Bain, 1945), biological age (Jackson et al, 2003), functional age (Sharkey, 1987; Graham et al, 1999) and cognitive age (Barak and Gould, 1985; Barak, 1987). Moreover, current cohorts of retirees appear to reject 'old age' as an identity. Increasingly, writers argue that subjective age is a more meaningful concept for understanding how older people see themselves (Barak, 2009). This is supported by empirical studies which show that age identity appears to be related to well-being. A youthful outlook has been shown to be a predictor of 'successful' ageing and, among women at least, older age identity is associated with a more pessimistic outlook towards cognitive ageing (Schafer and Shippee, 2010). Studies of life-course transitions and age-related identity have shown that conceptions of the timing of old age are related to chronological age, gender, health and social roles (Kaufman and Elder, 2002). Subjective life expectancy, for example, has been found to be associated with social class, with people in lower socio-economic groups being found to perceive an earlier end to middle age and having shorter subjective life expectancies and older identities (Barrett, 2003; Toothman and Barrett, 2011). Furthermore, studies addressing people's sense of the ideal ages for life-course transitions also show that these vary by age, gender, race and socio-economic status (Bowling et al, 2005). Subjective age also appears to be related to life events and transitions into social roles across the life course (Mathur and Moschis, 2005). Research indicates that age identities may be related to generational effects, particularly associated with the rise of the so-called 'baby boomer' generation, and the increasing emphasis on youthfulness as a driver of consumption in late modernity. It is further suggested that there are differences between countries that can be measured in cross-cultural studies (Barak, 2009).

Theories of identity change

One of the ways in which researchers have tried to explain and understand changes in human values and identities is by relating these to the extent to which human needs are met in modern societies. The post-materialist thesis (Inglehart, 1987) is based on the idea that in modern and late-modern societies, there is a decline in conditions of scarcity (where people tend to place greater value on materialist goals) and an increase in conditions of prosperity (where people tend to prioritise values that emphasise self-expression). Thus, it is argued, social class identities become diminished in importance because of improvements in living standards and rising affluence. The thesis, however, is based around more complex processes than a simple correspondence between development and values. Inglehart's socialisation hypothesis proposes that individual values form as a result of the environment and social interaction in early life, and although values can change as people age, the likelihood of change decreases as we move towards later life. There are, therefore, potentially important generational effects, as a sustained period of prosperity and economic development would lead one to expect differences in values and identity formation between younger and older cohorts. Indeed, Inglehart has pointed to stronger post-materialist values among generational groups born in the golden age of welfare capitalism compared to older groups (people born before 1950) and younger groups (people born after 1975) (Inglehart and Welzel, 2005).

It is important to have comparative studies to address the question of what factors influence perceptions of class interest and class identity. To date, comparative studies have presented differing results. Some studies have found class consciousness at similar levels in different countries (Wright, 1989), while others have found cross-national differences (Robinson and Kelley, 1979; Wright, 1997). Economic prosperity appears to strengthen upper-class identity (Evans and Kelley, 2004). A recent analysis of the World Values Survey covering 44 countries found household income to be positively correlated with class identity, with significant variations between countries (Andersen and Curtis, 2012). Lower levels of class identity were found in poorer countries. The study also found that the relationship between household income and class identity was stronger in countries with high income inequality. In contrast to commentators who have argued that class identities are dead, these researchers argue that people do locate their class positions on the basis of income. Thus, they argue, increasing income inequality may have a polarising effect.

To date, therefore, the literature appears to indicate that there are significant changes in class and age identities over time and that these changes may be related to economic development and generational or cohort effects. The evidence also suggests that class identities may present in different ways in different contexts – cross-culturally and across different social locations. Finally, we should not exclude the possibility that changes in identity forms may also be related to individual life-course transitions.

Issues in cross-national research

As this chapter is based on cross-sectional and time series data on how older people construct their identities, it is important to note a number of methodological issues. Comparing and contrasting any phenomena across time and/or space raises a number of challenges. These range from the abstract, conceptual level to the more practical and applied level.

An often-noted problem in cross-national research is the lack of precision in defining the basis of the comparisons. There can be conceptual and methodological slippage between cross-*national* and cross-*cultural* research. These terms are frequently and wrongly seen as synonymous, when, in fact, there is often a poor fit between culture(s) and nation(s) (Denton, 2007; Tung, 2008). The conflation of these terms can lead to an inappropriate generalisation from the unit of observation (that which is measured) to the unit of analysis (that which forms the theoretical basis of the research). It is, therefore, important that the unit of analysis in any comparative research is both theoretically grounded and matches the unit of observation. The approach taken in the following analyses is to compare nations, rather than cultures. This is for both practical reasons – for example, Gross Domestic Product (GDP) per capita is only available at the national level – and conceptual reasons – for example, nation-states set policies, such as the retirement age, which are likely to impact on the sense of identity for older people.

Another central issue in this type of comparative analysis relates not to what is being compared, per se, but to what is being measured, or ought to be measured, within each country. It is possible to identify two broad approaches to, or clusters within, cross-national research. The first of these is concerned with particular/local/internal/ subjective knowledge, while the other seeks to identify universal/ global/external/objective social phenomena. This distinction has been (re-conceptualised as 'emic' and 'etic' perspectives (Spiers, 2000; Higgins and Bhatt, 2001; Karasawa, 2002). This typology derives from Pike's work on linguistics (Pike, 1954; Helfrich, 1999) and provides a useful model for exploring some of the methodological challenges associated with this type of research. According to this distinction, an emic account is a description of behaviour or beliefs in terms that are, consciously or unconsciously, meaningful to the actor. Emic accounts are, therefore, seen as particular, internal and culture-specific (Helfrich, 1999). For researchers who adopt such a perspective, it is impossible to impose meanings from one culture on to the next. Writing questionnaire items, for example, is a cultural practice and the final product, the question and/or the questionnaire, will bear the imprint of the writer's culture (Miller et al, 1981). Thus, one cannot simply transfer or translate a question or concept derived from one culture to another and expect it to carry the same meaning. This is what Berry (1999) defines as an 'imposed etic'. Even the most rigorous translation and back-translation process cannot overcome the problem that meanings are relational. In contrast, etic accounts aim to describe behaviour or beliefs in terms that can be applied to other cultures. Hence, etic accounts are seen as universal and culturally neutral. Researchers from this perspective hold that with proper methodological procedures, it is possible to control for these cultural differences, termed measurement (in)variance or differential item functioning, and therefore produce comparable, objective, data (Sharma and Weathers, 2003). Nonetheless, the principle focus of emic research is question validity. In order to ensure that the answers that are given are meaningful, researchers need to ensure that the question wording or phrases used are understood within the cultural context in which the research takes place. The principal concerns of etic researchers, on the other hand, are item, construct and sample comparability. Inter-individual variation in responses to, say, a questionnaire item is seen, from an etic perspective, to come from three sources: real differences between individuals; differences in cultural norms or values; and measurement error. Thus, in order to truly be able to compare like with like and make international comparisons, the latter two sources of variation need to be reduced or removed. In the context of the data presented in the following, these debates force us to question whether class or age mean the same thing to people in different national contexts or at different points in time. It is arguable that within Europe, with its history of class politics, notions of class are broadly similar. However, it is debatable whether American or Japanese respondents, who have had a different political and social history, would understand this term in the same fashion. Likewise, age is open to multiple interpretations. One could see it as time since birth, how old/young you feel or in generational terms, as a parent or grandparent.

A final, more technical, set of issues relates to sample comparability when making international comparisons. It is important to ensure that the sampling methods employed in different national surveys are the same. A lack of sample comparability and/or the misapplication of sample weights could again lead to erroneous estimates (Kiecolt and Nathan, 1985; Lee and Forhofer, 2006). These issues are more commonly associated with research that employs data collected in independent studies in different countries where the sampling methods are not standardised a priori. The way to avoid such issues is to ensure that, whenever possible, data are taken from truly cross-national studies with universally applied sampling techniques within the participating countries and to ensure that study weights are applied to correct for the unequal probability of selection where stratified sampling methods are used (Lee and Forhofer, 2006). This is an issue to bear in mind when examining the results, as there is no uniform approach to sampling in the ISSP, whence some of the data are drawn.

Data and analyses

In the following sections, we present an analysis of data from the ISSP for 2003 and for four waves of the Citizenship Survey in the UK. The ISSP is a continuous programme of cross-national collaboration running annual surveys on topics important for the social sciences. The 2003 survey addressed issues of identity (ISSP Research Group, 2007). These data provide an unequalled opportunity to explore these issues cross-nationally. However, they tell us little about how retirees' sense of identity might have changed over time. To this end, we use time-series data from the Citizenship Survey in the UK (Department for Communities and Local Government, 2012).

Our aim was to address the importance of social class identity and age group identity among retired populations. We also wanted to examine differences in identity among different countries and to look in more detail at these patterns in the British case. A further step was to look at the relationship between GDP per capita and the proportion of those who say class or age is important – to test the post-materialist hypothesis – and the proportion aged 65 and over – to test the 'third age' hypothesis.

Age identity and class identity in later life: a global view

To get a global perspective on the salience of class and age for identity in later life, the initial analyses are based on the pooled data from all the countries in the ISSP. In order to directly test the hypothesis that class and/or age are more or less important sources of identity in a post-working population, we restricted the analyses to those respondents who said that they were retired. Notwithstanding concerns about the (in)comparability of concepts in cross-national research, we feel that retirement is commonly understood in most countries as the withdrawal from the labour market in later life (see Back, 1977). As such, these respondents should not have an occupation and, in line with the hypothesis advanced earlier, should therefore have a weaker attachment to (occupationally based) social class. Conversely, as they identify themselves as retirees, which is an age-based status, we ought to expect to see higher levels of identification with age or 'life stage'. Respondents were asked to choose from a list of around 12 different dimensions, including family, gender, local area and so on, and say which were important for their sense of identity. They were able select up to three different dimensions and rank them in order of most important, second most important and third most important. In these analyses, we have focused solely on those respondents who said that social class and age or life stage were important.

The data presented in Figure 5.1 show the proportion of retirees from all the ISSP countries combined who rank either social class or age as important. This is broken down by the relative importance, that is, first, second or third, and finally whether either was mentioned at all. Overall, the data show that age appears to be more important for retirees' sense of identity than class. Just over a quarter mentioned age as at all important whereas just under a fifth said that class was at all important. However, it is clear from closer inspection that neither age nor class feature predominantly in the identities of the retirees. Only 7% of the sample said that their age was the most important source of their identity and just 2% identified class as the most important. The proportions for both do rise somewhat when looking at the second and third most important features of identity and the gap between class and age narrows considerably. This suggests that class still lurks in the background of people's sense of who they are, perhaps related to a habitus that informs or influences other more proximal factors, such as family and friends. Unfortunately, it is not possible to directly test these arguments in these data. We do not have information on their social networks or cultural practices and because the data are cross-sectional, we cannot see whether attachment to class has weakened upon retirement. Class may never have been a dominant feature of their identity or class identity may have declined sharply with retirement.

The data in Figure 5.2 explore the interrelations between class and age identities among the retirees. Whereas the previous analyses looked at the two separately by using the data from all the rankings, it is possible to construct combinations of age and class identities. Based on whether the respondent said that age or class was at all important (regardless of order), one could report that neither was important, only one factor

Figure 5.1: Importance of social class and age group for retirees' identity throughout the world

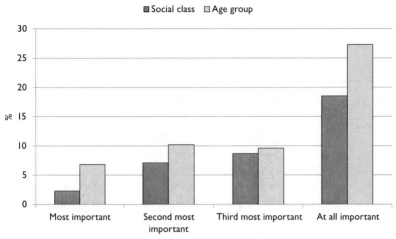

Source: ISSP (2007).

Figure 5.2: The relative importance of age and class for retirees' identity throughout the world

Source: ISSP (2007).

was important or that both were important.[1] The results show three things: (1) that the overwhelming majority of the sample see neither age nor class as important; (2) that age and class are considered as largely separate factors and only a very small proportion identify with both (4%); and (3) that there is a greater proportion of people (21%) who say that age alone is important compared to those who say that class alone is important (13%).

Cross-national comparisons of age and class identity

Thus far, the analyses have been based on the pooled data from the whole ISSP sample. However, while this gives us a rough insight into the 'global' picture of the salience of age and class for the identity of retirees, it masks any, potentially interesting, cross-national differences. In order to explore whether there were any such international differences, respondents from a number of countries were selected from the sample. Nationalities, for example, Russians, were picked if there were 100 or more retired respondents from that nationality with valid responses on any of the 'identity' questions. However, a number of other countries with fewer than 100 retired respondents, such as the US, the UK and Japan, which have around 90 valid respondents, were also included as these are important countries in terms of their international position and ageing populations.

The data presented in Figure 5.3 show a wide range in the proportions who report that class, age or both are salient factors in their identity. In Taiwan, over 60% say that at least one of these factors is important, while in Finland, only around one fifth report that they are important. The pattern for the relative importance of age and class separately or in combination is also rather varied. In some countries, such as Spain, age is clearly much more important than class. However, in others, such as Uruguay and the Netherlands, class appears to be more important than age. Nonetheless, age appears to be more important in more countries, 15 of the 22, than class. What is much clearer is that very few people in any country, with the possible exception of Taiwan (14%), say that both age and class are important. In fact, in Austria and South Africa, none of the respondents reported this combination. These analyses suggest that there might be macro-level factors, at the national level, that influence these differences. Thus, it could be that some countries have a greater level of 'age consciousness' or 'class consciousness' than other countries. This could be due to a number of potential factors, such as the degree of attention paid to these issues in the media or the type of party that is in power. However, we will focus here on two very basic sets of analyses that reflect key indicators of the post-materialist and third age theories. These are GDP per capita, as a measure of the general level of material well-being in a country, and the proportion of the population aged 65 and over, as a measure of the demographic critical mass of an ageing population. These analyses are presented in Figures 5.4 and 5.5 using data from the World Bank (2012) published online in 2012.

Figure 5.3: The relative importance of age and class for identity for retirees from selected countries

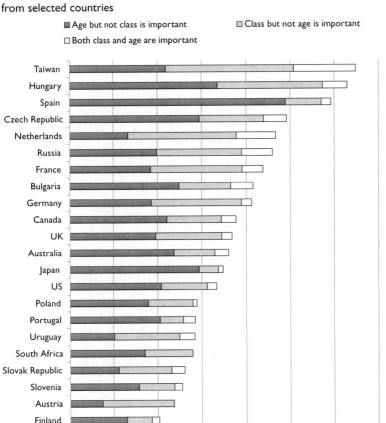

■ Age but not class is important   □ Class but not age is important
□ Both class and age are important

Source: ISSP (2007).

Figure 5.4 shows the proportion of retirees in the previously selected countries[2] reporting class as important for their identity by the GDP per capita for that country in 2003. The data show some interesting patterns. Overall, for the sample as a whole, there is no clearly identifiable relationship between the two measures.[3] However, there appear to be two clusters of countries, those below US$10,000 per capita, where there is no relation whatsoever, and those countries where GDP per capita is around US$15,000 and over. In this second group, there appears to be a strong relationship. But it is in the opposite direction to that which one would expect if the 'post-materialist' hypothesis were true. What these data seem to show is that (within Europe at least) the greater

Figure 5.4: The relationship between GDP per capita and the proportion of retirees who say that class is important for their identity

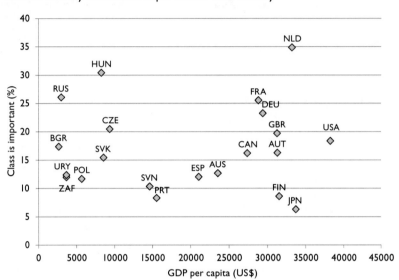

the degree of economic development, the greater the proportion of retirees who say that class is important for their sense of identity.

Turning to the 'third age' hypothesis, the data in Figure 5.5 show the relationship between population ageing and the degree of age identification among the retired population. As with the previous analysis, the data fail to show a clear pattern. Even when the data for South Africa are removed, as a clear outlier, no discernible relationship emerges.[4]

Comparisons of age and class identity over time

While the results from the ISSP give an important 'global' view of the salience of age and class for identity in later life, they were collected a decade ago and, as this question will not be asked again until 2014, they do not allow us to look at the development of this issue over time. Thus, to address this, we turn to the final set of analyses, which cover 10 years of the Citizenship Survey in the UK. This is important as not only do the data cover a sufficiently long period to detect any changes, but they also capture the 'credit crunch' and the beginning of the global recession. To some extent, therefore, they act like a natural experiment and ought to allow us to see whether the accompanying financial hardship felt by many and the austerity measures that were

Figure 5.5: The relationship between the proportion of the population that is aged 65+ and the proportion of retirees who say that age is important for their identity

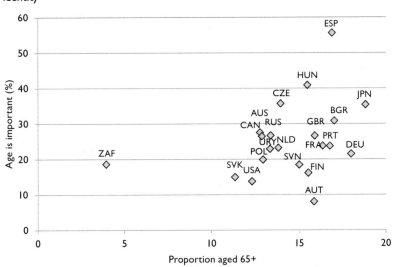

introduced post-2007 led to a return of materialist concerns and a heightened sense of class identification among British retirees.

On a practical note, unfortunately, the questions on 'importance for identity' were not asked in the 2003 or 2005 waves. Also, it is worth repeating that the data are cross-sectional, not longitudinal. Hence, it is not possible to look at how the relative importance of class and age for identity changes as a person ages. The data do show that from 2001, there has been an increase in the proportions of those in retirement who say that neither class nor age are important for their sense of identity.

In 2001, around 45% of retirees did not feel that either of these was important for their identity. By 2010, this had risen to 55%. Beyond this, the data appear to show a number of interesting things. First, at all time points, the proportion of retirees who say that class alone is important to their sense of identity is much smaller than those for whom age alone is important. At its highest in 2008/09, around 9% of retirees felt that class alone was important. However, this compares to just under a quarter of retirees in the same year who thought that age alone was important. Although within each year, age seems to be more important than class, the proportion of retirees who say that age is important has declined most sharply over the period, notably, between 2001 and 2007. Conversely, the proportion for whom class alone is important has remained remarkably stable. Another interesting feature of these data, compared to the ISSP data, is the much larger proportion of retirees who say that both age and class are important. This ranges from 12% in 2001 to 16% in 2007. There are a number of possible methodological reasons for this difference. The questions were somewhat different in the two surveys. In the ISSP, respondents were simply given a list and asked to identify the first, second and third most important thing for their sense of identity. In the Citizenship Survey, respondents were asked about each facet individually and invited to say whether they were very important, quite important, not very important or not at all important.

Figure 5.6: The relative importance of age and class for the identity of British retirees from 2001 to 2010

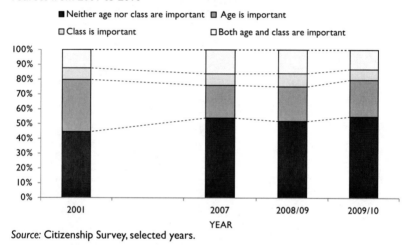

Source: Citizenship Survey, selected years.

Discussion and conclusion

This chapter has discussed the relationship between social class identities and age identity in later life. We have illustrated our discussion with an analysis of global comparative data at national state level and compared data sets over time in the UK context. We have highlighted some of the methodological issues relating to cross-national comparative work, and the limitations of the data and the methods used here mean that caution should be applied to any wider interpretations. There are, however, some interesting points that arise from these simple analyses that can be related to the literature on class identity and later life as well as some of the attempts to explain variations in class identity. Overall, the analyses presented in this chapter indicate that neither class nor age are salient features of identity in later life. While there is no evidence here of the 'death of class', there may be some support for elements of dis-identification, both of class and age. Moreover, there is some support for Gilleard and Higgs' (2005) argument that current cohorts of older people are actively rejecting age-based labels as they enter later life. Age and class identities appear to operate independently of each other, suggesting, from a relational sociology perspective, that other forms of identity and identification need to be examined. There is some evidence (in Europe at least) of a relationship between GDP and class identity, although this appears complex, but there is no evidence of a generational effect (although the data do not allow us to fully explore this question). Analysis of UK data suggests higher levels of class and age identity among this sample of retirees, raising both methodological questions and the possibility of greater variation within samples. Here, the possibility does arise of a decline in the salience of class and age identities over the last decade of the 20th century. More detailed work is required to examine which other forms of identification may have increased or whether there is a general trend towards more fragmented identities. In addition, there is scope for addressing questions relating different forms of identity in later life to political allegiances, civic participation and forms of engagement. If, as we believe, the changes associated with late modernity have led to a social context that is characterised by contingency and individual biographies driven by a reflexive imperative, the relatively low levels of class and age identity merit further exploration. It is important that social researchers study the experiences of older people in this respect and give consideration to the forms of identity (including class and age identities) that they take with them into later life or adopt in old age. After all, they in particular have lived through the key events that have led to conditions of nascent globalisation, the growth of consumer capitalism and its current crisis.

Notes

[1] It is worth noting here that these analyses include any respondent who had at least one valid answer on any of the three 'important for identity' questions. For example, if they said that family was the most important but then refused to give an answer for the second and third most important, they are still included in the 'neither age nor class' group.

[2] These analyses do not include Taiwan as the World Bank does not report national-level data for this area.

[3] A Pearson's correlation was used to test whether this was statistically significant. The result was $r = .06$ and $p > .05$.

[4] The result was $r = .34$ and $p > .05$.

References

Andersen, R. and Curtis, J. (2012) 'The polarizing effect of economic inequality on class identification: evidence from 44 countries', *Research in Social Stratification and Mobility*, vol 30, no 1, pp 129–41.

Archer, M. (2007) *Making our way through the world*, Cambridge: Cambridge University Press.

Archer, M. (2010) 'Routine, reflexivity and realism', *Sociological Theory*, vol 28, no 3, pp 272–303.

Archer, M. (2012) *The reflexive imperative in late modernity*, Cambridge: Cambridge University Press.

Atkinson, W. (2010) 'Class, individualisation and perceived (dis)advantages: not either/or but both/and?', *Sociological Research Online*, vol 15, no 4. Available at: http://www.socresonline.org.uk/15/4/7.html

Back, K. (1977) 'The ambiguity of retirement', in E.W. Busse and E. Pfeiffer (eds) *Behavior and adaptation in later life*, Boston, MA: Little & Brown, pp 78–98.

Bain, R. (1945) 'The ages of man', *American Sociological Review*, vol 10, no 3, pp 337–43.

Barak, B. (1987) 'Cognitive age: a new multidimensional approach to measuring age identity', *International Journal of Aging & Human Development*, vol 25, no 2, pp 109–28.

Barak, B. (2009) 'Age identity: a cross-cultural global approach', *International Journal of Behavioral Development*, vol 33, no 1, pp 2–11.

Barak, B. and Gould, S. (1985) 'Alternative age measures: a research agenda', *Advances in Consumer Research*, vol 12, no 1, pp 53–8.

Barrett, A. (2003) 'Socioeconomic status and age identity: the role of dimensions of health in the subjective construction of age', *Journal of Gerontology: Social Sciences*, vol 58, no 2, pp S101–9.

Bauman, Z. (2000) *Liquid modernity*, Oxford: Polity Press.

Beck, U. (2002) 'The cosmopolitan society and its enemies', *Theory, Culture & Society*, vol 19, no 1, pp 17–44.

Beck, U. (2007) 'Beyond class and nation: reframing social inequalities in a globalizing world', *The British Journal of Sociology*, vol 58, no 4, pp 679–705.

Beck, U. and Beck-Gernsheim, E. (2002) *Individualization: institutionalized individualism and its social and political consequences*, London: Sage.

Berry, J.W. (1999) 'Emics and etics: a symbiotic conception', *Culture & Psychology*, vol 5, no 2, pp 165–71.

Bourdieu, P. (1984) *Distinction: a social critique of the judgment of taste*, Boston, MA: Harvard University Press.

Bowling, A., See-Tai, S., Ebrahim, S., Gabriel, Z. and Solanki, P. (2005) 'Attributes of age identity', *Ageing & Society*, vol 25, no 4, pp 479–500.

Denton, T. (2007) 'Unit of observation in cross-cultural research – implications for sampling and aggregated data analysis', *Cross-Cultural Research*, vol 41, no 1, pp 3–31.

Department for Communities and Local Government (2012) 'Citizenship survey overview'. Available at: http://webarchive.nationalarchives.gov.uk/20120919132719/www.communities.gov.uk/communities/research/citizenshipsurvey

Desmond, H.J. (2000) 'Older and greyer: third age workers and the labour market', *The International Journal of Comparative Labour Law and Industrial Relations*, vol 16, no 3, pp 235–50.

Dex, S. and Phillipson, C. (1986) 'Social policy and the older worker', in C. Phillipson and A. Walker (eds) *Ageing and social policy. A critical assessment*, Aldershot: Gower, pp 45–66.

Donati, P. (2011) *Relational sociology, a new paradigm for the social sciences*, London: Routledge.

Elder, G. (1977) *The alienated. Growing old today*, London: Writers and Readers Publishing Cooperative.

Evans, M. and Kelley, J. (2004) 'Subjective social location: data from 21 nations', *International Journal of Public Opinion Research*, vol 16, no 1, pp 3–38.

Giddens, A. (1990) *The consequences of modernity*, Palto Alto, CA: Stanford University Press.

Gilbert, D. (2003) *The American class structure: in an age of growing inequality*, Belmont, CA: Thompson Wadsworth.

Gilleard, C. and Higgs, P. (2005) *Contexts of ageing: Class, cohort and community*, Cambridge, Polity Press.

Graham, J.E., Mitnitski, A.B., Mogilner, A.J. and Rockwood, K. (1999) 'Dynamics of cognitive aging: distinguishing functional age and disease from chronologic age in a population', *American Journal of Epidemiology*, vol 150, no 10, pp 1045–54.

Gubrium, J. and Holstein, B.A. (2000) 'Introduction', in J. Gubrium and B.A. Holstein (eds) *Aging and everyday life*, Malden, MA: Blackwell Publishers, pp 1–12.

Helfrich, H. (1999) 'Beyond the dilemma of cross-cultural psychology: resolving the tension between etic and emic approaches', *Culture & Psychology*, vol 5, no 2, pp 131–53.

Higgins, N.C. and Bhatt, G. (2001) 'Culture moderates the self-serving bias: etic and emic features of causal attributions in India and in Canada', *Social Behavior and Personality*, vol 29, no 1, pp 49–61.

Inglehart, R. (1987) 'Value change in industrial societies', *American Political Science Review*, vol 81, no 4, pp 1289–303.

Inglehart, R. and Welzel, C. (2005) *Modernization, culture change and democracy: the human development sequence*, Cambridge: Cambridge University Press.

ISSP Research Group (International Social Survey Programme Research Group) (2007) *International Social Survey Programme 2003: national identity II (ISSP 2003)*, Cologne: GESIS Data Archive (ZA3910 Data file Version 2.0.0).

Jackson, S.H.D., Weale, M.R. and Weale, R.A. (2003) 'Biological age – what is it and can it be measured?', *Archives of Gerontology and Geriatrics*, vol 36, no 2, pp 103–15.

Karasawa, M. (2002) 'Patriotism, nationalism, and internationalism among Japanese citizens: an etic–emic approach', *Political Psychology*, vol 23, no 4, pp 645–66.

Kaufman, G. and Elder, G.H. (2002) 'Revisiting age identity: a research note', *Journal of Aging Studies*, vol 16, no 2, pp 169–76.

Kiecolt, K.J. and Nathan, L.E. (1985) *Secondary analysis of survey data*, London: Sage.

Lee, E.S. and Forhofer, R.N. (2006) *Analyzing complex survey data*, London: Sage.

Mathur, A. and Moschis, G. (2005) 'Antecedents of cognitive age: a replication and extension', *Psychology & Marketing*, vol 22, no 12, pp 969–94.

Maule, A.J. (1995) 'Early retirement schemes: factors governing their success and how these differ across job categories', *Personnel Review*, vol 24, no 8, pp 6–16.

Miller, J., Slomczynski, K.M. and Schoenber, R.J. (1981) 'Assessing comparability of measurement in cross-national research – authoritarian-conservatism in different sociocultural settings', *Social Psychology Quarterly*, vol 44, no 3, pp 178–91.

Oddsson, G. (2010) 'Class awareness in Iceland', *International Journal of Sociology and Social Policy*, vol 30, no 5, pp 292–312.

O'Rand, A.M. and Henretta, J.C. (1999) *Age and inequality: diverse pathways through later life*, Boulder, CO: Westview Press.

Pakulski, J. and Waters, M. (1996) *The death of class*, London: Sage.

Phillipson, C. (1982) *Capitalism and the construction of old age*, London: Palgrave Macmillan.

Pike, K.L. (1954) 'Emic and etic standpoints for the description of behavior', in K.L. Pike (ed) *Language in relation to a unified theory of the structure of human behavior*, Glendale, CA: Summer Institute of Linguistics, pp 8–28.

Robinson, R. and Kelley, J. (1979) 'Class as conceived by Marx and Dahrendorf: effects on income inequality and politics in the United States and Great Britain', *American Sociological Review*, vol 44, no 1, pp 38–58.

Savage, M. (2000) *Class analysis and social transformation*, Buckingham: Open University Press.

Savage, M., Silva, E. and Warde, A. (2010) 'Dis-identification and class identity', in E. Silva and A. Warde (eds) *Cultural analysis and Bourdieu's legacy: settling accounts and developing alternatives*, London: Routledge, pp 60–74.

Sayer, A. (2011) *Why things matter to people, social science, values and ethical life*, Cambridge: Cambridge University Press.

Schafer, M. and Shippee, T. (2010) 'Age identity, gender, and perceptions of decline: does feeling older lead to pessimistic dispositions about cognitive aging?', *Journal of Gerontology: Social Sciences*, vol 65, no 1, pp 91–6.

Sharkey, B.J. (1987) 'Functional vs chronological age', *Medicine and Science in Sports and Exercise*, vol 19, no 2, pp 174–8.

Sharma, S. and Weathers, D. (2003) 'Assessing generalizability of scales used in cross-national research', *International Journal of Research in Marketing*, vol 20, no 3, pp 287–95.

Skeggs, B. (2004) *Class, self, culture*, London: Routledge.

Spiers, J. (2000) 'New perspectives on vulnerability using emic and etic approaches', *Journal of Advanced Nursing*, vol 31, no 3, pp 715–21.

Taylor, P. (2002) *New policies for older workers*, Bristol: The Policy Press.

Taylor, P. (2003) 'Older workers, employer behaviour and public policy', *Geneva Papers on Risk and Insurance – Issues and Practice*, vol 28, no 4, pp 553–7.

Toothman, E. and Barrett, A. (2011) 'Mapping midlife: an examination of social factors shaping conceptions of the timing of middle age', *Advances in Life Course Research*, vol 16, no 1, pp 99–111.

Tung, R.L. (2008) 'The cross-cultural research imperative: the need to balance cross-national and intra-national diversity', *Journal of International Business Studies*, vol 39, no 1, pp 41–6.

World Bank (2012) 'World Bank: data'. Available at: http://data.worldbank.org/

Wright, E. (1989) 'The comparative project on class structure and class consciousness: an overview', *Acta Sociologica*, vol 32, no 1, pp 3–22.

Wright, E. (1997) *Class counts: comparative studies in class analysis*, Cambridge: Cambridge University Press.

SIX

Class, pensions and old-age security

Elizangela Storelli and John B. Williamson

Introduction

Public old-age pension systems were originally introduced to reduce the risk of poverty and income insecurity in old age. Today, most elders in high-income countries[1] are covered by public pensions, and, as a result, in many high-income countries, older adults are less likely than the general population to be living below the national poverty line (Vos et al, 2008). Additionally, old-age inequality rates are significantly lower in countries with well-developed and resourced pensions systems (Barrientos, 2006; ILO, 2010). Such data support the *ageing-as-leveller* hypothesis, with public programmes 'rising the tide' of older adults to a more equal playing field with a narrowed distribution of income (Crystal and Shea, 1990). Other researchers have documented life-course continuities, suggesting post-retirement *status maintenance*, where inequalities remain stable with age (eg Henretta and Campbell, 1976; Hardy, 2009). Alternatively, the *cumulative advantage/disadvantage* hypothesis posits that social class origins have enduring positive and negative effects that accumulate over time, resulting in increased inequality with age (Dannefer, 2003; O'Rand et al, 2010). These three hypotheses are important to consider, as recent cross-cultural research has demonstrated the extent to which formal pension schemes provide income security and its effect on post-retirement inequality varies significantly among nations (Disney and Whitehouse, 2003). First, there are large disparities in terms of pension coverage. While high-income countries in North America and Western Europe have coverage ratios that range between 50% and 90%, large parts of Africa, Asia and Latin America have substantially lower coverage rates, often less than 20% of the elderly population (see Figure 6.1) (ILO, 2010). Coverage ratios also vary within countries, with disproportionate numbers of low-wage workers and other vulnerable groups being without coverage (Vos et al, 2008). Second, there are large disparities in benefit adequacy. Benefits are often tied to contributions and mirror the adequacy of pre-retirement income. Pensions in themselves do not guarantee old-age security. In addition to problems linked to coverage and adequacy, demographic changes are also contributing to the problem of pension system sustainability. In high-income countries, 21% of the population is aged 60 years or older (United Nations, 2009). By 2050, almost 33% of the population will be aged 60 or older and 26% will be aged 65 or older. Whereas middle- and low-income countries have had comparatively lower proportions of older adults, only 8% in 2009, by 2050, the proportion of the population aged 60 or older will reach 22%. Rapid population ageing is adding sustainability to the pressing issue of low coverage already facing many middle- and low-income countries.

Figure 6.1: Percentage of the working-age population effectively covered by old-age contributory pension programmes

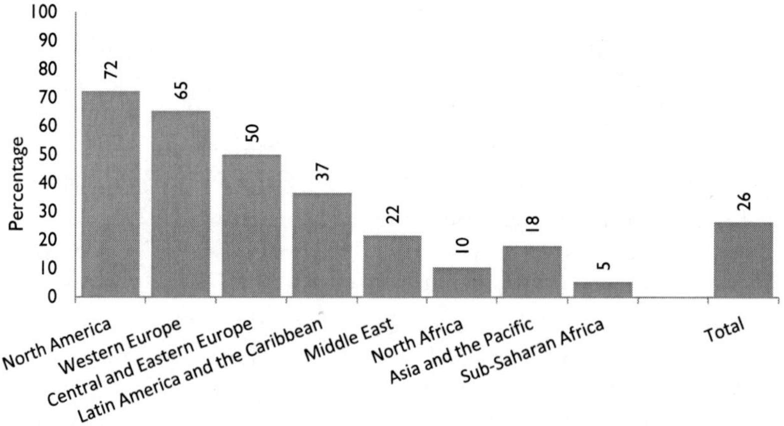

Source: Adapted from ILO (2010).

Such demographic and associated economic pressures have forced reforms that in many countries have reduced coverage and pension security while increasing inequality among older adults (Barrientos, 2006; Stewart and Yermo, 2009). The outcomes of these reforms, however, are not all negative: there have been both winners and losers, with variations depending largely on gender and class differences (Williamson, 2011). The political economy of ageing perspective can be used to argue that variations in the treatment of the elderly can be better understood by looking at country differences in social welfare policies, ideologies and social-structural factors, including power differences between class groups (Estes et al, 1996).Whether a country chooses a pension system that emphasises income replacement versus poverty prevention, or equal treatment versus equal outcomes, depends largely on the social values and ideals reflected in their political and welfare legacies (Kohli and Arza, 2010). In this way, class and income security outcomes also coincide with each country's social welfare political legacy. Different pension models emphasise different policies that reduce, maintain or exacerbate class differences in line with their political welfare legacies.

Pension models

Although there is great diversity among countries with respect to pension design, four basic public pension models are particularly relevant to the discussion presented in this chapter: (1) the pay-as-you-go defined benefit (PAYG-DB) model; (2) the funded defined contribution (FDC) model; (3) the notional defined contribution (NDC) model; and (4) the social pension model. These models vary in many ways, including funding, guaranteed benefits and risk outcomes. In the following, we discuss these important variations.

Table 6.1: Comparison of old-age pension schemes

	PAYG	**FDC**	**NDC**	**Social Pensions**
Financing	Taxes and contributions	Savings and contributions	Taxes and contributions	Taxes
Contributions	Variable	Defined	Defined	None
Benefits	Defined	Variable	Variable	Defined
Form	Social insurance	Personal savings	Personal savings	Social insurance
Management	Public	Private	Public	Public
Risks	State	Individuals	Individuals (state)	State

Source: Adapted from Calvo et al (2010).

Pension benefits can be financed on a PAYG basis, where contributions of active workers are used to pay for the benefits of present pensioners. As funds do not accumulate in these systems, they are referred to as 'unfunded'. In public, or government-managed, PAYG-DB models, pension benefits are usually funded by payroll taxes on the current working population and their employers. Benefits received at retirement are typically based on a pre-established formula using the number of years of contributions and a measure of average or final earnings.

As opposed to PAYG schemes, pension models where each generation finances its own pensions are described as 'funded' models. FDC models provide old-age security based on individual accounts typically funded by mandatory contributions from covered workers and/or their employers (James, 2005). Contribution levels are generally set by the government and benefits are based on accumulated funds and net annual returns of investment, minus the fees charged to manage account investments. FDC funds are usually invested by private sector money management organisations and are thus referred to as FDC private pensions, though, in reality, governments are still largely involved in supervisory and regulatory roles. Similar to the FDC model, with the NDC model, workers (and sometimes employers) make payroll tax contributions that are credited to their individual notional (unfunded) accounts, with their actual contributions going to the government, which, in turn, uses the money to pay pensions to current retirees. The eventual pension benefits are based on the total amount credited to the account over the working years. It is also based on the life expectancy of the worker's age cohort at the time of retirement (Börcsh-Supan, 2006).

As opposed to the other three schemes, old-age *social pensions* are not based on the contributions of individual workers. They are described as being non-contributory and are usually funded by the government's general tax revenues and provide flat-rate benefits. Social pensions can be 'universal', providing benefits to all residents (or citizens) of a certain age or industry, such as rural or agricultural workers, or 'means-tested', where coverage is provided only for those whose income falls below a specified level (Palacios and Sluchynsky, 2006).

Pension policy and old-age security

The structure of pension systems influences the exposure to and distribution of individual risk and, consequently, the degree of income security in old age. Pension models fall on a spectrum of high to low individual risk, coinciding with lower to higher degrees of income security (see Figure 6.2).

Figure 6.2: Individual risk and income security pension spectrum

Funded defined contribution plans

At one end of the spectrum are FDC privatised pensions, where funds are usually invested by private money management organisations in stocks, bonds and other securities. While FDC schemes are meant to encourage workforce participation, personal saving and individual redistribution (income smoothing) over the life course, they cannot guarantee income security in old age (Kingson and Williamson, 1999). Due to the connection between eventual benefits and individual contributions, those with low wages and infrequent contributions typically end up with inadequate benefits in old age (reflecting cumulative disadvantage). Contributions tied to employment in the formal sector lead to coverage problems for those working in informal sectors. The FDC model works best for workers who are fully employed in steady and well-paying jobs in the formal labour market, and it primarily benefits high-wage male workers (reflecting cumulative advantage) (Vos et al, 2008). Reliance on financial markets means that FDC schemes are subject to dramatic swings, leading to unpredictable and often inadequate benefits during retirement (Burtless, 2003). Current evidence suggests that shifting to an FDC scheme from PAYG-DB schemes reduces coverage rates (ILO, 2010). In general, FDC schemes are limited in their ability to provide poverty alleviation. In addition, they tend to foster increased inequality and decreased income security for older adults (Williamson, 2011). More than 20 pension schemes around the world include an FDC component (James, 2005).

Since NDC plans are also defined contribution schemes, they have many similar outcomes as FDC systems, though with less individual risk. As benefits depend on accumulated individual credit for payroll taxes paid in connection with formal employment, NDC schemes tend to favour higher-income and long-term workers and tend to penalise the frequently unemployed and low-income, temporary and informal workers (Fultz, 2006). Without redistributive elements, the distribution of income after retirement becomes a function of the combined inequalities of pre-retirement income and post-retirement pension adequacy, generally leading to greater inequalities among older adults than among younger workers (Arza, 2007).

However, unlike FDC plans, the 'interest' earned on NDC accounts is based on non-financial indexing mechanisms (eg changes in average wage levels). Thus, outcomes are less volatile than those in private markets. Further, some countries include measures that grant notional credit to certain groups of workers for time spent out of the paid labour force. For example, some countries grant credit to those who are receiving unemployment insurance benefits or mothers who are caring for small children. In such cases, the government contributes to the NDC system out of general revenue on behalf of the worker, whose NDC account is, in turn, credited for those contributions. Which groups are covered, as well as the size of the credit and the number of years a worker can receive credit, can vary from country to country, accommodating varied welfare preferences (Börcsh-Supan, 2006; Fultz, 2006). Although relatively new, NDC schemes have been introduced in several countries, including Sweden, Italy, Poland, Russia, Latvia, Slovakia, Croatia, Kyrgyzstan, Kazakhstan and Mongolia (Williamson et al, 2011).

Pay-as-you-go defined benefit plans

As defined benefit plans, PAYG-DB schemes guarantee certain benefits based on pre-established conditions, such as certain wage replacement levels, and thus do better at guaranteeing minimum pensions. However, as benefits are still tied to employment histories, pre-retirement status is generally maintained: low-income, temporary workers and those not in the formal workforce will have lower benefits than those with higher wages and full employment histories (Herd, 2009). In many cases, PAYG-DB models incorporate modest redistribution by providing greater replacement rates for lower-income individuals, though well-off individuals still receive greater absolute benefits. PAYG-DB systems are better at guaranteeing certain benefits than defined contribution systems, such as FDC and NDC pensions, but are less efficient than social pensions in terms of providing income security to the poor (Kingson and Williamson, 2001).

Social pensions

Social pensions are designed to redistribute income across population groups, with the goal of reducing poverty among the older population (Kohli and Arza, 2010). Since they are not based on contributions tied to employment, social pensions are able to increase coverage to include informal and irregular workers and the unemployed, and generally 'rise the tide', leading to reduced inequality and greater income security for poor older adults (Palacios and Sluchynsky, 2006). However, the effectiveness of social pensions in reducing old-age poverty depends on whether benefits are set above the poverty line. Typically, social pension benefits are set below the poverty line and are not sufficient to take older adults without other sources of income out of poverty (Barrientos, 2006).

Social pensions can be used as a country's primary pension system, or as a supplementary pension serving as a safety net to those who may have inadequate benefits from contributory pensions. For example, countries with NDC plans (which are generally not redistributive) often have a separate non-contributory social pension component (that is redistributive). Social pensions are generally funded in part or entirely from general government revenues and act as income insurance for individuals who would otherwise receive inadequate benefits due to low wages and/or irregular work histories. In such cases, the social pension is typically means-tested and, in many countries, eligibility requires payroll tax contributions for a specified period of time, ranging from five to 20 years. The effectiveness of social pensions in providing income security usually depends on both the eligibility requirements and the generosity of the benefit.

Although, in theory, universal social pensions have the potential to provide substantial income security in old age, in practice, the benefits are generally very low. In most poor countries, there is a lack of political support or the financial base needed to sustain social pensions at the level needed to bring poor elders up to the poverty line (Vos et al, 2008). Well-targeted, means-tested social pensions can have wide-ranging benefits, but are often limited by the lack of the administrative infrastructure needed to determine who qualifies (Holzmann and Hinz, 2005). Aside from cost and effectiveness, the choice between universal or targeted social pensions often reflects differences in underlying ideological values and the intended goals of each country's pension system (Barrientos, 2006).

Old-age security in high-income countries

FDC pensions, NDC pensions, PAYG-DB pensions and social pensions each favour different segments of the population. As such, a country's national pension system typically involves multiple pillars (tiers), and the distinct emphasis of each pillar is shaped in large part by welfare policy legacies that reflect societal preferences concerning the redistribution of resources within and among generations.

After the Second World War, several Anglo-Saxon and Scandinavian countries modified pensions that had originally been means-tested, making them universal. This group has been labelled 'the Beveridgean family', in recognition of William Beveridge's role in shaping the British welfare state at that time. During that same period, Continental and Southern European countries formed the 'Bismarckian family' of pension policy following the German model consisting of work-based earnings-related pensions (Kohli and Arza, 2010). By the end of the 20th century, it became common to group most of the pensions systems in the high-income nations into one of three groups using a typology outlined by Esping-Anderson (1990). Scandinavian countries had 'social-democratic' regimes characterised by high universal public benefits; Continental European countries had 'conservative' regimes, with public benefits aimed at preserving the status differentiation of the labour market; and Anglo-Saxon countries had 'liberal' regimes characterised by low public benefits coupled with private occupational schemes for many workers (Kohli and Arza, 2010). Although some argue that this typology is outdated today (Rhodes, 1996; Gough and Wood, 2004), recent analysis suggests that most high-income countries are still adopting social policies that align quite well with these three institutional and political legacies, especially during times of crises (Chung and Thewissen, 2011; Haynes, 2011). As outlined later, Esping-Anderson's threefold typology remains useful for categorising pension regimes in high-income countries.

Social-democratic countries

Countries with social-democratic regimes, such as Scandinavian countries, originally labelled as such for providing high public benefits, continue to choose a mix of pension policies that provide relatively high levels of income security and low levels of inequality. For example, though not generally associated with greater income security, the NDC scheme in Sweden includes benefit credits for those who are unemployed or temporarily out of the labour market, as well as a generous minimum benefit (Cichon, 1999; Williamson, 2011). By supplementing the NDC pillar with redistributive policy elements and a social pension pillar, income security among older adults in Sweden remains high and inequality remains low. In general, high levels of social benefits in Scandinavian countries have been associated with greater income replacement and lower levels of poverty and inequality among older adults throughout the region, especially when compared to countries with liberal (Anglo-Saxon) welfare regimes (ILO, 2010; Haynes, 2011).

Conservative countries

Countries with conservative regime legacies, such as those in Western Europe, have pension schemes that tend to maintain pre-retirement status. For example, in contrast to Sweden, Italy's NDC system provides generous benefits to contributors without generous minimum benefits (Cichon, 1999). Germany's pension system includes a large PAYG-DB pillar that closely ties benefits to individual contribution histories but, as opposed to the more social-democratic regime of Sweden, does not provide credits for periods of unemployment (Kohli and Arza, 2010). A distinction is sometimes made between the pension systems found in Southern Europe (Portugal, Italy, Greece and Spain), countries that put greater reliance on families for social assistance, the so-called Mediterranean model, and those in Germany and other Continental countries (Rhodes, 1996).

Liberal countries

Liberal regimes, typical of Anglo-Saxon countries, tend to emphasise a limited role for the state and a greater role for the market, including low public benefits topped with occupational and private schemes; a policy mix that tends to limit income security and exacerbate the effects of cumulative advantage and disadvantage in old age. For example, the US social security system (PAYG-DB), though slightly redistributive – replacing a higher rate of pre-retirement income for low-wage workers – provides relatively low replacement rates relative to the Scandinavian countries (ILO, 2010). When social security was first introduced, it significantly reduced poverty among older adults. However, stagnant benefits and an increased emphasis on employer-sponsored pensions (defined benefit and defined contribution pensions) and individual private pensions (voluntary FDC pensions) have led to increasing inequality among older adults in recent years (Engelhardt and Gruber, 2006). Legislated tax breaks used to encourage personal savings in individual pension accounts tend to benefit those with higher incomes, and employer-sponsored pensions are largely segregated by job and industry, disproportionately benefiting middle- and higher-income groups (Munnell and Sundén, 2004; Butrica et al, 2010).

As another example, the UK has recently passed new legislation mandating that as of 2012, every new employee earning over a specified amount must be automatically enrolled in either their employer's occupational pension plan or one of the new privatised account plans called 'personal accounts' (Williamson, 2011). This is just the most recent of a number of prior private sector individual account schemes promoted by the British government since the 1986 legislation that provided incentives for workers to opt out of the public PAYG-DB pension scheme in favour of privatised FDC personal accounts. Greater reliance on these private FDC pensions means that older adults in the UK face increased risks of inadequate benefits due to volatile markets and/or low contribution rates.

Although the tactic of limiting government involvement and using tax breaks to encourage supplementary employer and private pensions tends to absorb almost as much public revenue as the welfare policies of more conservative regimes, such as Germany and France, the outcomes tend to be less efficient and egalitarian (Kohli and Arza, 2010). Evidence suggests that old-age poverty is strongly associated with resources spent on social transfers. The poverty rates of older adults in the US are twice as high as those in Germany or France and four times as high as those in the Scandinavian countries, which spend an average of nearly 50% more on social transfers than do Anglo-Saxon countries (OECD, 2009; ILO, 2011). While outcomes are not necessarily uniform across countries, pension systems are effective in reducing income inequality and poverty among older adults when sufficiently endowed with resources.

In general, high-income countries have pension systems that affect income/class inequality and financial security in accordance with their political welfare legacies. Countries with social-democratic legacies have a policy mix that minimises income inequality and promotes retirement security for all. Countries with a conservative legacy tend to have policies that maintain pre-retirement class structures. Lastly, countries with liberal legacies have policy mixes that tend to exacerbate income inequalities and provide comparatively low retirement security.

Old-age security in middle- and low-income countries

Old-age security and pension outcomes in middle- and low-income countries are especially important to consider, as over 60% of the world's elderly population now live in these countries, a proportion that will reach nearly 80% by 2050 (United Nations, 2009). In most high-income countries, population ageing did not become an issue until economic and welfare structures were generally well-developed. Current middle- and low-income countries, on the other hand, are being forced to contend with population ageing in the midst of fragile economies, low levels of economic development and fierce economic globalisation (Vos et al, 2008). Pension programmes in lower-income countries are typically plagued by coverage rate problems, with mean coverage rates among the poorest countries generally under 20% (ILO, 2010). Although initially establishing pension systems that largely mirrored the European PAYG-DB schemes, faced with simultaneous population ageing and the need to promote economic development, many middle- and low-income countries have adopted developmentalist approaches to pension welfare. The developmental welfare approach regards economic development as the more essential element of social and economic advancement, and tries to use social policy as an agent to foster economic development (Ye, 2011). At early stages of development, the logic of the developmentalist approach suggests that pension policies should serve the most productive sectors of society, such as workers in large firms and urban areas or government employees.

The developmentalist welfare approach has generally resulted in poor outcomes, such as increased inequality between rich and poor or between urban and rural citizens (Kwon, 2009). Evidence from middle- and low-income countries suggests that developmentalist pension reforms – such as shifting from defined benefit to private defined contribution systems – generally failed to achieve their economic development objectives, and tend to reduce income security for both current and future retirees (Fultz, 2006; Arza, 2007; ILO, 2010). Disillusioned by the outcomes of privatised pensions, many middle- and low-income countries are now reviewing and reconsidering the role of income security in national development. Increasingly, income security among older adults is perceived as an effective and important means to facilitate and safeguard long-term economic growth and, rather than the developmentalist approach, many countries are now adopting reforms and policies that facilitate and encourage 'growth with equity' or 'pro-poor growth' (OECD, 2009; ILO, 2011). To this end, many middle- and low-income countries are enacting or considering a new wave of reforms aimed at increasing income security for older adults. For example, Chile has recently implemented social pension reforms designed to increase benefits for both low-income contributors and non-contributors (Calvo et al, 2010). Argentina and Bolivia have reversed their reforms based on funded individual accounts, and Croatia, Hungary and Poland are debating whether or not to reduce the size of the private tier of their pension systems (ILO, 2010). There have also been successful efforts to introduce universal and means-tested social pensions in several countries. In Botswana, Namibia and South Africa, for example, basic social pension schemes have had positive effects on poverty alleviation (Johnson and Williamson, 2006), and targeted rural social pensions in Brazil have also been very successful at reducing old-age poverty (Lloyd-Sherlock, 2006; Stewart and Yermo, 2009). We now discuss two country case studies to illustrate what may in the years ahead become a trend away from the prior developmentalist approach to pension policy reform in lower-income nations.

China

As in many middle- and low-income countries, the welfare system in China has gone through radical changes during the past few decades. Prior to 1995, China's pension system was a PAYG-DB scheme designed primarily to cover urban workers, particularly those employed in state-owned enterprises (Williamson et al, 2011). Under the developmentalist stage of its pension reform efforts, a number of changes were made (Ye, 2011). Between 1997 and 2005, China began the transition to a multi-pillar scheme by adding a substantial FDC pillar (Impavido et al, 2009). The urban system now includes a PAYG-DB pillar and a mandatory individual FDC pillar. In addition, there is a new government-regulated FDC occupational pillar available for workers in some of the most profitable large firms. Despite these reforms, as of 2008, only an estimated 33% of the Chinese labour force was covered by pension programmes (Impavido et al, 2009), including only about half of urban workers, but efforts are underway to greatly increase this coverage with a new social pension scheme for urban residents (Fang, 2012). China's rural population has historically had very little pension coverage (only 7% as of 2008; see Impavido et al, 2009); however, that will be changing rapidly as the government is making a major effort to extend pension coverage to the rural population (Williamson et al, 2011). With the goals of 'basic benefit' and 'broad coverage' the New Rural Social Pension Insurance (NRSPI), adopted in 2009, aims to cover all rural areas by 2020 (Ye, 2011: 688). NRSPI is a voluntary programme that combines a social pension financed by both local and central government with an FDC account financed by individual contributors. Older adults who contribute to the FDC part of the pension for a specified number of years become eligible for benefits that supplement the modest social pension component.

Although the establishment of the NRSPI demonstrates the Chinese government's new efforts towards sustainable 'development with equity' (Ye, 2011), there are a number of important limitations that may impact income security outcomes for older adults. Since the scheme is voluntary, it is unclear how well it is going to work with respect to both coverage rates and benefit levels. Further, many of the poorest workers may be unable or unwilling to contribute to the FDC component, and thus those most in need may not benefit. Lastly, central and particularly local (provincial) governments may not have enough tax revenue over the long run to make good on the pension benefits currently being promised (Williamson et al, 2011). Yet, despite these limitations, the NRSPI is crucial to bridging the urban–rural divide among older Chinese and has already increased income security for millions of older adults in rural China.

Chile

Chile's first pension system mirrored European PAYG-DB schemes based on employment contributions. With large agricultural and informal labour markets, coverage remained limited to government and urban workers and benefits were high (Barrientos, 2002). Due to increasing demographic pressures and pension system deficits, as well as the strong influence of developmentalist policy preferences from the World Bank and other economic consultants, in 1981, Chile began a transition from its old PAYG-DB system to a new scheme based on privately managed individual FDC accounts, making it the first country to implement a mandated FDC privatised pension system. Following the Chilean reform, 11 more countries in Latin America, as well as 13 countries in Central and Eastern Europe and Central Asia, have reformed their pensions systems to include full or partially privatised FDC plans (ILO, 2010).

The mandated individual contributions of the FDC plan pushed individuals into the informal sector and overall pension coverage declined (Arza, 2007). Additionally, the new privatised FDC plan had problems due to insufficient asset accumulation to pay adequate pensions at retirement to low-wage workers. Despite the high administration fees, the FDC pension plan worked quite well for high-income, steadily employed workers, but it has increased income inequality and has had a detrimental effect on income security, particularly among low-income older adults. Disillusioned with developmentalist welfare policy, Chile has recently introduced reforms designed to put greater emphasis on providing universal and equitable pension benefits. In 2008, the country passed comprehensive pension reforms that provide a non-contributory social pension, paid to the poorest 60% of the elderly population, and a supplementary pension benefit for those who are eligible for private pensions, but have inadequate benefits (Calvo et al, 2010). The reform also provides a tax credit for voluntary savings targeted specifically at low-income workers.

Beginning with PAYG-DB models, both Chile and China subsequently implemented developmentalist reforms that prioritised economic development and focused pension benefits on high-income and urban formal sector workers. Overall, these reforms had detrimental effects on coverage and benefit levels, reducing old-age income security in each country. In recent years, both countries have made policy shifts from a prior emphasis on developmentalist goals towards a new 'growth with equity' approach (ILO, 2011). Both have enacted social pension policies that aim to increase coverage and benefit adequacy for low-income and rural older adults. Although there are marked differences in pension policies and development trajectories among middle- and low-income countries, the examples of Chile and China illustrate how pension reforms can show functionally similar trends in different parts of the world while at the same time maintaining major structural differences reflecting country-specific policy legacies and differences in class, demographic, economic and political structures.

Looking to the future

Our analysis suggests that in the high-income countries, pension systems consist of a mix of policies that affect inequality and income security in accordance with their social welfare policy legacies. In middle- and lower-income countries, poverty, inequality and class-related pension outcomes have recently been shaped by policies designed more to foster rapid economic development than to deal with the current financial security needs of their economically vulnerable older citizens. We expect important, but relatively modest, policy changes over the next couple of decades in the high-income countries. While these countries will be experiencing rapid population ageing and increased pressures due to further economic globalisation, their welfare state cultures are likely to remain relatively stable, albeit with reforms tending towards less generous benefits.

Our conclusions are different, but necessarily more tentative, for the middle- and low-income nations. Their welfare states are emerging at a different point in history, and will be facing serious pressures due to dramatic population ageing and the exigencies of economic globalisation. The welfare state models that emerge in many of these countries may not fit well within any of the three categories of Esping-Anderson's typology. These countries each have their own class, cultural and institutional legacies that are likely to influence the shape of the pension policy institutions that emerge. It may be that different models will emerge in different parts of the world (Gough and Wood,

2004). It is possible that we will eventually see a degree of convergence around three new models: a Latin American model (greatly influenced by Chile) (Aspalter, 2011); an East/South East Asian model (greatly influenced by China) (Lee and Ku, 2007); and possibly an African model (greatly influenced by South Africa, or possibly Namibia). Yet, regardless of whether these three models converge, what seems most likely is that there will be an eventual shift away from the recent focus on developmentalist models promoted by the World Bank, towards new pension models that are more responsive to the immediate social welfare needs of the older populations in emerging economies around the world.

Note

[1] In this chapter, the differentiation of countries into low-, middle- and high-income is based on the World Bank's (2012) country classification system, which uses Gross National Income (GNI) per capita as its main criterion.

References

Arza, C. (2007) 'Pension reform in Latin America: distributional principles, inequalities and alternative policy options', *Journal of Latin American Studies*, vol 40, no 1, pp 1–28.

Aspalter, C. (2011) 'The development of ideal-typical welfare regime theory', *International Social Work*, vol 54, no 6, pp 735–50.

Barrientos, A. (2002) *Comparing pension schemes in Chile, Singapore, Brazil and South Africa*, Manchester: Institute for Development Policy and Management, University of Manchester.

Barrientos, A. (2006) 'Poverty reduction: the missing piece of pension reform in Latin America', *Social Policy & Administration*, vol 40, no 4, pp 369–84.

Börcsh-Supan, A.H. (2006) 'What are NDC systems? What do they bring to reform strategies?', in R. Holzmann (ed) *Pension reform: issues and prospects for non-financial defined contribution (NDC) schemes*, Washington, DC: World Bank, pp 35–55.

Burtless, G. (2003) 'What do we know about the risk of individual account pensions? Evidence from industrial countries', *The American Economic Review*, vol 93, no 2, pp 354–9.

Butrica, B.A., Murphy, D.P. and Zedlewski, S.R. (2010) 'How many struggle to get by in retirement?', *The Gerontologist*, vol 50, no 4, pp 482–94.

Calvo, E., Bertranou, F.M. and Bertranou, E. (2010) 'Are old-age pension system reforms moving away from individual retirement accounts in Latin America?', *Journal of Social Policy*, vol 39, no 2, pp 223–34.

Chung, H. and Thewissen, S. (2011) 'Falling back on old habits? A comparison of the social and unemployment crisis reactive policy strategies in Germany, the UK and Sweden', *Social Policy & Administration*, vol 45, no 4, pp 354–70.

Cichon, M. (1999) 'Notional defined-contribution schemes: old wine in new bottles?', *International Social Security Review*, vol 52, no 4, pp 87–102.

Crystal, S. and Shea, D. (1990) 'Cumulative advantage, cumulative disadvantage, and inequality among elderly people', *The Gerontologist*, vol 30, no 4, pp 437–43.

Dannefer, D. (2003) 'Cumulative advantage/disadvantage and the life course: cross fertilizing age and social science theory', *Journal or Gerontology, Social Sciences*, vol 58B, pp S327–38.

Disney, R. and Whitehouse, E. (2003) 'Cross-national comparisons of retirement income', in S. Crystal and D. Shea (eds) *Annual review of gerontology and geriatrics: focus on economic outcomes in later life*, New York, NY: Springer, pp 60–94.

Engelhardt, G.V. and Gruber, J. (2006) 'Social security and the evolution of elderly poverty', in A. Auerbach, D. Card and J. Quigley (eds) *Public policy and income distribution*, New York, NY: Russell Sage Foundation, pp 259–87.

Esping-Anderson, G. (1990) *The three worlds of welfare capitalism*, Princeton, NJ: Princeton University Press.

Estes, C.L., Linkins, K.W. and Binney, E.A. (1996) 'The political economy of aging', in R.H. Binstock and L.K. George (eds) *Handbook of aging and the social sciences* (4th edn), San Diego, CA: Academic Press, pp 346–61.

Fang, L. (2012) *Towards universal coverage: a macro analysis of China's public pension reform* (CISSS CASS Working Paper No 1), Beijing: Center for International Social Security Studies, Chinese Academy of Social Sciences.

Fultz, E. (2006) 'Discussion of NDC pension schemes in middle and low-income countries', in R. Holzmann and E. Palmer (eds) *Pension reform: issues and prospects for non-financial defined contribution (NDC) schemes*, Washington, DC: World Bank, pp 323–34.

Gough, I. and Wood, G. (2004) *Insecurity and welfare regimes in Asia, Africa and Latin America*, Cambridge: Cambridge University Press.

Hardy, M. (2009) 'Income inequality in later life', in P. Uhlenberg (ed) *International handbook of population aging*, New York, NY: Springer, pp 493–518.

Haynes, P. (2011) 'Are Scandinavian countries different? A comparison of relative incomes for older people in OECD nations', *Social Policy & Administration*, vol 45, no 2, pp 114–30.

Henretta, J.C. and Campbell, R.T. (1976) 'Status attainment and status maintenance: a study of stratification in old age', *American Sociological Review*, vol 41, pp 981–92.

Herd, P. (2009) 'Women, public pensions, and poverty: what can the United States learn from other countries?', *Journal of Women, Politics & Policy*, vol 30, no 2, pp 301–34.

Holzmann, R. and Hinz, R. (2005) *Old-age income support in the 21st century: an international perspective on pension systems and reform*, Washington, DC: World Bank.

ILO (International Labour Organization) (2010) *World social security report 2010/11: providing coverage in times of crisis and beyond*, Geneva: International Labour Organization.

ILO (2011) *Social security for social justice and a fair globalization*, Geneva: International Labour Organization.

Impavido, G., Hu, Y.W. and Li, X. (2009) *Governance and fund management in the Chinese pension system* (IMF working paper WP/09/246), Washington, DC: International Monetary Fund.

James, E. (2005) *Reforming social security: lessons from thirty countries* (NCPA Policy Report No 277), Dallas, TX: National Center for Policy Analysis.

Johnson, J.K.M. and Williamson, J.B. (2006) 'Do universal non-contributory old-age pensions make sense for rural areas in low-income countries', *International Social Security Review*, vol 59, no 4, pp 47–64.

Kingson, E.R. and Williamson, J.B. (1999) 'Why privatizing social security is a bad idea', in J.B. Williamson, D.M. Watts-Roy and E.R. Kingson (eds) *Generational equity debate*, New York, NY: Columbia University Press, pp 204–19.

Kingson, E.R. and Williamson, J.B. (2001) 'Economic security policies', in R.H. Binstock and L.K. George (eds) *Handbook of aging and the social sciences* (5th edn), San Diego, CA: Academic Press, pp 369–86.

Kohli, M. and Arza, C. (2010) 'The political economy of pension reform in Europe', in R.H. Binstock and L.K. George (eds) *Handbook of aging and the social sciences* (7th edn), San Diego, CA: Elsevier.

Kwon, H. (2009) 'The reform of the developmental welfare state in East Asia', *International Journal of Social Welfare*, vol 18, pp S12–S21.

Lee, Y. and Ku, Y. (2007) 'East Asian welfare regimes: testing the hypothesis of the developmental welfare state', *Social Policy & Administration*, vol 41, no 2, pp 197–212.

Lloyd-Sherlock, P. (2006) 'Simple transfers, complex outcomes: the impacts of pensions on poor households in Brazil', *Development and Change*, vol 37, no 5, pp 969–95.

Munnell, A.H. and Sundén, A. (2004) *Coming up short: the challenge of 401k plans*, Washington, DC: Brookings Institute.

OECD (Organisation for Economic Co-operation and Development) (2009) *Pensions at a glance: public policies across OECD countries*, Paris: OECD.

O'Rand, A.M., Isaacs, K. and Roth, L. (2010) 'Age and inequality in global context', in D. Dannefer and C. Phillipson (eds) *The Sage handbook of social gerontology*, London: Sage, pp 127–37.

Palacios, R. and Sluchynsky, O. (2006) *Social pensions part 1: their role in the overall pension system*, Washington, DC: World Bank.

Rhodes, M. (1996) 'Southern welfare states: identity, problems and prospects for reform', *South European Society and Politics*, vol 1, no 3, pp 1–22.

Stewart, F. and Yermo, J. (2009) *Pensions in Africa* (Working Paper No 30), Paris: OECD.

United Nations (2009) *World population aging 2009*, New York, NY: United Nations.

Vos, R., Ocampo, J.A. and Cortez, A.L. (eds) (2008) *Ageing and development*, London: Zed Books.

Williamson, J.B. (2011) 'The future of retirement security', in R.H. Binstock and L.K. George (eds) *Handbook of aging and the social sciences* (7th edn), San Diego, CA: Elsevier.

Williamson, J.B., Price, M. and Shen, C. (2011) 'Pension policy in China, Singapore, and South Korea: an assessment of the potential value of the notional defined contribution model', *Journal of Aging Studies*, vol 26, no 1, pp 79–89.

World Bank (2012) 'How we classify countries'. Available at: http://data.worldbank.org/about/country-classifications

Ye, L. (2011) 'Demographic transition, developmentalism and social security in China', *Social Policy & Administration*, vol 45, no 6, pp 678–93.

SEVEN

Class and health inequalities in later life

Ian Rees Jones and Paul Higgs

Introduction

For over 60 years, significant research activity has addressed the extent to which the effects of social class over the life course have determined or contributed to an individual's economic and social fate in old age. This has led to the elaboration and discussion of a whole host of conceptual and measurement issues among a growing body of epidemiological and social researchers. In light of the social changes and accompanying theoretical developments over the same period, to these issues we must add questions about the viability of class as a means of understanding social relations and social inequality in contemporary society. In this chapter, we will interrogate these issues as they relate to the role of class in later life using the prism of health inequalities. We will seek to show how the relationship between class and later life, in terms of health inequalities, is more complex than would be expected. Furthermore, we will argue that this complexity demands that we need to think more creatively about how such relationships can work and whether the nature of contemporary retirement creates a more 'individualised' context for the operation of social class in all its different manifestations.

A major driver of our argument is that when examined in the round, much research on health inequalities in later life in North America and Western Europe has produced remarkably ambiguous results. While some studies have demonstrated a convergence in the health of those from different socio-economic positions as they enter old age, other studies have shown that class-related inequalities in mortality, morbidity and health behaviours continue deep into later life (Breeze et al, 2001). Researchers have focused on two competing hypotheses to explain these patterns: the cumulated disadvantage thesis, which suggests that the level of health inequality related to socio-economic status (SES) in a cohort increases as a cohort ages (Dannefer, 2003; Prus, 2007); and the 'divergence/convergence', or 'age as leveller', hypothesis, which suggests a widening of inequalities up to early old age but with a decrease in inequalities thereafter (Beckett, 2000). To date, much socio-epidemiological research interrogating these hypotheses has treated social class as a variable within standard log linear models. This has led to two key areas of difficulty emerging: first, *technical* questions about the utility of occupational class and other indicators of socio-economic position to study health statuses in a post-working population; and, second, *theoretical* questions about the role of social class in the lives of both working and retired people. In respect of the former, studies of later life have focused on a range of different measures of SES, incorporating indicators of class, status, income, wealth and deprivation and how these interact with other important factors such as retirement status, gender and ethnicity. Almost as a consequence of this, there has been a relative neglect of wider theoretical debates about class and class culture and how these might relate to the changing nature of later life. One effect of this is that the wider implications of the emergence of a relatively lengthy post-working life have not been fully incorporated into studies of class and health in old age. This is a major lacuna given that the generations entering retirement today in affluent countries are precisely those who have experienced the social changes that have seen both increased prosperity and the questioning of the salience of class in wider society. We therefore need to address two questions. First, how is it best to describe and explain patterns of social class inequalities in health over the life course? Second, what does class mean in later life and how can it be conceptualised in relation to a population that may have been out of the workforce for many decades?

Health inequality and the role of social class

Despite continued increases in life expectancy, there is now a large and overwhelming body of research that highlights the persistence of health inequalities across the life course (Marmot, 2010). Health gradients have been identified by SES (Marmot, 2006), geographic indicators of area and place (Dorling, 2012), race and ethnicity (Nazroo et al, 2009), income (Wilkinson, 2005), education (Eikemo et al, 2008), IQ (Batty and Deary, 2004), and, not least, social class (Muntaner and Lynch, 1999). The general recognition that inequalities persist and are deepening has not led to any general agreement over their cause or, indeed, over the nature of the interventions necessary to address them (Pickett and Dorling, 2010). However, it has pointed out the need to go beyond the simple collection of the facts of inequality and towards explanation. One particular challenge reoccurs, which is how do the relationships between social class, geography, lifestyle and behaviour interact to produce the well-adumbrated statistics that populate epidemiological journals (Higgs et al, 2004)? Rather than trying to identify one key factor, it is likely that explanations are to be found in the complex interactions between individual, group and environmental factors.

Hall and Taylor (2009) have argued that social relations are structured by collective representations (or social imaginaries) that foster social trust, give meaning to individual action, provide a sense of belonging to a community and inform what is expected from other members of that community. Such relations contribute to social cohesion and influence people's capabilities and potential for resilience at both individual and population levels. By doing so, they set the range of behaviours that are seen to be appropriate in different contexts and promote (or damage) the health of communities (Gatens, 2004). In these formulations, social relations structured by organisations, social networks and social hierarchies all play a role in the construction of health inequalities. Some notable writers have taken the lead from these approaches and emphasised either social hierarchies and status (Marmot, 2006) or the concomitant psychosocial mechanisms that follow on from the stresses of living in unequal societies (Wilkinson and Pickett, 2009). Others have continued to argue for the continued salience of occupational class (Goldthorpe, 2009; Muntaner et al, 2010) in providing an overarching context for understanding health inequalities. To this group needs to be added those researchers drawing on the non-reductive work of Bourdieu (1984) to focus on the impact of class relations on the production and reproduction of advantage (Atkinson, 2010). For this latter group, class position is constructed and maintained through accumulation of different forms of economic, cultural and social capital over the life course (Le Roux et al, 2008; Jones et al, 2011). How this is then transformed into inequality is therefore not simple, nor is it inevitable. Given the increasing sophistication of these arguments, it is odd that the more complex and contextualised understandings of class relations are not fully incorporated into research addressing inequalities in health in later life.

Health inequality and later life

As we pointed out earlier, in respect of the understanding of health inequalities in later life, research has produced ambiguous results. Although rates of disability and illness in older populations have fallen over the last 40 years, inequalities in health can be found both in the young old and at very old ages. But, in equal measure, researchers have found evidence for declining levels of inequality in the case of some health conditions. Some early studies suggested that the health status of different socio-economic groups in old age was becoming more equal (Fox and Goldblatt, 1982; Townsend et al, 1988; Arber and Ginn, 1993; Arber and Lahelma, 1993). This convergence has been generally explained in terms of mortality selection or survivor effects. Indeed, data from the UK shows life expectancy seemingly growing more equal for people from manual and non-manual occupational backgrounds, suggesting that differential survivorship in old age may have lessened (Office for National Statistics, 2007). Some studies do show that socio-economic inequalities remain as people age (Marmot et al, 2003) and that inequalities in morbidity appear to continue into later life (Grundy and Glaser, 2000; Breeze et al, 2001; Grundy and Sloggett, 2003). Analysis of Scottish data suggests that, taking account of selective mortality, inequalities persist in old age (Benzeval et al, 2011). Analysis of the British Regional Heart Survey has also shown that inequalities in coronary heart disease incidence persist in later life (Ramsay et al, 2008). Importantly, the same data show that almost a third of all deaths occurring during middle and older age can be attributed to the excess risks experienced by manual men over non-manual men, with over half of this accounted for by adult coronary risk factors, including smoking, alcohol and physical activity (Emberson et al, 2004). In contrast, analysis of the Health Survey for England (Asthana et al, 2004) found substantial variation in the relative importance of the age and class distributions of different diseases. The authors argued that age effects may be important even in conditions where an apparently strong social class gradient exists.

In comparative work, Bowling (2004) examined evidence across 11 European countries and found that absolute and relative inequalities in mortality by measures of housing tenure and education persist into old age, even in the oldest old. Pooled data show that absolute socio-economic mortality inequalities increased with age, while relative socio-economic mortality inequalities decreased with age. However, different measures of socio-economic location appear to behave differently with respect to health status. For example, in Germany, income was found to be the best predictor of health status in a 60+ population, while education, occupational prestige and wealth were not consistently related to health (Von Dem Knesebeck et al, 2003). Analysis of the Survey of Health, Ageing and Retirement in Europe (SHARE) data found quality of life in old age (as measured by the CASP-19) to be associated with socio-economic position (SEP) (measured by income, education, home-ownership, net worth and car ownership), but this association varied in strength between countries, with high variation in Germany and low variation in Switzerland (Von Dem Knesebeck et al, 2007). Once again, we are left with ambiguous results, which makes the task of addressing the role of social class in later life all the more difficult.

Class as a variable and other indicators

Occupational class as a variable is a problematic entity, which has important implications for the conduct of research into health inequalities. As Muntaner et al (2010) show, measures of employment relations as the basis for formulations of social class follow two basic frameworks: neo-Weberian (drawing on the National Statistics Socio-economic Classification (NS-SEC) and neo-Marxist (Wright, 1997). Their review of studies utilising these approaches found that associations between employment relations and health do not always follow a graded relationship. For example, small employers can show poorer health than skilled workers and supervisors can sometimes have worse health than front-line workers. The studies provide important support for Wright's (1978) theory of contradictory class locations. Such findings, based as they are on a relational approach to class, differ considerably from approaches based on stratification according to income or status. They consequently buttress critiques of the later work of Goldthorpe (2009) and have important implications for any policy recommendations, specifically, the extent to which policies should focus on the redistribution of income and wealth or on changes in workplace conditions and the provision of education and welfare services.

In the past, later life was often ignored or at least neglected by researchers undertaking class analysis, primarily because researchers needed to concentrate on adult working populations in order to operationalise their analyses of inequality. In recent years, however, the number of studies of ageing and inequality has rapidly grown given the greater availability of large high-quality studies and longitudinal data, such as the English Longitudinal Study of Ageing (ELSA) the Berlin Ageing studies and SHARE. Aratzcoz and Rueda (2007) have noted the neglect of older people in research on health inequalities and, in particular, in research on class and later life. Crucially, one of the explanations for this neglect has been that there has been no agreement on the best measure of SEP for older people among social epidemiologists. Using the past occupational status of individuals was seen as problematic for a number of reasons, including the time elapsed since exiting the labour market, the ambivalent nature of last occupation and differences in the extent and depth of the relationship between occupation and material resources in old age. As Hyde and Jones (2007) showed, time since labour-market exit appears to affect the strength of the association between SEP measures (largely derived for use in working-age populations) and measures of health status. Gender differences appear to become more important in later life and so family roles, household compositions and the household division of labour may also be important determinants of (ill) health in later life. Grundy (2005), in addressing status, highlights a number of measurement problems that occur at older ages. Status can be different for both men and women, reflecting different life courses. Factors associated with health include marital status, lack of social support, education, low income, housing tenure, adverse life events, social networks, loneliness, self-assessed age, frequency of contact with children and receiving help from and giving help to children. Grundy found different levels and directions of associations with different health indicators (self-reported health, cardiovascular disease (CVD), chronic illness, mental illness, use of services).

In an analysis of the Health Survey for England, Grundy and Sloggett (2003) used receipt of income support as a marker of poverty and housing tenure as a measure of socio-economic resources. They found a strong link between poverty in old age and poor health after controlling for other factors, including smoking. They found that marital status and perceived social support (their measures of social resources) had the largest effect on their indicator of health (the General Health Questionnaire (GHQ)). But they also found counter-intuitive associations between marital status and health indicators, particularly a lack of health advantage for married older women. One of the key findings of this research was the possible bias of older people in institutions being excluded from private household surveys, thus distorting the explanation of inequalities among older people.

It is perhaps understandable that because the retired are not in an occupational grouping, it has been assumed in many studies that class becomes less salient. A contrary argument is that the 'long shadow of work' ensures that work environment over the life course has effects on health in later life. This latter argument, however, needs a standardised or at least stable employment history to be plausible. The transformations in work relations since the 1980s make such an assumption increasingly doubtful. The last occupation prior to retirement may be an unreliable data point because of potential downward mobility prior to retirement.

Furthermore, gender differences in employment histories may have profound effects on gender inequalities in material circumstances in later life (Arber and Ginn, 1993). Income is related to employment and, therefore, also becomes problematic as a measure of SES in old age. In relation to health studies, the added problem of people with disability/ ill health being in receipt of income from benefits additionally makes causal analysis difficult. Income data in old age, given the variety of sources and methods of payment, also make it a complex variable to interpret. Many researchers use education as a proxy variable because it has the advantage of avoiding some problems of reverse causation (because it tends to be fixed in early life), but education may be a crude indicator because the percentage leaving school with no qualifications in the mid-20th century does not capture the fine grain of social hierarchies and is subject to periodisation effects that lead to generational differences. Some researchers opt for using household-based indicators as against individual indicators (eg access to a car, housing tenure, ownership of resources), but, once again, there are potential problems in terms of reverse causation and health, with, for example, increasing disability leading to decreasing car ownership.

Grundy and Holt (2001) compared different indicators of SES either singly or in combination to investigate their use in studies of health inequalities in older people. Using two waves of the Retirement and Retirement Plans Survey, they compared seven indicators of SES in terms of predictive power in relation to self-reported health. These were the Registrar General occupation classification, equivalised income, educational qualifications, household tenure, household resources (car and others) and the Townsend deprivation indicator. They found that all indicators were significantly associated. The highest predictive power was found in education and social class when paired with a deprivation indicator. They concluded that measures need to be theoretically grounded. They also emphasised the importance of generational effects. For example, home-ownership as an indicator is sensitive to the effect of 'right to buy' for certain cohorts so that for those in retirement, housing tenure becomes less sensitive as an indicator of a social gradient. Thus, indicators need to be seen as context-dependent. The utility of indicators may also vary with the explanatory approach used. For those looking for material explanations of health inequality, income and wealth may be important; for those looking at behavioural explanations, education may be considered significant; while psychosocial explanations may look for indicators of status.

Connolly, O'Reilly and Rosato (2010) argue that the ideal indicator of SES in older populations should be a measure of lifetime SEP. This, they suggest, could be wealth as measured by the value of the individual's house. Their analysis of census data for Northern Ireland constructed an indicator of accumulated wealth based on a combination of housing tenure and house value and they found that it was a good predictor of ill health as measured by current subjective health status and future mortality risk. Their indicator correlated strongly with other indicators of SEP, such as social class (NS-SEC) and educational level. The relationship was found to be strong after adjusting for other indicators, such as social support and indicators of environmental quality. House value may provide an indication of the accumulation of resources over the life course, thus providing a strong indicator of SEP for studies of older groups. Work by McMunn, Nazroo and Breeze (2009) throws light on the view that a declining relationship between SEP and health may demonstrate survivor effects. Using data from the first two waves of ELSA, where individuals were healthy at baseline, they found that wealth predicted functional impairment but that the wealth gradient declined with age for self-reported health, and selective mortality appeared to contribute to this. In their study, wealth was the value of property net of debt, savings and assets. Pension wealth was excluded as it was considered as income. They concluded that patterns of socio-economic inequality persisted for impairment but not for heart disease, so that while selective mortality is present, it may only explain some of the decline in health indicators. The size of the effect of selective mortality is not clear. For example, selection does not fully explain the diminishing relationship between education level and health in old age (Becket, 2000). Common variables used in studies of old age or retirement are class, income and education. Accumulated wealth may be a better indicator of lifetime economic status than income in retirement, past occupation or past education. So, McMunn and colleagues (2009) focus on wealth as a means of capturing financial and other resources in old age as opposed to class or education. Following their argument that the variable 'previous occupation class' was not considered to correspond with class per se but was used as a measure of financial and other resources, it is therefore not surprising that it does not perform well compared to a measure of wealth.

In response to such problems, many social epidemiologists have argued for multiple indicators of SEP in old age as a means of addressing the complexities involved. Reflecting the issues discussed earlier, Aratzcoz and Rueda (2007) have called for more theoretically informed analysis of the social determinants of health in old age, greater clarity over the best indicators of SEP, health status and household forms, as well as greater attention to individuals living in residential settings in studies of older people. However, although all of these are to be welcomed, they cannot address the more troubling question of what changes have occurred to the social and cultural aspects of class.

Class culture and the death of class?

It is now well recognised that in the most affluent nations, the proportion of those over retirement age has increased and will continue to increase. Furthermore, the proportion of people's lives spent in this post-work life stage is increasing. Within social gerontology, both structured dependency and political economy approaches to old age sought to make their approaches directly link with social class. This was done by means of drawing a direct line between the individual (or household) social position as defined by the individual's working life. Irwin (1999), among others, has argued that there has been a tendency within gerontology to construct older people as an essentialised marginalised group constituting 'the elderly'. She argued that later life should not be seen as a post-employment category, but as one influenced by the changing nature of welfare claims over the life course. Still defined by social policy, for Irwin, it is the continuities in class and gender over the life course that comprise the nature of the inequalities experienced by older people. However, we would argue that it is the connections (or lack of them) between work and post-work that are key to the understanding of how social class and inequalities in later life are linked.

To develop this argument, we must examine two concurrent and interconnected phenomena. One is that transformations in economic and social life have led to class positions, class cultures and class identities becoming more contingent and unstable. The other is the 'deinstitutionalisation' of the life course, which has transformed the ascribed status of old age into the more agentic and less homogeneous category of later life. Previous conceptions of the role of old age as a form of economic redundancy had led to the ignoring of class in old age (Gilleard and Higgs, 2005). The former has been memorably described as 'the death of class' (Pakulski and Waters, 1996) and similar ideas have been put forward by a number of theorists who have seen a steady decline in class identities. This has been seen as the consequence of the transformations associated with increasing uncertainty and risk (Lash and Urry, 1987; Giddens, 1990), the emergence of liquid biographies within post-modernity (Bauman, 1998), or the effect of increasing reflexivity eating away at class identity and class solidarity (Beck and Beck-Gernsheim, 2002). This is not to say that these approaches are unaware of inequality, but that they see it as a more multifaceted process. These views are echoed among writers working within the 'employment aggregate' approach, who identify occupational class-related unequal access to economic, social and cultural resources at individual and family levels (Goldthorpe, 1996, 2009). Chan and Goldthorpe (2007), for instance, argue that while an individual's position within the class structure (as defined by employment relations) has a strong influence on one's life chances (lifetime risk of unemployment and earnings), status is of key importance in terms of one's lifestyle and cultural consumption. This leads them to argue that studies of outcomes (health, education, well-being, etc) should be based on the recognition that stratification is multidimensional.

In a similar fashion, the neo-Marxist Wright (2009) appears to advocate a pragmatic realist approach, identifying classes with the attributes and material life conditions of individuals whose social positions facilitate control of resources and opportunity hoarding but work in the context of wider mechanisms of domination and exploitation. This has parallels with Tilley's work on categorical forms of inequality, which are established through primary mechanisms of exploitation and opportunity hoarding and then generalised through emulation and institutionalised through adaptation (Tilley, 1998). Other writers see class retaining its importance but nevertheless view it as a social category that now needs rethinking and re-theorising (Savage, 2000). Here, the wider transformations in social class in the last 40 years have led to greater engagement with the work of Bourdieu (1984) and, in particular, his focus on practices of distinction, habitus and field. This has meant a turn towards examining the role of cultural practices and consumption patterns in reproducing forms of social distinction and division (Bennett et al, 2009). In contrast to the employment aggregate approach, class is seen more in terms of personal trajectories and biographies; an important feature of which is the identification with ordinariness in everyday lives of individuals (Crompton, 1998). As Skeggs (2004) demonstrates, narratives of the 'everyday' are an important way in which class inequalities are maintained, reproduced and naturalised. Social stratification and inequality, in turn, has been increasingly linked to modes of consumer behaviour (Bauman, 2011). Such arguments have therefore emphasised lifestyles as the nexus of class distinction, with working-class lifestyles changing in response to the need to maintain distinctions within the social hierarchy (Scott, 1996). Consequently, there is an emphasis on the reproduction of social class through individual and group access to different forms of capital – what has been described as the Capitals, Assets and Resources

(CARs) model (Savage et al, 2005). Here, the argument is that forms of capital are not just aspects of antagonistic relations of exploitation, but have the potential to be accumulated over time and to be converted into other valuable resources: 'it is not the fact that some people may exploit others that is fundamental; it is the potential of certain CARs to accumulate, store, and retain advantages that allow us to distinguish the most important causes of stratification' (Savage et al, 2005: 43).

The incorporation of these approaches within health inequality research might help us better understand the persistence of forms of stratification by class and status related to health and lifestyles (Blaxter, 2004). For example, recent work in respect to lifestyles and cultural capital among older men indicates that lifestyles may be an important form of class distinction in later life, which has effects on people's health (Jones et al, 2011). Significantly, however, these ideas are underdeveloped in relation to later life and while they may have much to offer, particularly in terms of explaining people's capacity to respond to changing circumstances as they age (to adapt, accumulate and convert CARs, so to speak), there is still much work to be done.

What, then, can be said about the new circumstances of class and how do they relate to later life? One answer could be that the death of class might be premature but that how it is now constituted demands that we take more notice of its new contexts, which seem to be much more multifactorial and contingent. If employment relationships and cultural forms are no longer so clear-cut, then it is not surprising that their outcomes are more complicated. This can be seen in the review of the field of health inequalities that we have just undertaken. It is, therefore, going to be even more complicated when we seek to address how these processes play out at older ages. It is for these reasons that we turn to explanations that counter-intuitively focus on the processes of individualisation in locating modern social relationships.

Nascent globalisation and individualised class conflict without classes

The conditions of modernity were ones of clearer institutional boundaries, a standardised life course, combined with clear ascribed statuses of class and gender. These concrete and fixed institutional forms provided the bases for identity formation. In contrast, under the conditions of what Ulrich Beck (2007) has termed 'second modernity', individuals face institutional frameworks that increasingly assume a fluid and contingent nature. These frameworks assume reflexivity on the part of the individual 'quasi-subject', who is expected to produce his or her own identity, networks and boundaries. For Beck, the collective successes of class struggle based upon organised labour also contributed to institutionalised individualisation. The most obvious example of this is the creation of welfare states to overcome the pernicious effects of social inequality. By intervening across a whole swathe of social locations, from employment through education to social welfare, the welfare state placed more emphasis on the individuality of the citizen than on their collective membership of a social class. The consequence of this is the dissolving of classes and class conflict within contemporary society. Indeed, according to Beck, the normative dimension of second modernity is centred on the acceptance of diversity and difference at the institutional level (Jones and Higgs, 2010). In arguing that social processes have become individualised, Beck (2000; Beck and Beck-Gernsheim, 2002) appears to view class as a redundant concept, a 'zombie category'. In his formulation, individualisation uncouples class culture from class positions, with the effect that conflicts are no longer primarily collective in nature. Instead, he argues that there are multiple individualised class conflicts without classes – a process in which the loss of significance of classes coincides with the categorical transformation and radicalisation of social inequalities (Beck, 2007: 686). Beck makes a crucial and often-misunderstood distinction between class and inequality. In arguing that the social transformations of second modernity have resulted in the end of classes, he also suggests that this is accompanied by the beginning of radicalised inequalities.

Contrary to earlier arguments about the death of class, the end of classes is not the result of a levelling of class differences, but a crisis of individualisation, where the institutions of first modernity, including trade unions, welfare states, the family and social classes, are challenged, questioned and undermined by the transnationalisation of social inequalities. To paraphrase Marx's dictum: collective class struggle created the welfare state, but not in conditions of the levelling of access to resources and opportunities. In a globalised economy, this gives rise to radicalised inequalities, where all of the contingent factors that make up an individual's social context come into play in ways that might not have been expected or controlled for. There are voices of dissent to this formulation, of course. Will Atkinson (2010) takes issue with Beck's thesis, arguing that it is based on a caricature of class and class analysis and utilises a thin understanding of processes of individualisation. Drawing on the work of Bourdieu, he argues that his own empirical work reveals a both/and situation, where individualist and class accounts coexist and intertwine. Margaret Archer (2007) also questions Beck's view of individualisation as the social structure of second modernity itself and Bourdieu's notion of habitus as a structured and structuring framework. Her criticisms, however, are based on an acceptance that reflexivity plays an increasing role in contemporary social processes. Indeed, for Archer, the conditions of nascent globalisation are such that there have been unprecedented levels of social change (morphogenesis), a key feature of which is for 'variety to spawn more variety' (Archer, 2010: 284). While there are important theoretical distinctions here, there seems to be a consensus that as we enter a phase of second modernity where structural inequalities increase, individual capacities to perceive and challenge these inequalities in class terms decline and weaken (Nollmann and Strasser, 2007).

Implications for inequalities in later life

With respect to later life, it is possible to argue that many of the generation who participated in and benefited from the class-based structures and stability of first modernity have found their circumstances in later life subject to greater uncertainty and contingency. For many, this has not been a necessarily negative experience. Living standards in later life have improved massively when compared with the circumstances of those retiring in the 1960s and 1970s. Similarly, the connection with occupation and the world of work may have become less determining as other factors, such as property, have increased in value in ways that could not have been foreseen in the years when these assets were first purchased. Also, the institutional arrangements enjoyed by many of those in retirement now seem very favourable when compared with much younger cohorts. While some writers have sought to use these developments to fan the flames of intergenerational conflict (see Higgs and Gilleard, 2010), the same contingencies of nascent globalisation are faced by individuals from different cohorts. The clearest example of this is the ongoing global financial crisis, where dramatic changes in the value of financial instruments and investments have undermined the finances not only of corporations and nation states, but also of individuals trying to plan for the future, be they aged 30 or 70. These uncertainties have implications for theories of inequalities in old age. The picture is now one of a much more complex relationship between income, wealth, social-economic status and location, and health in old age. Both the accumulation of disadvantage and age as leveller hypotheses have to be rethought as, increasingly, researchers need to consider the extent to which different health outcomes in later life may be influenced by both distal and proximal influences. It is on the ways in which the individualised contingencies of a later life reproduce class inequalities without those affected being seen simply as cyphers of those larger classes that we should focus future research.

Conclusion

While arguments rage over the extent to which class culture has changed and institutionalised individualism can be said to be a key feature of second modernity, it is important to try to relate these ideas to health inequalities in later life. If class is still important for understanding the broad outlines of social relations at earlier points in the life course, it may still be the case that it is less salient in old age. There is now strong evidence to show that ageing has been transformed from a residual category of the economy and social policy, to an important cultural field in which practices of distinction are enacted and where inequalities can take root. These practices and inequalities will probably reflect the nature of the various capitals (social, financial and health) that are valorised by the third age. How these relate to the ideas of 'successful' and 'unsuccessful' ageing has become part of the research view of gerontology. These factors need to be integrated into the study of how social class interrelates with health inequalities and how this constructs the new generational field of ageing, where not only it is necessary to look good in order to feel good, but looking young can seemingly keep the status of being identified as a passive older person away. Social gerontology needs to reflect on how categories of 'successful ageing' may be being constructed on the basis of class-related forms of distinction and taste. This context to contemporary ageing also shifts our focus away from the notion that it is only distal processes that matter. The emergence of later life as a distinct part of the life course also raises the possibility of contestation and resistance. Struggles and resistance to the inevitability of ageing are conditioned by cultural narratives and these narratives have their roots in social processes and inequalities. There is a danger that the study of social class-based inequalities in health at older ages acts as if this context is not important. All of the key processes have occurred and it matters little what the lives of older people are now like; what happened decades ago is more important.

The very fact that the conclusions of this research tradition have been ambiguous is not seen to be a problem. Consequently, the connection between social class and later life becomes one of 'requiring more research to refine the variable' rather than an arena of examining the effects of social change in the context of a social group whose experiences and lives have also been radically transformed. The individualisation of the determining processes that lead to inequalities in the health experienced by older people may make the task of identifying such causes more difficult but it does have the advantage of starting with the reality of later life today rather than implying that older people are primarily outcome measures of an elusive variable.

References

Aratzcoz, L. and Rueda, S. (2007) 'Social inequalities in health among the elderly: a challenge for public health research', *Journal of Epidemiology & Community Health*, vol 61, no 6, pp 466–7.

Arber, S. and Ginn, J. (1993) 'Gender and inequalities in health in later life', *Social Science & Medicine*, vol 36, no 1, pp 33–46.

Arber, S. and Lahelma, E. (1993) 'Inequalities in women's and men's ill-health – Britain and Finland compared', *Social Science & Medicine*, vol 37, no 8, pp 1055–68.

Archer, M. (2007) *Making our way through the world*, Cambridge: Cambridge University Press.

Archer, M. (2010) 'Routine, reflexivity and realism', *Sociological Theory*, vol 28, no 3, pp 272–303.

Asthana, S., Gibson, A., Moon, G., Brigham, P. and Dicker, J. (2004) 'The demographic and social class basis of inequality in self reported morbidity: an exploration using the Health Survey for England', *Journal of Epidemiology & Community Health*, vol 58, no 4, pp 303–7.

Atkinson, W. (2010) 'Class, individualisation and perceived (dis) advantages: not either/or but both/and?', *Sociological Research Online*, vol 15, no 4. Available at: http://www.socresonline.org.uk/15/4/7. html

Batty, G.D. and Deary, I.J. (2004) 'Early life intelligence and adult health', *British Medical Journal*, vol 329, no 7466, pp 585–6.

Bauman, Z. (1998) *Work, consumerism and the new poor*, Buckingham: Open University Press.

Bauman, Z. (2011) *Collateral damage: social inequalities in a global age*, Cambridge: Polity.

Beck, U. (2000) *The brave new world of work*, Cambridge: Polity Press.

Beck, U. (2007) 'Beyond class and nation: reframing social inequalities in a globalizing world', *The British Journal of Sociology*, vol 58, no 4, pp 679–705.

Beck, U. and Beck-Gernsheim, E. (2002) *Individualization: institutionalized individualism and its social and political consequences*, London: Sage.

Beckett, M. (2000) 'Converging health inequalities in later life – an artefact of mortality selection?', *Journal of Health and Social Behaviour*, vol 41, no 1, pp 106–9.

Bennett, T., Savage, M., Silva, E., Warde, A., Gayo-Cal, M. and Wright, D. (2009) *Culture, class, distinction*, London: Routledge.

Benzeval, M., Green, M.J. and Leyland, A.H. (2011) 'Do social inequalities in health widen or converge with age? Longitudinal evidence from three cohorts in the West of Scotland', *BMC Public Health*. Available at: http://www.biomedcentral.com/content/pdf/1471-2458-11-947.pdf

Blaxter, M. (2004) *Health*, Cambridge: Polity.

Bourdieu, P. (1984) *Distinction: a social critique of the judgement of taste*, London: Routledge.

Bowling, A. (2004) 'Socio-economic differences in mortality among older people', *Journal of Epidemiology & Community Health*, vol 58, no 6, pp 438–40.

Breeze, E., Fletcher, A.E., Leon, D.A., Marmot, M.G., Clarke, R.J. and Shipley, M.J. (2001) 'Do socioeconomic disadvantages persist into old age? Self-reported morbidity in a 29-year follow-up of the Whitehall Study', *American Journal of Public Health*, vol 91, no 2, pp 277–83.

Chan, T.W. and Goldthorpe, J.H. (2007) 'Class and status: the conceptual distinction and its empirical relevance', *American Sociological Review*, vol 72, no 4, pp 512–32.

Connolly, S., O'Reilly, D. and Rosato, M. (2010) 'House value as an indicator of cumulative wealth is strongly related to morbidity and mortality risk in older people: a census-based cross-sectional and longitudinal study', *International Journal of Epidemiology*, vol 39, no 3, pp 383–91.

Crompton, R. (1998) *Class and stratification*, Cambridge: Polity.

Dannefer, D. (2003) 'Cumulative advantage/disadvantage and the life course: cross-fertilizing age and social science theory', *Journals of Gerontology Series B: Psychological Sciences and Social Sciences*, vol 58, no 6, pp S327–38.

Dorling, D. (2012) 'Inequality constitutes a particular place', *Social and Cultural Geography*, vol 13, no 1, pp 1–9.

Eikemo, T., Huisman, M., Bambra, C. and Kunst, A. (2008) 'Health inequalities according to educational level in different welfare regimes: a comparison of 23 European countries', *Sociology of Health and Illness*, vol 30, no 4, pp 565–82.

Emberson, J.R., Whincup, P.H., Morris, R.W. and Walker, M. (2004) 'Social class differences in coronary heart disease in middle-aged British men: implications for prevention', *International Journal of Epidemiology*, vol 33, no 2, pp 289–96.

Fox, A.J. and Goldblatt, P. (1982) *Longitudinal study: socio-demographic mortality differentials*, London: HMSO.

Gatens, M. (2004) 'Can human rights accommodate women's rights? Towards an embodied account of social norms, social meaning and cultural change', *Contemporary Political Theory*, vol 3, no 3, pp 275–99.

Giddens, A. (1990) *The consequences of modernity*, Cambridge: Polity Press.

Gilleard, C. and Higgs, P. (2005) *Contexts of ageing: class, cohort and community*, Cambridge: Polity.

Goldthorpe, J.H. (1996) 'Class analysis and the reorientation of class theory: the case of persisting differentials in educational attainment', *British Journal of Sociology*, vol 47, no 3, pp 481–505.

Goldthorpe, J.H. (2009) 'Analysing social inequality: a critique of two recent contributions from economics and epidemiology', *European Sociological Review*, vol 26, no 6, pp 731–44.

Grundy, E. (2005) 'Reciprocity in relationships: socio-economic and health influences on intergenerational exchanges between Third Age parents and their adult children in Great Britain', *The British Journal of Sociology*, vol 52, no 2, pp 233–55.

Grundy, E. and Glaser, K. (2000) 'Socio-demographic differences in the onset and progression of disability in early old age: a longitudinal study', *Age and Ageing*, vol 29, no 2, pp 149–57.

Grundy, E. and Holt, G. (2001) 'The socioeconomic status of older adults: how should we measure it in studies of health inequalities', *Journal of Epidemiology & Community Health*, vol 55, no 12, pp 895–904.

Grundy, E. and Sloggett, A. (2003) 'Health inequalities in the older population: the role of personal capital, social resources and socio-economic circumstances', *Social Science and Medicine*, vol 56, no 5, pp 935–47.

Hall, P.A. and Taylor, R.C.R. (2009) 'Health, social relations and public policy', in P.A. Hall and M. Lamont (eds) *Successful societies: how institutions and culture affect health*, New York, NY: Cambridge University Press, pp 82–103.

Higgs, P. and Gilleard, C. (2010) 'Generational conflict, consumption and the ageing welfare state in the UK', *Ageing & Society*, vol 30, no 8, pp 1439–51.

Higgs, P., Jones, I.R. and Scambler, G. (2004) 'Class as variable, class as generative mechanism: the importance of critical realism for the sociology of health inequalities', in C. New and B. Carter (eds) *Making realism work, realist social theory and empirical research*, London: Routledge.

Hyde, M. and Jones, I.R. (2007) 'The long shadow of work? Does time since labour market exit affect the association between socio-economic position and health in a post working population?', *Journal of Epidemiology & Community Health*, vol 61, no 6, pp 532–8.

Irwin, S. (1999) 'Later life inequality and sociological theory', *Ageing and Society*, vol 19, no 6, pp 691–715.

Jones, I.R. and Higgs, P.F. (2010) 'The natural, the normal and the normative: contested terrains in ageing and old age', *Social Science and Medicine*, vol 71, no 8, pp 1513–19.

Jones, I.R., Papacosta, O., Wannamethee, G., Whincup, P. and Morris, R. (2011) 'Class and lifestyle "lock in" among middle aged and older men: a multiple correspondence analysis of the British Regional Heart Study', *Sociology of Health and Illness*, vol 33, no 3, pp 399–419.

Lash, S. and Urry, J. (1987) *The end of organized capitalism*, Cambridge: Polity.

Le Roux, B., Rouanet, H., Savage, M. and Warde, A. (2008) 'Class and cultural division in the UK', *Sociology*, vol 42, no 6, pp 1049–71.

Marmot, M. (2006) 'Status syndrome – a challenge to medicine', *Journal of the American Medical Association*, vol 295, no 11, pp 1304–7.

Marmot, M. (2010) 'Fair society healthy lives: strategic review of health inequalities in England post 2010'. Available at: www.ucl.ac.uk/marmotreview

Marmot, M., Banks, J., Blundell, R., Lessof, C. and Nazroo, J. (2003) *Health, wealth and lifestyles of the older population of England: the 2002 English Longitudinal Survey of Ageing*, London: Institute of Fiscal Studies.

McMunn, A., Nazroo, J. and Breeze, E. (2009) 'Inequalities in health at older ages: a longitudinal investigation of the onset of illness and survival effects in England', *Age and Ageing*, vol 38, no 2, pp 181–7.

Muntaner, C. and Lynch, J. (1999) 'Income inequality, social cohesion, and class relations: a critique of Wilkinson's neo-Durkheimian research program', *International Journal of Health Services*, vol 29, no 1, pp 59–81.

Muntaner, C., Borrell, C., Vanroelen, C., Chung, H., Benach, J., Kima, I.H. and Ng, E. (2010) 'Employment relations, social class and health: a review and analysis of conceptual and measurement alternatives', *Social Science & Medicine*, vol 71, no 12, pp 2130–40.

Nazroo, J., Falaschetti, E., Pierce, M. and Primatesta, P. (2009) 'Ethnic inequalities in access to and outcomes of healthcare: analysis of the Health Survey for England', *Journal of Epidemiology & Community Health*, vol 63, no 12, pp 1022–7.

Nollmann, G. and Strasser, H. (2007) 'Individualization as an interpretive scheme of inequality: why class and inequality still persist', in C. Howard (ed) *Contested individualization: debates about contemporary personhood*, New York, NY: Palgrave Macmillan.

Office for National Statistics (2007) *Trends in life expectancy by social class 1972–2005*. Available at: http://www.ons.gov.uk/ons/rel/health-ineq/health-inequalities/trends-in-life-expectancy-by-social-class-1972-2005/trends-in-ons-longitudinal-study-estimates-of-life-expectancy-1972-2005.pdf

Pakulski, J. and Waters, M. (1996) *The death of class*, London: Sage.

Pickett, K. and Dorling, D. (2010) 'Against the organization of misery? The Marmot review of health inequalities', *Social Science & Medicine*, vol 71, no 7, pp 1231–3.

Prus, S.G. (2007) 'Age, SES, and health: a population level analysis of health inequalities over the lifecourse', *Sociology of Health and Illness*, vol 29, no 2, pp 175–296.

Ramsay, S.E., Morris, R.W., Lennon, L.T., Wannamethee, S.G. and Whincup, P.H. (2008) 'Are social inequalities in mortality in Britain narrowing? Time trends from 1978 to 2005 in a population-based study of older men', *The Journal of Epidemiology & Community Health*, vol 62, no 1, pp 75–80.

Savage, M. (2000) *Class analysis and social transformation*, London: Open University Press.

Savage, M., Warde, A. and Devine, F. (2005) 'Capitals, assets, and resources: some critical issues', *The British Journal of Sociology*, vol 56, no 1, pp 31–47.

Scott, J. (1996) *Stratification and power: structures of class, status and command*, Cambridge: Polity.

Skeggs, B. (2004) *Class, self, culture*, London: Routledge.

Tilley, C. (1998) *Durable inequality*, Berkeley, CA: University of California Press.

Townsend, P., Phillimore, P. and Beattie, A. (1988) *Health and deprivation inequality and the North*, London: Croom Helm.

Von Dem Knesebeck, O., Lüschen, G., Cockerham, W.C. and Siegrist, J. (2003) 'Socioeconomic status and health among the aged in the United States and Germany: a comparative cross-sectional study', *Social Science & Medicine*, vol 57, no 9, pp 1643–52.

Von Dem Knesebeck, O., Wahrendorf, M., Hyde, M. and Siegrist, J. (2007) 'Socio-economic position and quality of life among older people in 10 European countries: results of the SHARE study', *Ageing and Society*, vol 27, no 2, pp 269–84.

Wilkinson, R. (2005) *The impact of inequality: how to make sick societies healthier*, London: Routledge.

Wilkinson, R. and Pickett, K. (2009) *The spirit level: why more equal societies almost always do better*, London: Allen Lane.

Wright, E.O. (1978) *Class, crisis, and the state*, London: New Left Books.

Wright, E.O. (1997) *Class counts: comparative studies in class analysis*, Cambridge: Cambridge University Press.

Wright, E.O. (2009) 'Understanding class: towards an integrated analytical approach', *New Left Review*, vol 60, pp 101–16.

EIGHT

Class, care and caring

Christina Victor

Introduction

Not all older people enjoy equal chances to experience positive health levels. It remains the case that persons aged 65 years and over experience a variety of chronic conditions, ranging from physical ailments, such as arthritis, respiratory diseases and circulatory problems, to mental health issues, such as anxiety, depression and dementia (Victor, 2010). The prevalence of these conditions and multiple pathologies experienced by older individuals is largely age-related. One consequence of this increase in morbidity with age is that, singly or in combination, these chronic conditions can challenge the ability of older people to live independently in the community by compromising their performance of essential activities of daily living. Older people in middle- and high-income countries who need care to maintain their independence at home in later life have three potential sources of help and support, namely, the formal services provided by statutory/ voluntary agencies, paid services and informal care provided 'free' by family members. However, within the UK context, it is acknowledged that the boundaries between formal, semi-formal and informal caring systems are becoming increasingly blurred with the implementation of personalised care and individual budgets. This chapter focuses upon the role of the 'informal' network in supporting older people to live independently within the community. The first part briefly outlines the definition of 'care' and caring by enumerating the types of care needs presented by older people by examining problems encountered in performing essential activities of daily living. The subsequent parts consider the emergence of research examining the role of 'carers', while also discussing who cares, and their location within the broader care economy. Interwoven within such an analysis is the examination of the importance of class, gender and ethnicity for the provision and receipt of care in later life.

Care and caring

There is an extensive body of work looking at the definition of both care and caring, and this work needs to be located within broader debates about policies for older people (Fine, 2013). In terms of informal family based-care, this is clearly evident in the early studies of Sheldon (1948), who notes that of the 90% of older people who needed help with domestic matters, only 10% were aided by persons outside of the immediate family. Feminist concerns about the essentially sexist and exploitative nature of family care, together with policymakers' concerns about the demographic challenges of an ageing population due to decreasing family size, combined to stimulate research into this previously neglected area. There is now an extensive body of research that examines not just the basic epidemiology of caring, but also the links between paid and unpaid care, the development of home as a place of care work, and the issues arising from the development of foreign care workers. The focus upon informal care in this chapter covers one of the three key debates concerning the care of older people within the UK, the others being the enumeration of care needs, and the classification and evaluation of who provides care and the locations of care (Phillips, 2007).

There are a number of different conceptualisations of the notions of care and caring (Victor, 2005). Informal care may be defined as that provided by family, friends and neighbours – unpaid and deriving from family/friendship bonds of reciprocity, obligation or duty – and which is not organised via a statutory or voluntary agency, although this definition is being challenged by the personalisation/individual budgets agenda. One also locates a range of typologies of care that differentiate 'caring about' (concerned about individual provision of care, such as emotional support) and 'caring for' (which focuses upon direct provision of practical support, the organisational and managerial components of care, the relationship between the givers and receivers of care, and the relationships between carers and the formal sector) (see Victor, 2005, 2010). Recently, one witnesses other formulations of notions of caring that include not just the 'giving' of care, but also the 'receiving' of care, as well as the changing global context and national contexts in which caring occurs. Zechner (2008), for example, developed a typology of caring that differentiates between 'caring about', 'taking care', 'care giving' and 'care receiving', so as to encompass the diverse emotional/affective dimensions in late-life caring. In this context, care is broadly conceptualised as both 'caring for' (ie providing help with activities of daily living, personal care and other forms of direct practical support) and 'caring about' (ie providing emotional, material and practical help as required). Hence, although there are a range of typologies concerning the conceptualisation of caring, there is always a task-oriented perspective that, in effect, provides a tally of activities that would need to be absorbed by the state/voluntary bodies if families were not providing them.

Who needs care?

Following Ian Rees Jones and Paul Higgs' comprehensive overview of class health inequalities in later life (Chapter Seven, this volume), it is clear that, at least within the UK context, those from the most privileged backgrounds are most likely both to survive to old age and to enjoy the 'best' health in later life. However, we also know that gender and, increasingly, ethnicity are also linked with health inequalities and that these factors intersect with social class, so that the experience of health and the need for care in later life is dynamic. As a context to understanding the issues of care and caring, one needs to translate the health statistics presented in Chapter Seven into a format that enables us to quantify the 'need' for care by older people (and, indeed, other groups). We cannot simply transform details of the prevalence of, for example, arthritis or a measure such as long-standing limiting disability into an estimate of the number of people who need care or the type of care that they require. Typically, one has to try to enumerate (or quantify) the need for help with specific tasks considered necessary for the maintenance of independent community living expressed by older people. The tasks and activities considered essential to independence include those related to personal care, such as housework and shopping (often characterised as instrumental activities of daily living), and mobility. These types of measures originated with the classic works of Sheldon (1948) and Townsend (1961, cited in Victor, 2010) and, therefore, reflect the socio-temporal cultural context of Britain in the 1950s. For example, the index devised by Townsend focuses upon public transport, asking about difficulties getting on and off buses. More recent versions of these types of checklists, such as that included in the 2006 and 2008 waves of the English Longitudinal Study of Ageing (ELSA), have been updated to include activities such as using the phone, managing finances, finding one's whereabouts in unfamiliar locations and taking medications, as well as 'traditional' self-care activities, such as washing, dressing, shopping and cooking (Banks et al, 2008).

These questions and scales include items that relate directly to issues that are emblematic of a direct need for care and support – such as the inability to bathe, dress or go shopping – others are indicative of specific needs (eg taking medication). Yet, others are indirect proxies of need, such as, for example, tying a knot in a piece of string or picking up a small coin, which reflect problems with manual dexterity. Despite their theoretical usefulness, it is more problematic to link such scales to the need for care.

Table 8.1: Reported difficulties with selected activities of daily living, England 2006

Reporting difficulties (%)	Age 65–74		Age 75–84		Age 85+	
	M	F	M	F	M	F
Dressing or washing	20	19	25	27	41	41
Eating or preparing meals	3	6	8	8	15	21
Shopping or doing work around the house	12	19	21	30	42	56
Telephoning or managing money	3	4	7	5	18	19
Taking medication	1	2	3	2	4	6

Source: Banks et al (2008).

There is a hierarchy in terms of the prevalence of the types of problems just mentioned. Difficulties using medication are experienced by around 3% of those aged 65 and over, compared with around 10% for cooking, and 20% for shopping/housework (see Table 8.1). Reported rates of difficulty increase with age, and are greater for women as compared with men. When considering how these data translate into the need for care, two factors need to be borne in mind. These data describe difficulties in performing tasks, and do not indicate if individuals are unable to perform the task, or if they actually need care to deliver the activity. If one focuses upon eating and preparing a meal, 5% of those aged 65+ are unable to do this, compared with approximately 10% who have difficulty with this activity. Therefore, the prevalence of those unable to perform activities (and who clearly need an intervention from formal or informal care to sustain them) is approximately half of those who report difficulties completing activities (Victor, 2010). Moreover, even an activity where the relative percentage of people unable to perform them is small translates into a substantial number of people: the 5% of people with difficulty in taking their medication represents almost half a million people who may need help. Thus, when comparing across studies in order to examine changes in prevalence rates over time, there are methodological issues relating to how the activity limitation question suites are asked (eg self-completion versus direct interview, the use of filter questions, etc) (Vlachantoni et al, 2011). Taking the examples of people aged 65 and over needing help with bathing or dressing, and three data sets – the General Household Survey (GHS), the ELSA and the British Household Panel Survey (BHPS) – academics report the following prevalence rates for difficulties with bathing: 15.3% (GHS), 9.7% (ELSA) and 16.2% (BHPS). For difficulties with dressing, prevalence was as follows: 10.8% (GHS), 6.5% (ELSA) and 6.7% (BHPS). Hence, in any discussion of who needs care, there in no 'right' answer. Estimates will inevitably lack some degree of precision and will vary across studies and populations, making cross-national research especially challenging (Chan et al, 2012).

Is the need for care equally distributed?

The need for care, as measured by limitations in activities of daily living, increases with age and is broadly greater among women as compared to men. Changes in disability and disability prevalence among older people are strongly associated with socio-economic position, as measured by a range of variables (education, income and housing tenure) (Grundy and Glaser, 2000). Therefore, those from the least privileged socio-economic position demonstrate higher levels of difficulties with key activities of daily living. Taking men aged 65 and over as a single group, Victor (2010) reports that there is a 9% difference in reported rates of long-standing limiting illness between those in social classes 1 and 2 (36%) and the unskilled and semi-skilled occupational groups (45%). Similar differentials have been observed for women. The majority of the major causes of long-standing limiting illness – the exceptions being heart disease in the case of men and nervous system disorders in the case of women – show a similar socio-economic class differential in distribution, and these differences are significant (Glaser and Grundy, 2002). These differentials are far from trivial. For musculo-skeletal diseases, the differences by social class are 30% for men and 22% for women; while for respiratory diseases, the differentials are 52% and 32%, respectively. When one focuses upon the severe category of disability, results demonstrate strong differentials between different social groups. Bowling (2005) reports that severe disability (as measured by her 15 Activities of Daily Living and Instrumental Activities of Daily Living items) was higher among females than males (25% vs 17%), persons aged 75 years and older (31% vs 15%) and even by socio-economic status, where 3% of those in the highest social grouping were classified as having severe difficulties compared with 12% of those at the bottom of the class hierarchy. This pattern is consistent for other measures of social status, namely, education, income and housing tenure. Such is the magnitude of the differentials in disability that Melzer and colleagues (2000) consider that the eradication of these would ensure that the ageing of the population would not pose any additional demands on services. While this may be something of an overstatement, it highlights the magnitude of class-based inequalities in health status among older people in the UK, and serves as a testament to the enduring nature of class in shaping the experience of health across the life course.

Within a UK context, one finds limited empirical data on the health status and need for care among minority ethnic elders, predominantly among those who migrated to the UK from the Caribbean and South Asian from the 1950s onwards. The only available data are on the prevalence of disability, problems with activities of daily living and chronic health problems. Data from the 2001 census shows that for those aged 65 and over, the population from Asian countries have the highest rates of long-tem limiting illness at 60%, compared with 54% of black African/Caribbean groups, and 51% of the white British population. With the exception of the Bangladeshi group, women demonstrate higher reported rates of long-term limiting illness, with the Indian group showing the highest difference (22%), and the white British group the lowest (8%) (Victor, 2010). Taken at face value, these data suggest that chronic health problems are indeed greater among minority ethnic populations and that women are especially disadvantaged. However, one needs to be cautious in drawing this inference, so as to ensure that these differences do not reflect gendered and cultural variations in how these questions are answered, rather than 'real' differences in health status across populations (Chan et al, 2012).

The presence of clear class, ethnicity and gender differentials – within an overall gradient of age-related increases in chronic illness, disability and difficulties with activities of daily living – serves to draw attention to the importance of socio-demographic factors in the experience of health and illness. While there is no doubt that genetics and biology play a key part in shaping the health experience of older people, key dimensions of social structure – gender, class and ethnicity – remain important in influencing both the need for care and the resources we can access to respond to these needs. Due to a lack of multi- and inter-disciplinary data, this chapter could only consider each of these factors separately and independently of each other. This is problematic, as individuals do not experience these separately. Rather, age, class, gender and ethnicity all interact and link together, and are played out within an integrative socio-environmental and biological context.

Who provides care?

Wanless (2006) reports that if they needed care due to old age or disability, 62% of adults would prefer to receive this in their own home with support from family and friends (56% reported the same care location preference but to receive care from state/trained care workers), with only 14% opting to move in with their children. Therefore, central to the research and policy literature in the field of 'informal' care is the identification and classification of who provides this type of care. In this context, informal care is 'unpaid', unregulated and monitored, and provided by a 'workforce' that is recruited because of filial or social obligations and responsibilities, rather than being professionally trained. The notion of 'tending' – caring for individuals or providing help with specific activities of daily living tasks – has been central to the ways that surveys of the provision of informal care within the UK have been conducted. The first such survey was conducted in 1985 as part the GHS and constituted an attempt to undertake a large-scale nationally representative survey of the provision of informal care. This exercise was repeated in 1990, 1995 and 2000, while the central question on the provision of care was subsequently included in the 2001 and 2011 censuses. The 2001 and 2011 censuses asked the following question: 'Do you look after, or give any help or support to family members, friends, neighbours or others because of: (a) long-term physical or mental ill-health or disability, or (b) problems related to old age?' The GHS surveys asked about extra responsibilities resulting from the care of someone that was 'elderly' (or sick or disabled), and then differentiates between those who lived with the person they cared for and those who did not. This question required respondents to compare what they do against some hypothetical norm of family/friendship relationships and define whether this was 'abnormal' or outside of normal family/friendship roles and functions. Concerns, however, have been raised about this definition in that specific subgroups may systematically 'over-' (or under-)report their family responsibilities as caring. It has also been proposed that this definition is 'gender-biased': women will under-report what they do as caring, while, for men, the opposite case may hold. There may well be biases in how this question is answered in terms of age, class or ethnicity, but we do not have any evidence in either direction, and we may also presume that responses to such questions are also temporally and culturally situated.

Consistently, 13–16% of adults report that they are carers, and this has remained roughly stable over time (see Table 8.2). Given all of the conceptual and operational issues involved, it seems unlikely that

Table 8.2: Prevalence of informal care (% caring 20 hours a week), 1985–2001

	1985	1990	1995	2000	2001 census
Men	12	13	11	14	11
Women	15	17	14	18	14
Aged 16–29	7	8	6	8	
Aged 30–44	14	15	10	13	
Aged 45–64	20	24	20	24	20
Aged 65+	13	13	13	13	12
Same household	4	4	4	5	
Other household	10	12	8	11	
White					4
Black Caribbean					4
Indian					5
Bangladeshi and Pakistani					7
All adults	14	15	13	16	13

Source: Adapted from Victor (2010) and Young et al (2005).

there is a 'right' answer to the question of how many carers there are at a given time. Caring, like chronic disease and disability, probably forms a continuum of relationships between an individual and their family/social network, and where the line is drawn reflects a range of factors that are temporally, socially and historically contextualised. Women are more likely to report that they are carers than men, and the 45–64 age group has the highest reported prevalence of caring and caring for someone who lives in the same residence. However, one must remember that, for example, the balance between co-resident and extra-resident carers reflects many factors, including expectations of living arrangements in later life, house stock and policy incentives that support the establishment and maintenance of their own homes for older people, the nature of the relationship (spouse or parent), and class (Glaser and Grundy, 2002). The 2001 census provided important information on caring among minority ethnic communities and revealed that rates of caring for 20 hours or more a week are highest among Bangladeshi and Pakistani populations. Given the differing age profiles of minority ethnic groups, this is difficult to interpret. Young and colleagues (2005) calculated an age–sex standardised caring ratio (reference group of all carers is equal to 1) for those providing care for 20 hours a week. For the black Caribbean group, this index was 0.77 – hence indicating lower than expected levels of caring – while higher levels of caring were demonstrated by the Indian (1.36) and Bangladeshi/Pakistani groups (2.11). The white population had an index of 1.02. Therefore, it certainly seems the case that there is some prima facie evidence that informal caring is greater among those from South Asian backgrounds than the general population. However, it is not clear if this reflects elevated levels of need for care, lack of access to formal services, socio-cultural norms and expectations, or some combination of all of these.

Normative priorities governing who gives care for older people in the family have been demonstrated for the general population (Grundy, 2005), and reveal the complexity of how kinship responsibilities are negotiated in specific situations and across/between generations and places (Phillips, 2007). Socio-cultural norms are especially important within this context. The concept of care implicit within the census/ GHS questions emphasises the 'exceptionality' of caring, while focusing upon responsibilities over and above what is 'normal'. This may well fail to fully capture the extent to which caring activities form part of daily life within minority ethnic communities, where family care is both 'expected' and normal. However, one notes some empirical studies of how family obligations operate in minority ethnic families. Research in this area tends to be qualitative in nature (eg Merrell et al, 2006), has focused upon individual Asian minority ethnic groups and tends to look at 'theoretical' dimensions of support and/or service access issues (Stopes-Roe and Cochrane, 1990; Ahmed and Jones, 2008). Nevertheless, one must admit that we possess limited insight into current (and future) views about the care of older people from our 'minority ethnic communities', especially from younger and second-generation adult children. Preliminary data from Victor et al (2012) illustrate very strong expectations of family care, as expressed by older people from Bangladeshi and Pakistani backgrounds:

> "I have finished my duty of looking after my children and now my children have a duty towards me.... If I need care I believe my children will look after me when I cannot do things on my own.... I hope my children will look after me when I am old and dependent." (Informants, cited in Victor et al, 2012)

However, it remains unclear whether younger generations share these expectations as strongly as their (grand)parents (Butt and Moriarty, 2004). Another important perspective regards the examination of the socio-demographic characteristics of the population who self-identify themselves as carers. This analysis demonstrates that the majority (60%) of carers are women, with the highest levels of caring responsibilities reported by persons in the 45–64 age bracket (48%). As many as 20% of carers are aged 65 and over. The 2008 wave of the ELSA shows that 25% of men and 20% of women aged 65+ with at least one limitation in activities of daily living are receiving help from their spouse (Breeze and Stafford, 2010). Another 11% of men and 20% of women, also experiencing at least one limitation in activities of daily living, receive help from their children (Breeze and Stafford, 2010). However, one must not overlook other older people receiving care from friends and neighbours (53% of those aged between 65 and 74, and 35% of those aged 75+) (Breeze and Stafford, 2010). This reinforces the earlier point that older people are major sources of carers as well as being care recipients.

So far, this chapter has demonstrated that the study of caring in later life is intimately intertwined with a number of demographic characteristics, most notably, age, but also social class and ethnicity. The link with gender is more complex and linked to the relationship between carer and dependant. Where care is being provided to someone in the same household, carers are almost equally divided between males and females (approximately 50%), as these situations generally characterise the situation where a spouse is caring for their marital partner. In cross-generational care, however, where the carer is typically an adult child looking after their parent(-in-law), the majority of carers are women (approximately 60%) (Victor, 2010). The relationship with socio-economic status is unclear. Unfortunately, data from the GHS has failed to demonstrate any significant difference in the reported prevalence of informal caring by socio-economic position, although Grundy and Glaser (2002) demonstrate that there are class differences in spouse care. While those from manual backgrounds demonstrate higher levels of spouse care, which reflect class differences in disability, the ELSA data demonstrate a socio-economic gradient in terms of wealth in the percentage of older people providing care to others ranging from 43% (poorest quartile) to 53% (wealthiest quartile). Interpreting this differential is somewhat problematic, as it may represent the influence of material resources and/or better health status, thereby enabling more affluent older persons to provide care, rather than any differentials across social classes to provide care.

As regards what types of care informal carers are providing, the available evidence is framed by the questions asked in the specific surveys. Again, the most extensive data derive from the suite of GHS surveys, which reveal that 'other practical help' was the most frequently cited caring activity (reported by 71% in 2000), 'keeping company' and 'taking out' were activities reported by approximately 50% of carers, and with 'help with finances and paperwork' being undertaken by around 40% of carers. At the same time, help with physical mobility tasks was reported by 35% of carers, help with medication by 22% of carers and personal care tasks by about a quarter. This shows that informal carers perform a range of activities and that these are nuanced according to the type of caring context, especially the co-resident versus non-resident caring typology. Same generational caring relationships, as indicated by co-residence of carer and dependant, are characterised by high levels of provision of personal care (approximately 50% of carers provide this), with approximately 50% being predominantly 'sole' carers, which forces them to perform a significant amount of hours of care-giving (an average of 53 hours per week, with 60% caring for a minimum of 20 hours per week) (Victor, 2005). With the exception of the highly gendered nature of non-resident caring, which is a predominantly female activity, it is unclear as to how patterns of caring in terms of tasks, hours and care networks vary with ethnicity and socio-economic position.

The results also show that there is a significant subgroup of older people who do not receive help with identified problematic tasks. However, estimating the extent of this 'unmet need' from existing survey data is problematic because of differences in the way that questions are asked across different surveys. Vlachantoni and colleagues (2011) used three different sources and types of tasks to estimate unmet need for care. Focusing upon those who needed help with both bathing and dressing, they report that 32% of those who had 'difficulties' with this task in the ELSA survey reported receiving no help, compared with 39% of those who needed help with these tasks in the GHS survey. The BHPS did not include family-based care and reported that only 9% of those who needed help with these tasks did not receive it. Unfortunately, no finer-grained analysis is presented of the characteristics of those who report unmet need or of their socio-demographic profile. However, it is likely that, following Tudor Hart's (1971) 'inverse care laws', it is the least privileged members of the population who are more likely to be included in this category, but this requires verification by robust research.

Who receives care?

There has been much less attention focused upon who 'receives' care than who 'provides' care. The question here is: who is being cared for and what are their characteristics? The available evidence is that in the vast majority of cases, the person being cared for is a close relative or spouse (72%), either parents(-in-law), who represent 43% of this group, or spouses (19% of care recipients). Approximately a quarter of those receiving care are 'other relatives' (14%) and neighbours (14%). This reinforces the observations of Finch (1989) on the 'hierarchy' of caring responsibilities within families, which highlight the importance of the marital and filial relationships in the giving and receiving of care. One can stress this in another way by looking at 'hours of care' provided rather than simple prevalence. Although 22% of care-givers are looking after a friend/neighbour, this represents only 7% of total time spent caring, as compared with 81% for close family members (30% for a spouse, 40% for a parent and 11% for a parent-in-law) (Arber and Ginn, 1991). This again highlights that the provision of informal care outside of the family/kinship obligations is, comparatively, rare and probably confined to less 'personal' tasks.

As noted at the start of this chapter, informal care is only one component out of a number of potential sources of care and support, which also include paid help arranged privately and state/statutory services. In addition, it is highly likely that there are older people who require help with key activities of daily living that do not, for whatever reason, receive the appropriate care. Data from the 2008 ELSA help us to put the relative contribution of these three (potential) sources of care into perspective. Focusing upon those who report a limitation in at least one activity of daily living, approximately 35% receive help from informal sources, 5% from 'paid help' and 7% from state sources (Breeze and Stafford, 2010). These data also suggest that 25% are not receiving help, but given the nature of the question asked, this may be entirely appropriate. One can, of course, look at this in another way and evaluate the characteristics of the groups who receive no help and only help from the three main surveys. If we look at who receives state help, then approximately 60% of this group are aged 75 and older, 30% have a spouse and around 55% are in the poorest wealth quintile. The most wealthy participants are most likely to use paid help as compared with state or informal care, while 60% of those using informal care only are in the bottom two quintiles of the income distribution (Breeze and Stafford, 2010). This concentration of state and informal help among the poorest pensioners is not just a UK phenomenon. Similar results surfaced in a comparative study of four different countries, which demonstrated that those from the lowest socio-economic groups were more likely to receive informal care than their more affluent peers (in Great Britain, 21% and 7%, respectively)

(Broese van Groenou et al, 2006). The steepest socio-economic status gradient in the use of formal help was found in the Netherlands. However, it is not clear if this relationship reflects a greater sense of filial obligation among poorer older people or the lack of alternatives (or some combination of the two). It is also noteworthy to look at the relative contribution of the informal, state and private sectors in terms of particular activities that older people have difficulties with. As regards 'technical' care tasks, such as cutting toenails, the majority of these activities are undertaken by practitioners. Informal care only substitutes in part for these professional activities. The results also show that for (Instrumental) Activities of Daily Living tasks of older persons living at home, the role of the informal sector is paramount, with 90% of help with domestic tasks, such as shopping, cooking and house care, and 70% of help with personal care being provided by the informal sector. Thus, family and informal care is not marginal to older people living at home, but quite clearly both essential and central to their ability to remain living within the community.

Conclusion

A substantial proportion of the research evidence concerned with informal care is rooted in the 'apocalyptic' demography context of 'auditing' the activities undertaken by informal carers. This emphasis reflects the policy concerns of successive governments, who are troubled by the implications of family reconfigurations for the 'supply' of informal care. There are other areas where the research base is more limited. While one finds some evidence for the experience of potential gender inequalities in caring, there is much less evidence focusing upon social class and ethnicity. Furthermore, there is little research that integrates class, gender and ethnicity perspectives to provide a more realistic evaluation of the complexities of caring. It is clear that there are class, gender and ethnicity dimensions to the need for care, receipt of care and provision of care, but how these intersect remains unclear and problematic. It is also apparent that those with the greatest needs are from the least privileged groups, who tend to be more reliant upon family-based care (and state care) than their more affluent contemporaries. However, the derivation of these differential patterns is unclear, and determining which groups receive the 'best' care or have the best outcomes is unclear. One may make assumptions about the quality of care being received by older people from their family, state services and private providers, but evaluating differentials in both quality and outcomes of care remains a challenging research agenda. Furthermore, as Fine (2013) notes, the systems for providing care and support to older people are dynamic and under pressure from both the contemporary motif of austerity and the 'demographic' imperative. Within the UK, the landscape of care is subject to significant organisational change as well as philosophical changes in the principles underlying care delivery within the emergence of the personalisation agenda. This policy change has many implications for both the givers and receivers of care, including the shifting of 'risk' for the quality and provision of care to the family/individuals, and, potentially, the payment of families for what they currently provide 'free'. Will these policies differentially affect different subgroups of older people? Will they secure or undermine the complex web of family obligations and responsibilities that have been the bedrock of family care for older people? These are all legitimate and urgent questions that future research on the relationships between class and caring should undertake.

References

Ahmed, N. and Jones, I. (2008) 'Habitus and bureaucratic routines, cultural and structural factors in the experience of informal care', *Current Sociology*, vol 56, no 1, pp 57–78.

Arber, S. and Ginn, J. (1991) *Gender and later life: a sociological analysis of resources and constraints*, London: Sage.

Banks, J., Breeze, E., Lessof, C. and Nazroo, J. (2008) *Living in the 21st Century: older people in England (the 2006 English Longitudinal Study of Ageing – Wave 3)*, London: Institute for Fiscal Studies. Available at: http://www.ifs.org.uk/elsa/report08/elsa_w3.pdf (accessed 30 April 2012).

Bowling, A. (2005) *Ageing well: quality of life in old age*, Maidenhead: Open University Press.

Breeze, E. and Stafford, M. (2010) 'Receipt and giving of help and care', in J. Banks, C. Lessof, J. Nazroo, N. Rogers, M. Stafford and A. Steptoe (eds) *Financial circumstances, health and well-being of the older population in England (the 2006 English Longitudinal Study of Ageing – Wave 4)*, London: Institute for Fiscal Studies. Available at: www.ifs.org.uk/elsa/report10/elsa_w4-1.pdf (accessed 30 April 2012).

Broese van Groenou, M.I., Glaser, K., Tomassini, C. and Jacobs, T. (2006) 'Socio-economic status differences in the use of informal and formal help: a comparison of four European countries', *Ageing & Society*, vol 26, no 5, pp 745–66.

Butt, J. and Moriarty, J. (2004) 'Social support and ethnicity in old age', in A. Walker and C. Hennessey (eds) *Growing older: quality of life in old age*, Maidenhead: Open University Press, pp 167–87.

Chan, K., Kasper, J., Brandt, J. and Pazzin, L. (2012) 'Measurement equivalence in ADL and IADL difficulty across international surveys of aging', *The Journals of Gerontology: Series B Psychological and Social Sciences*, vol 67, no 1, pp 121–32.

Finch, J. (1989) *Family obligations and social change*, Oxford: Blackwell.

Fine, M. (2013) 'Individualising care: the transformation of personal support in old age', *Ageing & Society*, vol 33, no 3, pp 421–36.

Glaser, K. and Grundy, E. (2002) 'Class, caring and disability: evidence from the British Retirement Survey', *Ageing & Society*, vol 22, no 3, pp 325–42.

Grundy, E. (2005) 'Reciprocity in relationship', *British Journal of Sociology*, vol 56, no 2, pp 233–55.

Grundy, E. and Glaser, K. (2000) 'Socio-demographic differences in the onset and progression of disability in early old age: a longitudinal study', *Age and Ageing*, vol 29, no 2, pp 149–57.

Melzer, D., McWilliams, B., Brayne, C., Johnson, T. and Bond, J. (2000) 'Socioeconomic status and the expectation of disability in old age: estimates for England', *Journal of Epidemiology and Community Health*, vol 54, no 4, pp 286–92.

Merrell, J., Kinsella, F., Murphy, F., Philpin, S. and Ali, A. (2006) 'Accessibility and equity of health and social care services: exploring the views and experience of Bangladeshi carers in South Wales, UK', *Health and Social Care in the Community*, vol 13, no 3, pp 197–205.

Phillips, J. (2007) *Care*, Cambridge: Polity Press.

Sheldon, J.H. (1948) *The social medicine of old age*, Oxford: Oxford University Press.

Stopes-Roe, M. and Cochrane, R. (1990) 'Support networks of Asian and British families', *Social Behaviour*, vol 5, no 2, pp 71–85.

Tudor Hart, J. (1971) 'The inverse care law', *Lancet*, vol 1, pp 406–12.

Victor, C.R. (2005) *The social context of ageing*, London: Routledge.

Victor, C.R. (2010) *Ageing, health and care*, Bristol: The Policy Press.

Victor, C.R., Martin, W. and Zubair, M. (2012) 'Families and caring amongst older persons in South Asian communities: a pilot study', *European Journal of Social Work*, vol 15, no 1, pp 81–96.

Vlachantoni, A., Shaw, S., Willis, R., Evandrou, M., Falkingham, J. and Luff, R. (2011) 'Unmet need for social care amongst older people', *Population Trends*, vol 145, pp 1–17.

Wanless, D. (2006) *Securing good care for older people*, London: King's Fund.

Young, H., Grundy, E. and Kalogirou, S. (2005) 'Who cares? Geographic variation in unpaid caregiving in England and Wales: evidence from the 2001 Census', *Population Trends*, vol 120, pp 23–34.

Zechner, M. (2008) 'Care of older persons in transnational settings', *Journal of Aging Studies*, vol 22, no 1, pp 32–44.

NINE

Social work, class and later life

Trish Hafford-Letchfield

Introduction

Social work with older people in the UK has only relatively recently emerged as a separate and distinct area of expert practice and provision, mostly in response to government reforms, which, in the 1990s, laid the foundations of contemporary policy and practice following the implementation of the National Health and Community Care Act (DH, 1990). This led to the creation of specialist systems of assessment and care management, prior to which older people accessed a wide range of generic social care services. While this gave rise to new optimism and belief that social work could make a positive contribution to the lives of vulnerable people within a community-based framework, significant debates have since drawn attention to the increasing complexity and uncertainty about the direction of travel being taken in social work with older people. This has been influenced by wholesale structural change, the unquestioning acceptance of the free market, neo-liberalism, as well as the universal adoption of economic rationalism, managerialism and fiscal restraint. Not least, a notable change in the retreat of government from its traditional role of provider and funder of care has led to greater promotion of individualisation within care provision while, at the same time, reducing eligibility for services (Ferguson, 2007). These developments pose enormous challenges, tensions and ambiguities for the orientation of social work with older people, where evidence is beginning to emerge of ever-widening inequalities and social exclusion (Grenier and Guberman, 2009). Both Ian Rees Jones and Paul Higgs (see Chapter Seven, this volume) and Christina Victor (see Chapter Eight, this volume) have already provided analyses that document the importance of socio-demographic factors in the experience of health and illness, the relationship between class health inequalities in later life, and the use of social work services. Those from less privileged backgrounds are more likely to be subject to the assessment and instrumental measurement of tasks and activities considered essential to their independence and the inequities and hierarchies of resource allocation involved. Victor further documented the strong association between the prevalence of disabilities and socio-economic position, as measured by a range of variables such as education, income and housing tenure. How social work has contributed and engaged with debates about these differentials, many of which also highlight the continuing significance of class within access to social care services, and the subsequent position and roles taken up by social work within these debates, are key thematic issues tackled in this chapter.

The status of social work with older people has to some extent been reflected by the status of the service-user group itself and the relative prestige given to this area of practice. Within social care, older people are often conceptualised as a problem of demography (Townsend, 2006) and practice has become focused on the challenges associated with supporting those living with disabilities and long-term conditions. Attention has been given to the growing incidence of dementia (DH, 2009) and the need to develop and sustain realistic alternatives to institutional care (HMG, 2009). Further, globalisation and structural influences continue to disadvantage older people as the ideologies of economic rationalism have radically shaped the organisational and professional landscape of social work practice. In their introduction, Formosa and Higgs noted how both these 'structured dependency' and 'political economy' approaches to old age make direct links to conceptualising social class, particularly in later life. Social work, however, has unique insight into the genuine connection of class to current circumstances and illuminates a more nuanced understanding of the socio-economic factors that underpin the connections between consumption, lifestyle and class identity currently obscuring the trajectories of those using social care but which are more than likely structured by previous opportunities in earlier life. As these political-economic environments take hold, they have served to slowly move social work away from a structural analysis or critical exploration of the social problems that people face in later life, such as those associated with a range of structural factors, for example, race, gender and class. Instead, practice has tended to become more preoccupied with delivering services against increasingly detailed government guidance. Within statutory provision for older people, some have asserted that social workers are merely working to a policy rhetoric that focuses on helping people to adjust to personal and social circumstances in a reductionist approach, thus reducing complex socio-economic factors to pathology or individual failings (Ferguson, 2007; Lymbery, 2010).

The move towards 'personalisation', 'individualised budgets' and 'self-directed care' within UK social policy, in which the older person is allocated resources up front to meet their needs and given options for how they might direct these resources, is now expected to become embedded in social work's role with adults (HMG, 2007; Law Commission, 2011). This policy directive has sought to promote a discourse of user engagement and co-production. The latter 'relates to the generation of social capital, the reciprocal relationships that build trust, peer support and social activism within communities' (Needham and Carr, 2009: 1). On the surface, this potentially gives more weight to the quality of partnerships between social workers and service users at the practice level by focusing on outcomes that are capable of bridging policy, administration and accountability with the aspirations, goals and priorities identified by older people themselves. These may include the commissioning of services with attention to leisure, learning and opportunities for community cohesion, where older people might be more active participants. The current state of consumerism with social care, however, rests on an uneasy synergy between a highly influential, articulate, 'bottom-up' movement from service users themselves and the 'top-down' ambitions of successive governments to increase the penetration of market-related mechanisms into the support and care for older people (Glendinning, 2009). One of the key concerns has been the financial levels being set for direct payments and individual budgets, with evidence to suggest that some local authorities have taken the opportunity to cut costs behind the mask of personalisation.

Such tensions are quickly picked up by front-line staff, who can sometimes feel trapped between its empowering rhetoric and the severely constrained nature of how this is actually being operationalised. Social work has yet to firmly grapple with these competing tensions by taking a stand or playing it safe. A number of questions have been raised as to how far social work is able to maintain its social justice orientation with older people within these specific policy and practice environments. The literature is beginning to document how the changing nature and characteristics of social policy is impacting on older people by taking into account their cultural capital and their potential for purchase in this new field of care provision. From a life-course approach, there are clear associations between the backgrounds of people and how they go on to interact with social care in later life, and the different identities taken up in relation to acting as consumers and co-producers. As we will see in the following section, specific factors in relation to class, identity or lifestyle tend to have a direct relationship with the roles expected from both service users in later life when using social care services and their subsequent relationships with social work professionals. These raise questions as to how social workers themselves might continue to work proactively and positively with issues associated with poverty and class alongside active promotion of the principles of choice, control and well-being.

Social work and its position to structural determinants in later life

Relatively little is known about the effect of socio-economic status on the take-up of social work services as, unlike other equality and diversity characteristics, 'class' is not routinely conceptualised or evaluated and so remains relatively unexplored in relation to social care. The regulations under the Health and Social Care Act (HMG, 2008) require providers to have 'due regard' to the needs of people using their services in relation to their age, sex, religion, sexual orientation, ethnicity, cultural and linguistic background, and disability. These equality and diversity characteristics are usually captured during information-gathering at the point at which older people access social care services and by those commissioners and providers when reporting on and evaluating trends in contracted provision. Conceptualising and analysing class in social care has been explored to some extent through research that explores associations between the use of formal and informal help and socio-economic status (Broese van Groenou et al, 2006). Given that health status appears to be a strong predictor of the potential for older people using social care, examination of health inequalities and other proxies, such as education and home-ownership, in relation to age alongside other demographic factors has provided further sources of evidence. Socio-economic status is particularly relevant when social workers are considering the older person's ability to pay for care during the process of assessment and provision. For example, there has been a growing concern about the impact of statutory charging policies on the take-up of care provision of older people (Keen, 2008), and these challenges have become more imperative since the introduction of and reliance on the computerised resource allocation systems (RAS). These have been developed to support the setting of personal budgets, in which older people are told their financial allocation and decide afterwards what level of control they then wish to take over their budget.

Insights about prejudice, discrimination and privilege have always been given importance within social work practice, which strives to recognise and respond to extremely divergent life experiences. However, despite a growing awareness of the importance of poverty issues (Becker, 1997), social work has yet to develop a significant anti-poverty perspective. It is well known that gender, race, ethnicity and social class are crucial factors that structure different experiences of ageing and its relationship with social care services. Even within a wide range of social work knowledge, research and practice on discrimination and oppression, significant gaps remain on some of the other issues faced by marginalised communities and hard-to-reach groups (Mantle and Backwith, 2010). For instance, most of the literature rarely makes sexual orientation and heterosexism explicit or addresses it specifically. Among older people, lesbian, gay, bisexual and transgender service users still have very low expectations of social care services, based on both individual and institutional prejudice, stereotyping and invisibility (Cocker and Hafford-Letchfield, 2010).

Research by Stoller and Gibson (2000) has illustrated discernible patterns in the different experiences of older service users from diverse backgrounds that reflect social-structural arrangements and cultural blueprints in relation to the use of care services. Debates about the future of social welfare, such as universalism versus targeting, the concept of fairness and, particularly, intergenerational fairness, have questioned the role and stance social workers are expected to take up in the administration of policy. Social work traditionally comes from a radical position. Indeed, the International Federation of Social Work, in its statement on the purpose of social work, asserts that:

> The social work profession promotes social change, problem solving in human relationships and the empowerment and liberation of people to enhance well-being. Utilising theories of human behaviour and social systems, social work intervenes at the points where people interact with their environments. Principles of human rights and social justice are fundamental. (International Federation of Social Work, 2012)

In practice, however, this explicit focus on challenging both the structure and its systems around the older person, rather than focusing on the individual, has been difficult to achieve within mainstream social work thus far. According to Strier and Binyamin (2010), this requires giving concerted attention to long-term strategies associated with lobbying, advocacy, coalition-building, increasing social awareness and supporting social movements that increase community participation in political processes. They also refer to the different perceptions that social workers and service users might hold about their social problems, which is fundamental to the types of assessment undertaken, interventions offered and outcomes expected. Research by Hafford-Letchfield (2011) into the experiences of older people using social care services and their perception of opportunities for self-directed care identified that service users generally felt disengaged from high-level policy and had minimal knowledge of, or understanding about, the government's policy objectives for ageing and their own roles within it. They also expressed a strong perception of age discrimination in society, which was sometimes internalised by participants themselves and accompanied by reduced optimism about their potential engagement and participation at both the individual and collective level. As Higgs and Formosa will remind us in the concluding chapter of this book, achieving change is also about the capacity of older people to participate in a social and cultural world where such participation in the construction of lifestyles is both expected and used as a form of distinction. This is not just about capitalising on physical resources, which cumulative disadvantage contributes to, but also about the richness afforded in the capacity to choose how to use them when locked into an institutionalised approach often featured in social care.

This potential 'dumbing down' of more activist approaches within social work is also discernible in more recent reviews of its role in society and subsequent efforts to reform the profession in response to public enquiries into its perceived failings. In England, for example, which has seen the creation of a new national college of social work (The College of Social Work; TCSW) in 2011, the task of social work is described as helping people to face 'difficulties as a result of disability, including feeling isolated within the community and experiencing practical problems with money or housing' (TCSW, no date: 1). Further, it describes social work as 'the safety net of society in which it promotes human development and security, social inclusion and participation across the lifespan' (TCSW, no date: 1) and suggests that it should use 'creative ways of working to resolve the challenges people face and aims to promote empowerment, enabling people to take action to improve their lives' (TCSW, no date: 3). While it is suggested that the profession works with people in a variety of different ways appropriate to their individual circumstances to help them achieve independence and exercise their human and civil rights, specific references to poverty, class and other structural determinants of access and use of social care appear to be relatively silenced. The core tasks of aiding people to improve their financial position, inform them about their entitlements and help them to access training or volunteering opportunities and welfare benefits, while not disputed, are much more in tune with the perpetuation of government policy on individualisation than challenging structural oppression. On the surface, therefore, social work appears to be coming from a position where there is less sensitivity to class differences and poverty and lower identification of one's issues with social inequality. Where these are not upfront and embedded in everyday approaches to working with older people, social workers are less likely to make important connections between these different layers of support, which can ultimately jeopardise the potential for addressing poverty and social inequality, or even perpetuate these.

Tracing some of this historical significance, Ferguson (2007) and Lymberry (2010) assert that social work's uncritical acceptance of the personalisation agenda has resulted in actual neglect of poverty and inequality. This, they argue, follows a flawed conception of the people who use social work services, leading particularly to the deprofessionalisation of social work, with social workers now seen simply as brokers, personal advisers or support workers, and the subsequent fragmentation of provision. To complicate matters, the cautiousness and alleged insensitivity of social work towards poverty and class has also been associated with its own middle-class values, creating class conflict between service users and themselves – another pillar of social oppression (Strier, 2009). Fenge (2012) has highlighted the distinct lack of understanding of social workers of the actual experiences of older people during times of financial crisis and recession to make better use of their economic resources, and the paucity of research in this area. In Chapter Eight, Victor also highlighted some of the 'exceptionalities' that could be considered by social workers in relation to the historical significance of migration, racism and gender, for example, in relation to caring within minority ethnic communities. Social workers might fail to fully capture the extent to which caring activities form part of daily life within minority ethnic communities, where family care is both 'expected' and normal, particularly from younger and second-generation adult children; nor may they question assumptions that value the relative contribution of these sources of care where there are few alternatives. There is also little in-depth exploration of how destabilisation in the economy can impact on some older people on fixed incomes and the routine management of their finances (Bornat and Bytheway, 2010). What we do know is that the expressed humiliation of older people in applying for and accepting care becomes emphasised through the nature of its bureaucratised exchange with social work (Grenier, 2007; Hafford-Letchfield, 2011). Before exploring these different dynamics in more detail, some of the specific issues facing people using social care in later life are summarised, with questions raised as to whether the proposed 'transformation' of social welfare in the form of increased control, choice and personalisation might offer any solutions.

Key issues for social care in later life

In the UK, social care has seen a continued rise in demand for services. The Care Quality Commission (2011) estimated that the reduction in social care budgets and increased demand has led to local authorities tightening their eligibility criteria for people to receive state-funded community care. In 2009/10, only 10% of people aged 65 and over receiving state-funded social care were using personal budgets and self-directed support. At the same time, the number of National Health Service (NHS) hospital beds for older people has reduced further, despite a rapidly increasing proportion of very elderly people with health and social care needs. Therefore, an anticipated trend for a diminishing proportion of long-term care for older people being provided directly by the NHS, and a rising proportion to be provided in care homes and community settings, highlights the potential inadequacy of the resource base. Consequent reprioritising of how resources are allocated has given rise to 'a situation of more complexity which is allowed for in official accounts' (Lymberry, 2010: 10). The sector has also seen expansion in models of provision such as extra care housing and short-term nursing care in homes to replace extended stays in hospital.

There are a number of factors that highlight potential patterns around the interrelationship of these challenges with older people's own resources and access to services. Long-term residential care is subject to a means test, which takes into account the capital value of people's homes if they are home-owners. According to the Association of Directors of Adult Social Services (2011), first, an estimated 45% of care home places in England are occupied by people who are self-funding, meaning that their costs are met privately rather than by the state. In addition, some people funded by local authorities have their care home fees 'topped up' by relatives or other third parties to bridge the gap between income received from their local authority and the fees charged by residential homes. Across England, around a quarter of local authority care home placements may be co-funded in this way. Second, it is estimated that 168,700 older people pay privately for care in their own homes, and this increases to over 271,500 if widened to include those who pay for support with things like housework and shopping. Third, there is evidence that local authorities are tightening their eligibility thresholds in the face of social care budget reductions and demographic pressures, which has restricted support only to those whose needs and risk factors are identified as 'critical' and 'substantial'. A further complication is that each local authority decides for itself how much to spend on older people's care. This means that levels of care and the qualification criteria vary by region. Age UK (2012), for example, has estimated that there are currently 800,000 older persons with needs for care but without any state support, a number anticipated to increase to 1 million by 2014.

Undoubtedly, access to material resources affects the quality of support received by someone attempting to use personalised care. Poverty is a combination of the lack of not only basic requirements such as food and shelter, but also a range of goods considered to be necessities of daily living, and has a negative impact on health, well-being and material security (Burtholt and Windle, 2006). Once people move into material deprivation, there is very little they can do about their position in later life. Higgs and Formosa (see Chapter Ten, this volume), for example, argue that the capacity to maintain health and fitness in later life is one of the key areas where distinction and access to positions of cultural and social hierarchy can be maintained. There is also likely to be a cumulative impact of material disadvantage if they become subsequently dependent on care (Bullock and Limbert, 2003). Mobility, both physical and social, is impacted by limited resources, for example, through the provision of transport and the ability to fund alternatives where there are unmet needs. For example, those whose needs are not deemed as 'critical' and 'substantial' are least able to take any action to meet their 'moderate' needs (DH, 2003) or take preventive action until they reach crisis point. It is estimated that, in England, there are 1.4 million older people with low-level care needs and 0.9 million with high dependent needs. The majority (5.5 million) do not require care. The starting point on social care, then, is substantial under-provision at the high end of need on the one hand, and virtually nothing of a preventive nature at the lower end on the other (Walker, 2010). Given that one third of local authorities have charging policies that can leave users with less to live on than basic income support levels, there is a potential for escalating or reinforcing deprivation. Not least, older people are particularly likely to be sensitive to the stigma associated with means-testing (Wanless, 2006). As a corollary to budget reductions in social care, it is inevitable that self-funding by older people will rise alongside further impact on informal caring. In Chapter Eight, Victor discussed the extensive body of research that examines not just the basic epidemiology of informal caring, but also the links between paid and unpaid care, the development of home as a place of care work, and the issues arising from the development of foreign care workers. Her focus upon informal care is relevant to key debates concerning the material resources available to older people requiring alternative sources of care within the UK, including the enumeration of care needs and the classification and evaluation of who provides care and locations. These cumulative factors are embedded within the broader care economy. A consultation with service users about future proposals for funding social care (Beresford, 2010) revealed a perceived sense of failure to ensure fairness and equity in the options put forward by the UK government (DH, 2009). A key concern for UK policymakers has been to improve the integration of health and social care, thought to increase efficiency and cost-effectiveness. Social care is means-tested whereas health services are currently universal and free at the point of access. Divisive and inaccurate arguments about the burden of people in later life have perpetuated the myth that intergenerational transfers are solely from younger to older people and have failed to acknowledge that many people remain subject to taxation in later life. There are situations where some service users are paying twice by both funding their own social care or meeting charges levied for care while continuing to pay tax on their private income.

In relation to quality of care, some studies (Hill et al, 2009) have demonstrated that service users sometimes resisted paying for formal help even where this was deemed essential. This was often related to the justification of costs, where the perceived service was not seen as representing value for money. In some cases, social services provision was seen to be making excessive money from older people, who chose to manage without as they perceived themselves as being subject to 'rip-off' rates from the local authority. Hill et al (2009) revealed that some older people cut back on their use of social care in response to low-quality services or an increase in the costs of certain services, such as day care. An increase in seeking private help by participants in this particular study was related to the desire of the older person to see salaries go directly to the person performing the service and to seek a greater element of control. At the more extreme end, a number of dependent older people may be at risk of various forms of abuse from carers, including financial abuse. Advice, information and education are central to preventing financial abuse and between 0.5% and 2.5% of all older people living at home admit to experiencing some form of financial abuse (Help the Aged, 2008). Finally, there is a failure to take account of the way in which social care support could prevent problems, reduce costs and enable people in later life to contribute to society, particularly from different backgrounds and cultures.

Older social care users' experiences are not shaped by one aspect of their identity alone, but by a combination of factors, such as gender, age, religion, disability, health location, sexual identity, migration history and ethnicity. Within broader poverty research, Barnard and Turner (2011) have identified two key informal processes that occur within care-giving situations that shape outcomes for those living with poverty. These include the texture of day-to-day life, the decisions and assumptions that people make as individuals, in families, as managers, employers and service providers, and the interactions between people. Economic vulnerability can lead to insecurity and sensitivity in the well-being of individuals, households and communities in the face of the changing environment and, implicit in this, their responsiveness and resilience to risks that they face during such changes. Social capital can provide assets through an array of social contacts that give access to emotional, social and practical support through the older person's informal networks and connections within their communities (Fenge, 2012). Within rural areas, allocations for individual local authorities have failed to recognise the costs of delivering services over long distances in sparsely populated areas. Older people are particularly at risk because of a combination of isolation, poverty and increased costs arising from rural life (Burtholt and Windle, 2006).

There are a number of specific issues for informal carers in relation to poverty and class. Families need to have enough income to be out of poverty as well as to care for older family members in a way that all parties feel is appropriate. Chapter Eight by Victor has provided a useful analysis of these issues, which is valuable for social work. Research shows that older people are significant providers of care. A longitudinal study done by Young et al (2006) also found that care-giving is associated with disadvantage. Their analysis of the characteristics of people who provide unpaid care to family and friends found that people providing care for 20 or more hours per week are more likely to have health problems themselves and live in poorer areas, and less likely to have educational qualifications. People from certain ethnic groups may be less likely to access professional care services due to a lack of cultural sensitivities in the services and a lack of information and networks connecting them to the services. Independent living following the death of a partner may be further exacerbated by low levels of financial literacy combined with lack of experience in managing family finances. A policy discussion paper by Carlton et al (2002) notes the move towards more technologically based financial transactions. Hafford-Letchfield's (2011) research also noted that the complexity of managing savings and investments in a recession often lies outside the range of knowledge and support available to those providing care. Living on a low income in later life and dealing with the financial implications of entering residential care require targeted support and a particular set of skills. The need for support in managing financial and administrative demands was identified as crucial in making direct payments work for older people and funding brokerage or payroll schemes (Clark et al, 2004).

In summary, current trends in social care with older people demonstrate a reduced emphasis on structural and institutional approaches to the provision of effective care. Given that the social welfare systems in the UK were originally designed to act as a safety net, particularly for poorer people in the population, it would seem that developments over the last decade, have only served to create a framework that lacks equity and has consequences for key groups of people, notably, the poorest older people who need care, and the poorest carers supporting them. Fenge (2012) has argued that it is vital for social work practitioners to develop an increased awareness of financial literacy as just one of the mechanisms for empowering older people to have more knowledge and control over their own financial well-being.

Towards increasing choice, control and personalisation

Radical revision of the principles underpinning the provision of effective care is exemplified in UK government policy emphasis on the use of personal budgets and user-directed and controlled services (HMG, 2007). A personalised service involves the older person in determining what services are required to meet their individual needs and recognises a broader diversity of provision by looking beyond the immediate social care environment to the wider community, so that choices can be linked to the older person's own desired outcomes. Lymbery (2010) identifies the complexities and contradictions that characterise the implementation of the personalisation agenda for older people. He highlights the changing relationship to resource-based adult social care, already grossly inadequate in relation to demographic changes even before the need for an improved focus on outcomes was considered. The UK government circular on 'transformation' (DH, 2008: 7) repeatedly specified that the development of adult social care 'must be set in the context of the existing resources and be sustainable in the longer term', and reiterated that the rationing of scarce resources remains a priority in any new developments.

Choice has been argued to be vitally important in social care, accompanied by control, which is fundamental to self-determination, citizenship, social inclusion and human rights. Wider citizenship debates assume that individuals have the capacity for free choice and that full citizenship involves the exercise of autonomy. Although articulated well by the disabled service users' movement, for older service users, these principles may involve considerable levels of responsibility for others, for example, engagement in becoming an employer of personal assistants and in making a distinctive contribution to the production of social care (Glendinning, 2009). Being able to take individual responsibility in such circumstances depends heavily on having an adequate income, having access to affordable local services, living in a safe neighbourhood with good social networks and accessing quality health care. It also requires frank and honest exchange about how espoused policy is enacted and experienced and how policy actually enables challenges in the political and socio-economic environment to be meaningfully transgressed. Finally, some have expressed concern that some service users, particularly those more educated, articulate and middle-class, will be more able to take advantage of the opportunities offered through direct payments than others (Ferguson, 2007).

Hafford–Letchfield (2010) argues that more participative approaches have the potential to transform relationships between social workers and older people, as they introduce new knowledge, particularly lay and user-derived knowledge, to the procurement and delivery of services. Other commentators have identified core problems when seeking to apply the principles of consumerism to social care, asserting that mechanisms of choice can often replicate rather than amend inequality because more attention is paid simply to 'the capacity to *make* choices rather than the capacity to *realise* choices' (Clarke et al, 2000: 249, italics in original). Clarke et al (2000) also highlight that while there is much rhetoric around the redistribution of power, it actually lacks a political dimension. This is where social work may play a more active role. Current bureaucratised and individually based interventions may erode earlier traditions of care, such as those found in communities, with the loss of informal networks. The perceived failure of personalisation is its inability to engage with the effects of structural inequalities and its potential to undermine collective community provision through its emphasis on moving people away from dependency, whereas interdependence is perhaps a more useful and less stigmatising concept. Victor has provided a rich source of evidence in relation to the potential for interdependency in her analysis of formal and informal caring within minority ethnic communities. She highlights the paucity of research that integrates class, gender and ethnicity perspectives to provide a more realistic evaluation of the complexities of caring and how different roles and responsibilities combine and intersect so that they might be valued or supported. Some have gone further in locating the introduction of personalisation as epochal rhetoric deployed to smooth the way for the transfer of risk from the state to the individual (Lymberry, 2010).

There are complexities to consider and barriers to overcome when implementing self-directed support with older people using care. Some messages from research, policy and practice have so far suggested that with the right approach, self-directed support and individualised budgets can work (Glendinning et al, 2008; Hafford–Letchfield, 2010, 2011). Co-production with older people requires interdependence and the reclaiming of social work skills, knowledge and resources with the reassertion and revaluing of relationship-based practice traditionally co-located within community social work. How social workers and older people achieve change perhaps requires more explicit and conscious questioning of what they can learn from the practice wisdom of front-line staff and managers, and the lived experiences of older people using services. Emphasis on learning and sharing experiences, for example, might well offer a positive model in which older people take up a more active role.

Developing class- and poverty-aware social work in an individualised world

As stated at the beginning of this chapter, formal discourse in social work explicitly emphasises the profession's commitment to confronting the problems associated with class and to aiding those living in poverty. These are embedded in its aims and mission statements, although there have been some indications of potential dilution of these within the current climate. Examination of some of the problems faced by some older people using social care also illustrates such contestation, given that there is surprisingly little research on social work's position on class in later life. Davis and Wainwright (2005) and, more recently, Krumer-Nevo et al (2011) have both identified characteristics of poverty-aware social work as being that which understands its role in the broader socio-economic context as linked to a range of policies, structures and institutions. Formosa and Higgs, in Chapter One, highlight how the concept of class constituted a fundamental touchstone of gerontological scholarship, a discipline from which social work might borrow. Indeed, an analysis of social work job descriptions in Israel by Krumer-Nevo et al (2011) found that references to poverty or economic distress were very rare and considered how these concepts were mainly used to define the service user population, to define the direction for assessing their situation or to determine the aims of interventions and directions for action. This 'taxonomy of textual silence' (Krumer-Nevo et al, 2011: 326) included neutrality or the ignoring of class and poverty, as well as manipulative silence. They attributed this to an unconscious internalisation of the ideological pressure of the organisation to work with policy by those managing the organisation. Neglecting references to poverty can be seen as an expression of the emerging conservative ideological attitude of a profession that performs its task in such a way that it conceals the existence of social problems and the government's responsibilities for it. Earlier, Formosa and Higgs (see Chapter One) problematised this implicit moral argument and highlighted the reactionary nature of government reform. Such a situation offers a discourse that emphasises personal problems and pathology instead. It is acknowledged that both poverty and social class are highly value-laden theoretical and methodological constructs, the discussion of which, however, does bring into sharp focus the role of the state and social work in addressing oppression in relation to poverty and social class and achieving social justice (Strier and Binyamin, 2010). Examination of sub-topics of poverty, such as homelessness, reveals that the goals and directions for professional interventions are more likely to become limited in their scope as we move towards a more individualistic culture. Ferguson (2007) goes so far as to say that the implications of the way in which personalisation and self-directed care is being implemented clearly merits much more critical scrutiny as it may be less benign for both those who provide social work services and even more so for those who use them. He elaborates that to continue ambiguously may allow social work to retain a semblance of loyalty to its own values, while carrying out the bidding of political masters with very different ideas and purposes.

Hafford-Letchfield (2011) argues that the growing imperative for personalisation, welcome though it may be, requires older people – often at a time when they may have to make other adjustments – to acquire a greater repertoire of techniques to learn and understand and to use complex information. She suggests that the exploration of the nature of learning, and nurturing of more pedagogical approaches within care provision, could be examined from a more critical paradigm than formerly, so that it can have the potential for the true emancipation of older people, the transformation of their consciousness and the reduction of their disempowerment. From a social work perspective, this requires social workers to take a more reflexive and creative approach, even perhaps a Freirean viewpoint, in their direct work with older people. It also raises questions as to why established social services are not more involved with poverty work and what form of social work would best be suited to such an endeavour. This does depend on whether social workers take a systems or individualised approach, and begs the question of what social workers can actually do to address class and poverty in their day-to-day work. Advocates of community-oriented perspectives on social work are largely aligned with radical social work theory and practice, and in the UK, there may be signs that radical social work could be experiencing something of a revival (Lavalette, 2011). Community social work has also become a contested concept, which has more recently been associated with the Big Society. Social work that aligns itself with structural issues rather than with the individual older person and that uses systemic methods may be difficult to achieve but can be advanced through long-term strategies such as advocacy, lobbying, coalition-building, increasing social awareness and supporting social movements that increase community participation in the political process (Strier and Binyamin, 2010). Other strategies may include tackling practice within the organisational domain. At an individual level, developing interventions that do not pathologise and that address the older person's underpinning issues while working with their strengths helps to recognise the contextual nature of their issues and the unjust nature of resource allocations by addressing their rights and entitlements in a multilayered approach. Strier and Binyamin (2010) recommend making connections between these layers which acknowledge that class and poverty result from power differences in society and can be exacerbated in later life.

References

Age UK (2012) *Care in crisis*, London: Age UK.

Association of Directors of Adult Social Services (2011) *Models for funding allocation in social care: 'the £100 million project'*, London: Association of Directors of Social Services.

Barnard, H. and Turner, C. (2011) *Poverty and ethnicity: a review of evidence*, York: Joseph Rowntree Foundation.

Becker, S. (1997) *Responding to poverty: the politics of cash and care*, Basingstoke: Macmillan.

Beresford, P. (2010) *Funding social care: what service users say?*, York: Joseph Rowntree Foundation.

Bornat, J. and Bytheway, B. (2010) 'Late life reflections on the downturn: perspectives from the oldest generation', *21st Century Society*, vol 5, no 2, pp 183–92.

Broese van Groenou, M., Glaser, K., Tomassini, C. and Jacobs, T. (2006) 'Socio-economic status differences in older people's use of informal and formal help: a comparison of four European countries', *Ageing & Society*, vol 26, no 5, pp 745–66.

Bullock, H. and Limbert, W. (2003) 'Scaling the socioeconomic ladder: low-income women's perceptions of class, status, and opportunity', *Journal of Social Issues*, vol 59, no 4, pp 693–709.

Burtholt, V. and Windle, G. (2006) *The material resources and well-being of older people*, York: Joseph Rowntree Foundation.

Care Quality Commission (2011) *The state of social care in England*, London: CQC.

Carlton, S., Soulsby, J. and Whitelegg, D. (2002) *Old money, financial understanding for adult learners*, Leicester: National Institute for Continuing Education.

Clark, H., Gough, H. and Macfarlane, A. (2004) *It pays dividends: direct payments and older people*, York: Joseph Rowntree Foundation.

Clarke, J., Gewirtz, S. and McLaughlin, E. (2000) 'Reinventing the welfare state', in J. Clarke, S. Gewirtz and E. McLaughlin (eds), *New managerialism, new welfare?*, London, Sage.

Cocker, C. and Hafford-Letchfield, T. (2010) 'Critical commentary: out and proud, social work's relationship with lesbian and gay equality', *British Journal of Social Work*, vol 40, no 6, pp 1996–2008.

Davis, A. and Wainwright, S. (2005) 'Combating poverty and social exclusion; implications for social work education', *Social Work Education*, vol 24, no 3, pp 269–73.

Department of Health (DH) (1990) *National Health Service and Community Care Act*, London, DH.

DH (2003) *Fair access to care services – guidance on eligibility criteria for adult social care*, London: DH.

DH (2008) *Transforming Social Care (LAC 2008)*, London: The Stationery Office.

DH (2009) *Living well with dementia (National Dementia Strategy)*, London: DH.

Fenge, L.A. (2012) 'Economic well-being and ageing: the need for financial education for social workers', *Social Work Education*, vol 31, no 4, pp 498–511.

Ferguson, I. (2007) 'Increasing user choice or privatising risk? The antinomies of personalisation', *British Journal of Social Work*, vol 37, no 3, pp 367–403.

Glendinning, C. (2009) 'The consumer in social care', in R. Simmons, M. Powell and I. Greener (eds) *The consumer in public services: choice, values and difference*, Bristol: The Policy Press, pp 177–96.

Glendinning, C., Challis, D., Fernandez, J.-L., Jacobs, S., Jones, K., Knapp, M., Manthorpe, J., Moran, N., Netten, A.M., Stevens, M. and Wilberforce, M. (2008) *Evaluation of the Individual Budgets Pilot Programme*, York, Social Policy Research Unit: Individual Budget Evaluation Network.

Grenier, A. (2007) 'Constructions of frailty in the English language, care practice and the lived experience', *Ageing & Society*, vol 27, no 3, pp 425–45.

Grenier, A. and Guberman, N. (2009) 'Creating and sustaining disadvantage: the relevance of a social exclusion framework', *Health and Social Care in the Community*, vol 79, no 2, pp 116–24.

Hafford-Letchfield, T. (2010) 'The age of opportunity? Revisiting assumptions about the lifelong learning needs of older people using social care services', *British Journal of Social Work*, vol 40, no 2, pp 496–512.

Hafford-Letchfield, T. (2011) 'Grey matter really matters: a study of the learning opportunities and learning experiences of older people using social care services', *International Journal of Education and Ageing*, vol 2, no 1, pp 23–40.

Help the Aged (2008) *The financial abuse of older people: a review of the literature*, London: Help the Aged.

HMG (Her Majesty's Government) (2007) *Putting people first: a shared vision and commitment to the transformation of social care*, London: HMG.

HMG (2008) 'The Health and Social Care Act', HMG, Crown Copyright.

HMG (2009) 'Shaping the future of care together', Green paper, HMG, Crown Copyright.

Hill, K., Sutton, L. and Cox, L. (2009) *Managing resources in later life: older people's experience of change and continuity*, York: Joseph Rowntree Foundation.

International Federation of Social Work (2012) 'Definition of social work'. Available at: http://ifsw.org/resources/definition-of-social-work/

Keen, J. (2008) *Does anyone care about fairness in adult social care?*, York: Joseph Rowntree Foundation.

Krumer-Nevo, M., Weis-Gal, I. and Levin, L. (2011) 'Searching for poverty-aware social work: discourse analysis of job descriptions', *Journal of Social Policy*, vol 40, no 2, pp 313–32.

Lavalette, M. (2011) *Radical social work today: social work at the crossroads*, Bristol: The Policy Press.

Law Commission (2011) 'Adult social care: Law Commissions report'. Available at: www.justice.gov.uk/lawcommission/docs/lc326_adult_social_care.pdf

Lymberry, M. (2010) 'A new vision of adult social care? Continuities and change in the care of older people', *Critical Social Policy*, vol 30, no 1, pp 5–26.

Mantle, G. and Backwith, D. (2010) 'Poverty and social work', *British Journal of Social Work*, vol 40, no 8, pp 2380–97.

Needham, C. and Carr, S. (2009) *Co-production: an emerging evidence base for adult social care transformation* (Research Briefing no 31), London: Social Care Institute for Excellence.

Stoller, E.P. and Gibson, R.C. (2000) *Worlds of difference: inequality in the aging experience*, Thousand Oaks, CA: Pine Forge Press.

Strier, R. (2009) 'Class-sensitive social work: a preliminary definition', *International Journal of Social Welfare*, vol 18, no 3, pp 237–42.

Strier, R. and Binyamin, S. (2010) 'Developing anti-oppressive services for the poor: a theoretical and organisational rationale', *British Journal of Social Work*, vol 40, no 6, pp 1908–26.

The College of Social Work (no date) 'The contribution of social work'. Available at: http://www.collegeofsocialwork.org/uploadedFiles/TheCollege/CollegeLibrary/College_produced_documents/The%20contribution%20of%20social%20work.pdf

Townsend, P. (2006) 'Policies for the aged in the 21st century: more "structured dependency" or the realization of human rights?', *Ageing & Society*, vol 26, no 2, pp 161–80.

Walker, A. (2010) 'Older people', in N. Yeates, T. Haux, R. Jawad and M. Kilkey (eds) *In defence of welfare: the impacts of the spending review*, York: Social Policy Association, pp 21–2.

Wanless, D. (2006) *Securing good care for older people: taking a long-term view*, London: Kings Fund.

Young, H., Grundy, E. and Jitlal, M. (2006) *Care providers, care receivers: a longitudinal perspective*, York: Joseph Rowntree Foundation.

TEN

The changing significance of social class in later life

Paul Higgs and Marvin Formosa

The theme around which this volume has been organised is the continuing utility of the idea of social class for the understanding of contemporary later life. Within the chapters published in this book, we have seen many different ways in which social class continues to be a valuable concept for researchers, as well as constituting a critical aspect of old age. Elizangela Storelli and John B. Williamson's chapter on the global implications of changes to pensions policy both in the US and abroad not only demonstrates that pension policies create or maintain class differences in later life, but that different models based upon different contributory principles can have different implications for providing financial security in later years. That these alternatives are not pursued is seen as one of the consequences of the salience of social class and of the interests implicated in its existence. The chapter on social work among older people in the UK by Trish Hafford-Letchfield also points out that evidence of widening inequalities is emerging as a result of changes to social policy, such as the introduction of direct payments, and that this is affecting those who have the poorest health and the lowest capacity to take advantage of formal and informal sources of support. Christina Victor's chapter extends our understanding of how the formal and informal care sectors, in terms of both providers as well as recipients, are connected to social class, as well as being affected by gender and ethnicity. These chapters provide valuable analysis regarding the connections between social class and old age that are ever-present in contemporary social policy directed towards later life. They demonstrate that the issues faced by the oldest sections of the population are not just issues of age and dependency, but also structured by many of the same forces that influence younger sections of the population. This point is made more directly in Chris Phillipson's chapter, which addresses the topic of globalisation and its effects on both later life and social class. Starting from a position that accepts that class has both been neglected in social gerontology and also has a major impact on the lives of older people, Phillipson also acknowledges that social changes brought about in the wake of globalisation are changing some of the coordinates of old age and not just around changes in pension policy. These he sees as connecting to processes of 'individualisation', which have disaggregated the sphere of community from the sphere of work, with a concomitant decline in assumptions of social inclusivity. It is in this context that growing class inequalities now find their expression in much more individualised circumstances. For Phillipson, these changes present a new challenge for researchers utilising class as an explanatory mechanism for understanding the structuring of later life in contemporary circumstances.

It is therefore not surprising that one theme that has run through many of the chapters in this book has been that our theorisation of social class has not developed sufficiently to keep up with the task of understanding the linkage between old age and social class in the modern world. We would argue that there are two reasons for this. The first reason is that contemporary sociological enquiry into the operationalisation of social class has generally concentrated on people of working age or younger. So, as Wendy Bottero's chapter in this volume shows, while there have been many attempts to understand how social and cultural changes have made the delineation of social class more difficult, these preoccupations have overlooked the way that social class operates in old age. The second reason for this lack of development has been the reluctance of many researchers to situate possible linkages between old age and social class in changes to the nature of later life in North America and Western Europe. Alexandra Lopes, in her chapter, points out that while there is support for the argument that social class has a direct effect on financial resources in later life, such causality could not be seen in relation to social relations and networks. Similar difficulties in extending social class to issues such as class identity in later life can be seen in the chapter by Martin Hyde and Ian Rees Jones, where they demonstrate that the evidence for such identities is limited. These difficulties are often compounded by many writers who use class interchangeably with inequality (Walker, 2009). For many such researchers, life after retirement is still a residual category created by social and health policies (Gilleard and Higgs, 2000). We would argue that it is important to acknowledge the need for rethinking social class under new conditions, because without it, research about later life and retirement will become less and less convincing as to the role of social class in older people's lives.

Old age and social class

Bringing all of this together, we feel that it is appropriate to offer more than just an overview of the book that we have just edited. It is also necessary to offer our own assessment of the direction of approaches to social class and later life and suggest some solutions to the issues raised. This is not done in order to create a magisterial assessment of the field, but rather to suggest a way out of some of the impasses that contemporary social changes have placed in the way of using the category of class effectively. Some of what we write might seem too critical of the concept, while others may argue that we have not gone far enough; however, we feel that over the course of a number of interventions around social class (Higgs and Gilleard, 2006; Formosa, 2009), we have been constantly trying to address the issues in a realistic way.

A starting point for our intervention is the acknowledgement that the position of older people in the class structure has always been a problematic issue in sociology. Not only have the 'founding fathers' of sociology – Marx, Durkheim and Weber – had little to say on the topic, but few theorists of note have had much to say on the nature of old age as a separate dimension of social structuring. There are, of course, some exceptions to this rule. Both Talcott Parsons (1942) and Matilda White Riley (1971), as leading American sociologists of their time, tried to understand the effect of ageing on social structures but made little explicit connection to approaches based on social class. As we noted in Chapter One, both the 'structured dependency' and 'political economy' approaches to old age did make direct links to social class, but, in general, they saw old age as determined by the class position occupied by individuals during their working lives rather than being connected to current circumstances. While such a position was relatively unproblematic in the period between 1950 and 1980 in the UK, where occupation, wealth and retirement income were closely related, such a connection was not so easy to demonstrate in later decades or, indeed, in other nations (see Lopes, Chapter Four, this volume), where the unique formulation of 'flat-rate universalism' was not the chosen model for social policies around old age. Where attempts were made to establish a Marxist (or *Marxisant*) sociology of old age, the model that resulted was often one that still defined the retired population as victims of social policy instead of seeing them as individuals occupying a distinct position in the class structure. Class analysis was far from alone in treating old age as a residual status. Other areas of sociological enquiry that could have been expected to have a more nuanced approach, such as research into health, consumption and politics, also failed to locate older people in categories that did not reduce them to their pasts. It could be argued that there were very good theoretical reasons for this residual status. After all, this conclusion reflected the fact that from the emergence of modern retirement in the early 20th century through to the last few decades of that century, there was very little dynamism in the social activities of the retired other than the continuation of past practices in more straightened circumstances. Moreover, while some parts of US sociology tried to understand this state of affairs in terms of cohort and age stratification, more attention was given to the impact of younger generations on social structure than to how older ones were also transforming society. Ironically, it was the cultural impact of these younger cohorts making up the youth culture of the 1960s who first polarised the status of 'the old' as an impediment to social change and then later created the opportunities for newer cohorts of older people to get away from these definitions of later life as a residual category.

Consequently, another reason for the inadequacy of conventional accounts of the linkages between old age and social class was that there has been a reluctance to situate older people in processes of social change that affect wider society. The cultural and social changes that occurred in the 1960s had, and still continue to have, effects on the way that societies and individuals function in ways that sociologists are still coming to terms with (Chaney, 2002). The focus on consumption and identity is just one aspect of this change, but less noticed has been the way that in its rejection of old age in favour of youth, it also helped create a new social space for later life, one not primarily defined by dependency and exclusion. Part of how this occurred is connected with how social institutions became redefined around consumption rather than production, and how this, in turn, was structured by, as well as structuring, social class itself (Sassatelli, 2007). As many researchers (particularly those influenced by Pierre Bourdieu's [1984] work on distinction) came to assert, relationships between the economy and consumer society are also class relationships, with all of its concomitant complexity. Having access to participation in the culture of consumption became a larger and larger part of the social interactions and distinction common to an understanding of social stratification. Obviously, while there have been many debates and positions taken about the nature and extent of the changes that have occurred, as well as disputes about nomenclature, there is now widespread acceptance that the social and cultural terrain on which social class is now operating has greatly changed from the classical period of modernity in which many approaches were situated. Consequently, our understanding of class needs to match contemporary circumstances and provide us with useful explanatory accounts of the social world. These accounts may differ considerably from earlier, more familiar, ones, where social class was a condensate of occupation, lifestyle and resources.

Returning to the subject of old age, the view that social class in old age was an epiphenomenon of earlier points in the life course has become less and less tenable as an explanation of class relationships in the retired population. Post-working life has been subject to many of the changes that have occurred for people of working age, without necessarily being reducible to them. The connections between consumption, lifestyle and class identity, which have made simple inferences of class membership more difficult to assert, are multiplied in later life. It could be argued that the nature of post-working life lifestyles and consumption are more defining of the statuses of retired people than their class identities. Although participation in leisure may be more structured by previous opportunities, which reflect more closely occupational class (Scherger et al, 2011), it is still difficult to see how this constitutes a separate dimension of class rather than resources and dispositions. Much more significant to the discussion of class is that retirement from paid employment has become increasingly contingent in terms of when (or how) it occurs and how it is to be financed. Again, this is not to argue that retirement is free of the influences of the past, but rather to accept that in countries such as the UK, notions of early retirement have impacted on when post-working life begins and how much participation in the cultural arena of the third age is possible.

Class, generation and lifestyle

Shifting our focus to participation in the cultural field of the third age serves to problematise further the conventional connections between social class and later life, given that under these circumstances older people are subject to a multiplicity of sources through which they are expected to construct their lives in retirement. Phillipson, in his chapter, cautions against seeing the issues as ones principally of choice, but as the upcoming members of the baby boom cohort move into retirement, their generational habitus, as Gilleard and Higgs (2005) point out, implicitly valorises leisure and choice rather than being wedded to a potentially dependent relationship with the welfare state. Again, whether this is an elective affinity or an imposition of neoliberal individualisation is a matter of considerable debate (Polivka, 2011). It still remains that the cultural transformations that are brought about in its wake not only help to undermine class identities, but also bring into prominence the idea of the citizen-consumer as the true description of the various relationships that now situate contemporary social policy. Such a formulation, with its emphasis on consumption, could be seen as providing a better fit for the interests of some older people than approaches that give priority to achieving the status of being a citizen, senior or otherwise. However, this is not to underplay the extent to which the cultural space of the third age, by being dependent on consumerism, may construct or exacerbate forms of structural inequality resulting from the intertwining of ageism, globalisation and the processes of individualisation.

Consequently, an inevitable criticism of any approach based upon individualisation is that it allows little role for social class (Atkinson, 2010). Rising to the accusation, Ulrich Beck (2007: 686) argues: 'individualisation uncouples class culture from class position' and, as a result, 'status, consumption and social security choices ... become progressively independent of income'. Beck argues that the stability of social class and its linked inequalities, as well as collective responses to inequalities, are features of a 'First Modernity' in which social processes are bounded by a nation-state. He points out that it is the 'irony and paradox of the welfare state' that it is the collective success of class struggle that has not only institutionalised individualisation, but also dissolved class culture through its campaign to eradicate inequalities. In a 'Second Modernity', not only are these processes individualised and dominated by contingency, but so too is class conflict. As he writes, 'many individuals may still be in the same position. But there is no common and unifying explanation for their suffering, even more: they have to blame themselves' (Beck, 2007: 686).

As we have seen in the chapter by Ian Rees Jones and Paul Higgs in this volume, from such a perspective, class can only come back into the equation through the medium of 'individualised' class struggle. This is an arena where social inequalities become more obvious but do not seem to reflect the operation of easily identified processes. An important feature of this change is the way that labour force participation loses its pivotal role in the ordering of society. Not only is consumption therefore less stratified by age or status, but the complex entitlements of welfare policy create opportunities for de-commodified lives in ways that were previously not possible and very possibly were not intended. In relation to the welfare state, it is no longer acceptable to assume the superiority of the nuclear family or the gendered division of labour. The issue of de-commodification, which has been at the heart of social policy debate for many decades, has now become a reality, with its own attendant problems.

For Beck and colleagues (2003), it is no accident that lifestyle has become a major focus of both personal and social activity in what he terms 'Second Modernity'. The institutional boundaries of the life course that dominated the First Modernity of the early and mid-20th century were ones that connected the ascribed statuses of social class with both work and gender, and therefore provided stable bases for identity. In a Second Modernity, the individual can no longer be posited as a stable and unchanging subject. Instead, he or she is forced to become a 'quasi-subject', the result as well as the producer of his or her own networks, situation, location and form. Lifestyle – which might seem to be an anodyne term to have so much importance thrust upon it – therefore becomes an important facet of negotiating Second Modernity.

This negotiation lies at the heart of Gilleard and Higgs' (2005) arguments about the nature of contemporary ageing. They argue that the Third Age is a cultural field that needs to be understood as an expression of the generational habitus of those cohorts who came of age in the 1960s and after, for whom consumption and lifestyle, rather than work and class identity, were inextricably linked together. Significantly, for Gilleard and Higgs, the dispositions of these post-Second World War cohorts went hand in hand with a reluctance to accept the ascriptive social locations of the past, whether these were of gender, race or even class. As we have seen, this led to what Beck and his colleagues have described as the 'revolution through side effects', creating a situation where ascription in terms of identity has been replaced by a greater reflexivity on the part of individuals as to who they are and how they want to be seen by others.

Social class as a 'zombie category' in later life

Does this therefore mean that we have to adapt another of Beck's formulations, that class in later life is a 'zombie category' (Beck and Beck-Gernsheim, 2002)? Certainly, as many writers in this volume and others have pointed out, the constant injunction to include class in our understanding of later life has not been matched by its rigorous application. Are we therefore compelled to see the connection between social class and old age as a rhetorical device rather than as a part of an analysis of the structures that influence later life? One way of avoiding this conclusion is to utilise some of the rethinking that has being going on in connection with cultural studies of class. Here, we return to the work of Pierre Bourdieu and his notions of distinction, reproduction and habitus, which have been frequently called upon in attempts to understand the newer cultural processes of social class. In particular, Bourdieu's work has been used to think about how dispositions emerge out of social distinctions and help reproduce them. This is particularly true of the practices of consumption and how they may play a powerful role in reproducing social divisions.

Recent work utilising his insights has therefore repositioned social class in terms of individual identity or in terms of personal trajectories, rather than seeing people existing within an all-embracing class culture (eg Savage, 2000; Bottero, 2004). The significance of class for these writers is manifested in the importance of hierarchy and social position in individual narratives. An important aspect of this is the notion of 'ordinariness' or authenticity regarding the class identity that people use in their everyday life. Some commentators, such as Beverley Skeggs (1997), see these narratives as leading not only to individualisation, but also to the maintenance and reproduction of inequalities. However, as Méndez (2008) points out, most applications of Bourdieu's work have been focused on the distinctions between the middle class and the working class, and relatively less work has been done examining horizontal differentiation and the symbolic boundaries that are used in everyday life by members of the same class. This is particularly important in relation to processes of consumption, where intersubjective assessments and judgements are made using notions of authenticity, and where Méndez points out that individuals are 'compelled to be themselves'.

Taking up and adapting these arguments can do much to counter the idea that social class is a zombie category in relation to later life. As many writers have pointed out, there has been considerable debate about the utility of Bordieusian approaches for groups that do not easily fit into his schema, such as women. As a result, this has led to a renewed emphasis on how gender interrelates with distinction and habitus, as well as with reproduction. A similar shift of focus can be applied in relation to later life, where older people do not share in an undifferentiated old age mediated by social and health policy, and neither do they simply live out their retirements determined by the constructs of a pervasive social class. This may have been the case for much of the 20th century, but the arguments about the influence of the culture of the Third Age and the role of the post-war cohorts outlined earlier make this position relatively untenable. Equally, it must be emphasised that the cultural dynamics of the Third Age should not be considered another form of social stratification whereby the middle classes are able to engage in 'a Third Age' while the working classes are condemned to fall into a situation of structured dependency. Such formulations fail to understand the important dynamics unleashed in contemporary society in the form of individualisation and the transformation of post-working life as a cultural field. As Gilleard and Higgs (2000) point out, the change is about the capacity to participate in a social and cultural world where such participation in the construction of lifestyles is both expected and used as a form of distinction. The distinction between a Third and a Fourth Age does not lie in the possession of resources, but rather in the capacity to choose how to use them. For those whose physical and mental capacities have been used up and for whom social or nursing care is needed, entry into a fourth age is not alleviated by class or by the resources associated with it; rather, it is the capacity to actively construct and maintain a lifestyle that demarcates the Third and the Fourth Age (Gilleard and Higgs, 2011). However, as Jones and Higgs (2010) underline, there is now an expectation that normal ageing contains an invocation not only to 'age well', but also to have 'a will to health' in later life. This can be seen to set up 'projects of the self' that extend from middle age through retirement into old age. Distinctions between individuals whose ageing 'fitness' is to be applauded and those whose perceived lack of 'engagement' with these activities is bemoaned abound in the health promotion literature. Such engagements are, according to Zygmunt Bauman, part of the culture of 'fitness' that underlies modern consumerism, and partially account for its focus on the body (Higgs, 2012). The capacity to maintain health and fitness in later life is one of the key areas where distinction and access to positions of cultural and social hierarchy can be maintained. When this wanes and entry into the Fourth Age seems possible, many of the assets associated with this form of capital also seem to dissipate. Consequently, the connection to social class can be maintained, but within different circumstances and under different articulating principles.

Social class in later life as a normative structure

These circumstances have, as we have seen, transformed the nature of what class can mean in wider society. However, as a number of writers have been at pains to argue, class still has a resonance, which relates to its normative significance. As Andrew Sayer writes:

> Sociology may not have given up on class altogether, but it often tracks and represents class in ways that miss its normative significance. We will understand class better if we stop reducing people to occupants of positions, or bearers or performers of class, etc., and attend also to their normative

> dispositions and beliefs, even though these only contingently affect the reproduction of class. Lay normativity is not reducible to habit or the pursuit of self-interest and power, but has a crucial moral dimension, relating ... to a feel for how actions, events and circumstances affect well-being. (Sayer, 2005: 225)

Social class in later life probably exemplifies this dimension better than any other aspect of class society because it relates to the relative inequality that the old have felt in many societies when their capacity to secure their existence has become dependent upon either their own resources or the benevolence of others. From the early modern period in Europe, the issue of the aged poor has been at the centre of social policy concerns. Indeed, it can be argued that the introduction of universal pensions has been as much the foundation of modern welfare states as has any other programme. The connection between social class and pensions is one that has been made in this volume as well as elsewhere, but in current circumstances, it is the controversies surrounding current arrangements that reconnect the moral dimension of class and later life. In a globalised world dominated by financial institutions, are the retired no longer deserving of their benefits negotiated in decades past? Should there be a retrenchment of the idea of a retirement pension? All of these questions problematise the implicit moral argument concerning the status of older people. They may be posed in new guises, but the fundamental argument is that the contingencies being experienced by other sections of the population render unfair the arrangements that exist for the older population (Higgs and Gilleard, 2010). It is hardly surprising that there have been many negative responses to the idea that reform is necessary and, indeed, they have often been positioned as unfair, if not reactionary, in nature. The moral argument around social class in relation to later life is one that accepts that many people in what would have once been deemed the working class have seen that their entitlements to a secure old age are both fair and militate against the potential inequalities created by growing older. Under present circumstances, these insecurities seem to be growing larger. While it is the case that many retirees have benefited from the structures and stability of a standardised life course, their current circumstances are much more contingent on Beck and colleagues' notion of 'side effects' (Beck et al, 2003), where decisions that affect them are often the consequences of decisions and structures placed well outside nation-state boundaries. Nowhere has this been truer than in the financing of retirement, where shifts in the global economy have had dramatic effects on the values of stocks and shares that underpin the profitability of pension funds, as well as reducing the rates of return on savings, which many older people rely upon for important parts of their retirement income. It is not only at the level of the private pension that these effects are felt. The retirement pensions underwritten by nation-states have been problematised for a number of decades by bodies such as the World Bank as they have sought more market-oriented reforms. For many years, most European Union nations have worried about the long-term viability of their own schemes in the context of demographic decline and the need to reduce public expenditure. Different solutions or compromises have emerged, but the general conclusion has been that even current arrangements and levels of support need to be reformed and ideally reduced. This has been further exacerbated by the financial crisis that has beset the world economy since 2008. All of this creates a line of antagonism that affects nearly all in retirement, whether they have done well out of previous arrangements or wish for better times.

It is under such changing social circumstances that opposition and resistance become more important, but unlike in the past, such resistance takes on more individualised forms. The idea that the social institutions of the labour movement or social-democratic parties can comprehensively undertake this task has declined along with the demise of corporatist social policies such as the 'social wage'. Consequently, in an era of austerity, resistance is now more particularised and seemingly more concerned with the maintenance of historic arrangements than it is with the advancement of a more egalitarian agenda. However, Bourdieu's (1998) later work, which was concerned with these changes, pointed out that these forms of resistance were often about opposition to capitalist social relations and the disregard for the individuals who make up society. In *Acts of resistance*, Bourdieu (1998) went beyond the analysis of distinction and the reproduction of power to examine how it was possible to resist the imposition of system requirements on ordinary individuals, particularly in the realm of social rights. Nowhere are these rights more obvious than in relation to those resources for sustaining an engagement with the Third Age. The behaviour of the global economy and of the financial institutions within it, which play an increasingly directive role, creates a normative demand for stability that places many people at odds with the unregulated 'freedom' of an unfettered capitalism (as well as possibly those who markedly benefit from this state of affairs). This suggests that resistance is not random or arbitrary; rather, it is conditioned by a wider and more volatile set of processes that have made understanding contemporary capitalism more difficult. The relationships of individuals to the economic system in terms of interests may, therefore, have become more complex (and sometimes more contradictory) than they were in the past (Higgs and Gilleard, 2006), but it is also the case that as the structuring processes of social class have become more individualised, later life and its cultures have become more and more a part of these structures. The tension created by these different forces leads to a variety of outcomes and increases the range of inequalities that can, in turn, be compounded by the role of health and disability or the role of social support. The danger of focusing on these differences, however, is that the power of the idea of social class is lost in the attempts to operationalise it. If, however, we think of class in terms of its moral significance instead of its positioning of individuals into a class schema, we can concentrate our attention on the combined political, moral and cultural issues that have always been at the centre of the idea of class. Adopting this approach will not only open up promising avenues for research and thinking about old age, but also help to ensure that the concept of social class keeps its place in the sociological lexicon.

References

Atkinson, W. (2010) 'Class, individualization and perceived (dis) advantages: not either/or but both/and?', *Sociological Research Online*, vol 15. Available at: http://www.socresonline.org.uk/15/4/7.html

Beck, U. (2007) 'Beyond class and nation: reframing social inequalities in a globalizing world', *British Journal of Sociology*, vol 58, no 4, pp 679–705.

Beck, U. and Beck-Gernsheim, E. (2002) *Individualization*, London: Sage.

Beck, U., Bonss, W. and Lau, C. (2003) 'The theory of reflexive modernisation, problematic, hypotheses and research programme', *Theory, Culture and Society*, vol 20, no 2, pp 1–33.

Bottero, W. (2004) 'Class identities and the identity of class', *Sociology*, vol 38, no 5, pp 985–1003.

Bourdieu, P. (1984) *Distinction: a social critique of the judgment of taste*, Cambridge, MA: Harvard University Press.

Bourdieu, P. (1998) 'Neo-liberalism, the utopia (becoming a reality) of unlimited exploitation', in P. Bourdieu (ed) *Acts of resistance: against the tyranny of the market*, Cambridge: Polity, pp 94–105.

Chaney D. (2002) *Cultural change and everyday life*, Basingstoke: Palgrave.

Formosa, M. (2009) *Class dynamics in later life: older persons, class identity and class action*, Hamburg: Lit Verlag.

Gilleard, C. and Higgs, P. (2000) *Cultures of ageing: self, citizen and the body*, Harlow: Prentice Hall.

Gilleard, C. and Higgs, P. (2005) *Contexts of ageing: class, cohort and community*, Cambridge: Polity Press.

Gilleard, C. and Higgs, P. (2011) 'Aging, abjection and embodiment in the Fourth Age', *Journal of Aging Studies*, vol 25, no 2, pp 135–42.

Higgs, P. (2012) 'Consuming bodies: Zygmunt Bauman on the difference between fitness and health', in G. Scambler (ed) *Contemporary theorists for medical sociology*, London: Routledge, pp 20–32.

Higgs, P. and Gilleard, C. (2006) 'Departing the margins: social class and later life in a second modernity', *Journal of Sociology*, vol 42, no 3, pp 219–41.

Higgs, P. and Gilleard, C. (2010) 'Generational conflict, consumption and the ageing welfare state in the UK', *Ageing and Society*, vol 30, no 8, pp 1439–51.

Jones, I.R. and Higgs, P. (2010) 'The natural, the normal and the normative: contested terrains in ageing and old age', *Social Science and Medicine*, vol 71, no 8, pp 1513–19.

Méndez, L. (2008) 'Middle class identities in a neoliberal age: tensions between contested authenticities', *The Sociological Review*, vol 56, no 2, pp 220–37.

Parsons, T. (1942) 'Age and sex in the social structure of the United States', *American Sociological Review*, vol 7, no 5, pp 604–16.

Polivka, L. (2011) 'Neoliberalism and postmodern cultures of aging', *Journal of Applied Gerontology*, vol 48, no 5, pp 564–72.

Riley, M.W. (1971) 'Social gerontology and the age stratification of society', *Gerontologist*, vol 11, no 1, pp 79–87.

Sassatelli, R. (2007) *Consumer culture: history, theory and politics*, London: Sage.

Savage, M. (2000) *Class analysis and social transformation*, London: Sage.

Sayer, A. (2005) *The moral significance of class*, Cambridge: Cambridge University Press.

Scherger, S., Nazroo, J. and Higgs, P. (2011) 'Leisure activities and retirement: do structures of inequality change during old age?', *Ageing and Society*, vol 31, no 1, pp 146–72.

Skeggs, B. (1997) *Formations of class and gender: becoming respectable*, London: Sage.

Walker, A. (2009) 'Why is ageing so unequal?', in P. Cann and M. Dean (eds) *Unequal ageing: the untold story of exclusion in old age*, Bristol: The Policy Press, pp 141–58.

Index

Page numbers followed by the letter "n" indicate tables.

V

W

Y

Z